THE WORLD'S GREATEST IDEAS

AN ENCYC
SOCIAL IN

THE WORLD'S GREATEST IDEAS

AN ENCYCLOPEDIA *of* SOCIAL INVENTIONS

Edited by
NICHOLAS ALBERY, RETTA BOWEN,
NICK TEMPLE, STEPHANIE WIENRICH

Preface by **Jay Walljasper**

Foreword by **Brian Eno**

Introduction by **Kirkpatrick Sale**

 NEW SOCIETY PUBLISHERS

Cataloguing in Publication Data:
A catalog record for this publication is available from the
National Library of Canada.

Cover art and design by Diane McIntosh. Earth image © PhotoDisc, 2001.

Printed in Canada by Friesens Inc.

New Society Publishers acknowledges the support of the Government of
Canada through the Book Publishing Industry Development Program
(BPIDP) for our publishing activities,
and the assistance of the Province of
British Columbia through the British
Columbia Arts Council.

**BRITISH
COLUMBIA
ARTS COUNCIL**
Supported by the Province of British Columbia

Paperback ISBN: 0-86571-443-6

Inquiries regarding requests to reprint all or part of *The World's Greatest
Ideas* should be addressed to New Society Publishers at the address below.

To order directly from the publishers, please add $4.50 shipping to the
price of the first copy, and $1.00 for each additional copy (plus GST in
Canada). Send check or money order to:

New Society Publishers
P.O. Box 189, Gabriola Island, BC V0R 1X0, Canada

New Society Publishers' mission is to publish books that contribute in fundamental ways to building an ecologically sustainable and just society, and
to do so with the least possible impact on the environment, in a manner
that models this vision. We are committed to doing this not just through
education, but through action. We are acting on our commitment to the
world's remaining ancient forests by phasing out our paper supply from
ancient forests worldwide. This book is one step towards ending global
deforestation and climate change. It is printed on acid-free paper that is
100% old growth forest-free (100% post-consumer recycled), processed
chlorine free, and printed with vegetable based, low VOC inks. For further
information, or to browse our full list of books and purchase securely, visit
our website at: www.newsociety.com

NEW SOCIETY PUBLISHERS   18 95   www.newsociety.com

TABLE *of* CONTENTS

ABOUT THE EDITORS

NICHOLAS ALBERY died in a car accident after this book's completion, on June 3, 2001. Nicholas was the founder and chairman of the Institute for Social Inventions, the charitable project which collects socially innovatory ideas from around the world and aims to put the best of them into practice. The ideas that you read about in this book were gathered together in this way.

This belief in the power of ideas to change society led Nicholas to starting projects such as the ApprenticeMaster Alliance, the Global Ideas Bank, the Natural Death Centre, the Poetry Challenge, and www.DoBe.org. Some arose from ideas sent in to the Institute, and others came from Nicholas' own fertile and creative imagination. Indeed, many of his own ideas are included in this Encyclopedia — an enduring testament to his vision and creativity.

He never doubted that a small group of committed people could change the world, and he proved this most effectively with his involvement in the Republic of Frestonia in which a small group of West London residents declared their independence from Britain (see under 'F'). He was also ahead of the game on green issues, suing the oil companies in 1979 for the lead in their gasoline adversely affecting children's health. Not many years later, it was the same oil companies who began marketing lead-free gasoline back to us. As a prolific social inventor, writer, publisher, and activist, Nicholas touched the lives of thousands of people. The evidence is all around us — schoolchildren learning poetry for charity, woodland funerals being organized, apprentices being taken on, and more and more people submitting ideas to the Global Ideas Bank every day. What he achieved will not be forgotten, and his work will continue through the people he inspired.

RETTA BOWEN began working at the Institute in October 2000 directly after leaving university, where she co-founded Muchos Theatre, a company which has disbanded temporarily to seek out gainful employment. She continues to learn a poem a day by heart as part of the Institute's lunchtime ritual that is paving the way for its second poetry collection, *Poem for the Day 2*, to be published in October 2003.

NICK TEMPLE has been working at the Institute for Social Inventions for a year now, having come to work there directly after finishing his studies. He came away from university with a Masters in Literature, Culture, and Modernity, an ailing poetry magazine, and the ability to work into the dead of night. His main duties, aside from typesetting and proofreading, include keeping coffee supplies low and recollecting useless facts of trivia.

STEPHANIE WIENRICH has a Master's degree in Culture and Social Change from the University of Southampton, UK, and has been working as a writer and editor for the Institute for Social Inventions since 1998. She has co-edited a number of ISI publications, including *Seize the Day; Social Dreams &*

Technological Nightmares; The Book of Inspirations; Ways To Go – Naturally; 1,001 Health Tips; and The New Natural Death Handbook.

→ Readers are invited to submit their socially innovative ideas and projects for future volumes and for possible awards to the non-profit Global Ideas Bank at <www.globalideasbank.org> or by e-mail to <rhino@dial.pipex.com>. Fuller references and further details for many of the entries in this present encyclopedia can be found on the Global Ideas Bank website by using the search engine there.

→ The website of the Institute for Social Inventions is <www.globalideasbank.org>.

→ See also <www.DoBe.org>, <www.apprentice.org.uk>, <www.poetrychallenge.org.uk> and <www.naturaldeath.org.uk> for some of Nicholas Albery's many projects.

→ There is a memory board with links to obituaries of Nicholas at <www.globalideasbank.org/nicholas/wwwboard>.

DEDICATION

This book is dedicated to its co-editor Nicholas Albery,
who died in a car accident after the book's completion,
on June 3, 2001. Nicholas was the founder and chairman of the
Institute for Social Inventions, the charitable project which
benefits from sales of **The World's Greatest Ideas**.
He will be greatly missed.

PREFACE

A cornucopia of wisdom

JAY WALLJASPER

Jay Walljasper is editor of *Utne Reader* magazine.

JOURNALISM, as most practitioners of the form readily acknowledge, is a profession based upon the fine art of appropriation. Good journalists are the wily ones who track down interesting and insightful people from whom to draw ideas. A mark of accomplishment in the field is locating and raiding especially rich sources of information that are unknown to most other writers and editors.

With the publication of this splendid book, jam-packed with brilliant ideas and illuminating suggestions, I fully expect my own rank in the journalistic standings to descend. The truth is, in many years of editing *Utne Reader* magazine I have lifted stories from London's Institute for Social Inventions on a frequent basis. I can think of few other organizations, including major media corporations with planeloads of expert reporters and travel budgets in the multimillions, that have so consistently dazzled me with the freshness and worthiness of their ideas. But now my secret has crossed the Atlantic, and curious North Americans (including many journalists, I fear) can feast their imaginations on the Institute's cornucopia of wisdom.

One of the most valuable services provided by Nicholas Albery and his colleagues is to pull bright ideas from places most journalists wouldn't think of looking: Asian villages, obscure community groups' handbills, remote corners of the worldwide web, as well as postcards and e-mails from around the world that come flooding into their London office. I'm pleased that on occasions *Utne Reader* has provided them with the germ of an idea, thus making long-distance borrowing a two-way street.

Antidotes to the vexing annoyances and melancholy moments of modern life

---

But even when the institute's sources are as well-known as *The Times* of London, there is a clear sense that these ideas arise not from abstract theorizing in a think tank or university office, but out of the direct experience of everyday people meeting the challenges of a complicated yet ultimately joyful world. You'll find answers to major international problems here, but also antidotes to the vexing annoyances and melancholy moments of modern life. The vision of the Institute for Social Inventions, distilled into this volume, is broad enough to incorporate both outrageous flights of fancy that can inspire our dreams of a better world, and down-to-earth common sense with eminently practical applications for our everyday lives — sometimes at the same time.

There's something here to brighten everyone's day and bring hope for tomorrow.

FOREWORD

An incrementalist strategy for changing the world

BRIAN ENO

Brian Eno — musician, producer, artist, and author — is a patron
of the Institute for Social Inventions.

JUST AS CHEETAHS have a talent for speed, humans have a talent for imagining — for wondering how else things might be. This means that, unique among animals, we can rethink our social arrangements. Although such a talent is a mixed blessing — we are capable of manufacturing arrangements that enslave us as well as ones that liberate us — we nonetheless have no choice but to use it. We can't withdraw from the imagining game, just as cheetahs can't withdraw from the running game. It's our niche, our living.

It's strange, then, that our new media — the instruments charged with reporting back to us how we are doing — should be so much more fascinated by bad ideas — or the failure of good ones — than by successes. We drown in bad news, in tales of how things went wrong, but we have only the most cursory discussion on how they might go right.

Is this because we still won't — or can't — accept our own astonishing powers? Is it more comforting to see ourselves as victims of uncontrollable complexities than to take some responsibility for the way things are and make some decisions about how else they could be better? Or are we just frightened of getting it wrong — paralyzed by the long history of Utopian ideas gone bad?

Scanning the world for signs of more successful and humane ways of doing things

---

This book, and the approach to world-changing it espouses, is not Utopian. It doesn't say, "We'll build a whole New World from scratch, and if everyone does what they should it will all be perfect." It offers a much more pragmatic, much more incrementalist strategy. Instead of an all-embracing ideological overview from which correct behavior is supposed to flow, it takes a case-by-case approach to changing the world. It says, "Given what we have and what we now know, wouldn't it be better if we did this particular thing in this other way?" Primarily, this book is a work of research — scanning the world for signs of more successful and humane ways of doing things, and then re-presenting them in new mixes and matches. In that sense, it's The Good News, the stuff that doesn't make the headlines, the material of human success.

This approach constitutes the proposal that a better world will be achieved not by smashing everything up, but by accumulating systems and arrangements that work a little better. It arises out of the expectation that, given the choice, people will make rational and even generous decisions. And it says, "It's our responsibility to look after the future."

INTRODUCTION

Ideas at the human scale

KIRKPATRICK SALE

Kirkpatrick Sale is the author of nine books, including *Human Scale* and
*Rebels Against the Future: The Luddites and Their War on the Industrial Revolution:
Lessons for the Computer Age*. His latest work is *The Fire of His Genius:
Robert Fulton and the American Dream*. He is a founding board member
of the American E.F. Schumacher Society.

WHAT PRESUMPTION, you're thinking, what effrontery. These people claim to
have come up with the world's best ideas? The *world's best?*! How arrogant!

Wait, though. Consider just this one: a Hippocratic oath for scientists,
binding them to ethical principles for judging their life works, to be sworn,
as with doctors, when they begin their careers. If that doesn't rank up there
with the great thoughts of our time, it's hard to know what would. Just imagine if, say, Robert Oppenheimer had taken it, or Wernher von Braun: " I will
abstain from all intentional wrongdoing and harm," as Hippocrates put it.
What a different — and much safer — world this would be.

I would not argue that all of the ideas in this volume rank quite on that
level. But there are many that come close. "Cantonizing the USA," for example, a proposal put forth by Gore Vidal, arguing (unarguably) that the Swiss
system of government works "superbly" and that an American form of
regional groupings might do as well. Or developing local currencies on a city
or regional level, bypassing the national currencies and their dangerous fluctuations and keeping money circulating in a small area where it promotes
local jobs and a community economy rather than chainstore mallification.

Finding sparkling ideas,
seeing them through, and making them real

You get the picture. These really *are* great ideas, picked by people who
have a clear sense of what makes an idea important and how it can penetrate
and resonate when presented right. Indeed, the people who compiled this
book have a long history not only of finding and offering sparkling ideas, but

in many cases of seeing them through and making them real. The Institute for Social Inventions, begun by Nicholas Albery and colleagues in London in 1985, has pioneered in the business of searching for "social inventions" — new and imaginative ways of tackling social problems — and then putting them into action with independent centers, local committees, professional networks, counseling circles, national competitions, circulated petitions — and whatever else that works. This present volume represents the best of these "inventions" they've encountered over the years.

Social inventions address issues at a human scale, often on a neighborhood level.

The reason that they have succeeded — the reason, in fact, why these really are the world's best ideas – is that they address issues, and operate artfully on them, at a human scale, often on a neighborhood level. There are no grand government schemes and bureaucracies involved here, no global problem-solving arrangements or UN interventions. All of the ideas are born out of hands-on, community-based, face-to-face experience and ask for their accomplishment only human ingenuity and dedication, elementary settings and tools (well, some do use computers and faxes), and easy-to-see, easy-to-learn principles and procedures.

Use rockdust to "remineralize" a depleted garden. Build houses with straw bales, cheap and durable. Liberate streams long buried beneath a city's concrete. Create permaculture forest gardens and get your neighbor to do so as well. Practice random kindness and senseless acts of beauty.

All the ideas, you see, are simple, really, though most have profound ramifications. All can be envisioned and enacted at a small, doable level, though some have implications for saving the world. Simple and small, cheap and safe: Schumacher's notion of what is truly beautiful.

Just skim through this volume for a few minutes. I guarantee you will come across an idea that will startle and engage you, possibly even inspire and energize you. And if after going through the whole catalog you don't agree that these really are the world's greatest ideas, well then, come up with a few of your own and send them in to the Institute for Social Inventions. They'll be added to the next volume. And that, of course, is the point.

What presumption, indeed.

A

Addicts receive $200 to get birth control

Summarized from an article by Margot Hornblower in *Time* and an article by Eli Sanders in the *Seattle Times* — both monitored by Roger Knights — and from the CRACK website <www.cracksterilization.com>.

BARBARA HARRIS FOUNDED CRACK (Children Requiring a Caring Kommunity) to offer drug addicts $200 cash incentives in return for reliable birth control.

The USA sees the birth of 500,000 drug-exposed children annually, many of whom suffer from brain damage and HIV.

In poor areas, prostitution is often seen as an easy way of making money to pay for drug habits, and careless contraceptive protection frequently leads to unwanted births. The USA sees the birth of 500,000 drug-exposed children annually, many of whom suffer from brain damage and the human immune deficiency virus (HIV). Having adopted four children from the same drug-dependent mother, Harris lobbied the police, the district attorney, social workers, and local politicians about the way this particular mother was constantly endangering the lives of the children she brought into the world.

"Finally I realized," she said, "that if I wanted these women to take birth control, I'd have to do it on my own."

The proposition she came up with was to pay addicts $200 to get sterilized or take long-term birth control. Since its establishment in 1997, CRACK has paid approximately 200 women and one man to follow her program. The majority of them opted for sterilization, although less-radical birth control measures are on offer, such as a one-year program of Depo Provera injections.

Besides approaching addicts directly, CRACK has set up a toll-free phone line as well as a website.

Opposition has come from civil liberties lawyers and bioethics academics, who are concerned that the scheme may be unethical since many of the women are not in a position to give their informed consent. Giving up their reproductive rights in exchange for a bribe of $200 "could lead these people to make a decision they would later regret," comments Gloria Feldt, president of the Planned Parenthood Federation of America. The program has also been presented as a eugenic assault on society's marginalized groups.

Harris is happy to defend herself against cries of racism and social planning. She has three of her own biracial children with her African-American husband, and the four children she has adopted are black. From her point of view, CRACK acts to prevent unwanted babies by making birth control accessible: "We're not about sterilization, we're about birth control, and I don't see why an alcoholic or a drug addict shouldn't use birth control."

"The people who yell the loudest aren't the ones raising the kids," she complains. "Unless you're willing to take these babies into your home for 18 years, your opinion matters nothing to me."

Jason is one example of a baby who was born addicted to drugs and who weighed less than two pounds. He lived three short years. He was totally vent-dependent — he could not breathe on his own without a tube in his throat. He could only eat formula through a tube in his stomach. Because of his condition, nurses had to be paid to attend to him 24 hours per day, seven days a week. The cost for those nurses was over four million taxpayer dollars. In addition, there were substantial costs for foster caretakers, numerous hospital stays (including a seven-month stay at birth), much surgery and medication, and many social workers.

Between the time Jason was born and died, his drug-addicted parents had another baby. That baby, who was also vent-dependent, did not live as long. He showed no sign of brain waves, and the doctors made the painful decision to remove his life-support systems.

Women and men who use or are addicted to drugs are often responsible for an extraordinary number of pregnancies (five to ten or more) that they are in no position to take care of. Babies of women who use cocaine during pregnancy are two to six times more likely to be born with a low birthweight. Low-birthweight babies are 40 times more likely to die in their first month, and those that do survive are at an increased risk of lifelong disabilities, including mental retardation, cerebral palsy, or visual and hearing impairment. For this reason, the March of Dimes Birth Defects Foundation advises women who use cocaine to stop before they become pregnant or to delay pregnancy until they believe they can avoid the drug completely throughout the pregnancy.

The children of drug addicts also run a higher risk of exposure to HIV. The babies require long, difficult, and expensive hospital stays before they are released into the overburdened foster care system. The tiny newborns struggle with drug withdrawal and are commonly abandoned at birth. The children are also at a high risk of neglect, further physical or sexual abuse, and, later, homelessness, institutionalization, and worse.

Barbara Harris does not have the answers about how to get people off drugs and alcohol and will refer any person who wants help to one of many other organizations that offer drug- and alcohol-related rehabilitation services. The sole focus of CRACK's Project Prevention is to offer options that will result in a decrease in drug- or alcohol-saturated pregnancies.

→ *CRACK, PO Box 74, Stanton, CA 90680 (Phone: 714 236 0217; Fax 714 236 0111; E-mail: Luvbabies@aol.com).*

Adopt-a-Planet

THE ADOPT-A-PLANET PROJECT WAS PILOTED IN THE UK in the 1990s and deserves to be copied internationally. It consists of a national publicity campaign, sponsored by a charitable foundation, that encourages every class in every school to adopt its own particular piece of Planet Earth to caretake on a permanent basis — adopt-a-street, adopt-a-pond, adopt-a-park, adopt-a-river, etc.

Students adopt a particular piece of Planet Earth to caretake on a permanent basis.

The students, as "Planetary Guardians," design and carry out imaginative projects to improve their adopted spot. The area chosen should be one that has been vandalized or suffers from graffiti or is similarly damaged or derelict. Prizes of money are awarded to the most successful adoptions.

Past winners have included George Farmer School in Holbeach, Lincolnshire, where the students adopted a disused pond that had become a dumping ground. They got a local contractor to excavate the pond. The students cleared the area and planted shrubs, trees, and wild flower seeds. Police and local farmers helped to keep watch over the area to prevent future dumping, and the students spent their prize money on a bird table, nesting boxes, and benches.

Five- and six-year-olds at Longstone Infants School in Saltash, Cornwall, adopted a local playground that had been vandalized, clearing up the rubbish, sanding off the graffiti, painting a mural, planting daffodils, and fundraising through carol-singing for a new waste bin.

To enter the Adopt-a-Planet competition, a class simply registers its project with the organizing body as soon as possible after it has chosen a spot to adopt. Then it sends progress reports, saying how it has improved the area chosen, and includes before - and after - pictures.

The idea is that each class adopts its spot on a permanent basis, with the class teacher passing the project on to newcomers year by year.

The criteria according to which winners of prize money and certificates are chosen include the following:

- How imaginative has the class been in designing and carrying out its project?
- How successful have the students been in focusing on the anti-vandalism aspect?
- To what extent have they shown perseverance?
- How successful have they been in gaining support locally or in fundraising for their project or in lobbying the authorities if required?
- To what extent have they developed their Planetary Guardian image (badges, clothes, signs, etc.) or put their work in a wider context?
- What evidence is there of coverage of their efforts in the local media?
- How good is the material submitted (drawings, progress reports, etc.)?

➔ *Adopt-a-Planet is run by the Council for Posterity (an environmental organization that tries to protect the interests of future generations), 20 Heber Road, London NW2 6AA, UK (Phone: Int.+44 [0]20 8208 2853; Fax: Int.+44 [0]20 8452 6434; E-mail: rhino@dial.pipex.com). The pilot project was launched with initial funding from the Gulbenkian Foundation and seeks long-term funding.*

Aids – Why I survive it

Nina Markoff Asistent

Summarized from *Why I survive AIDS: One woman's inspiring recovery — and the techniques she uses to help others* by Nina Markoff Asistent with Paul Duffy (published by Simon and Schuster/Fireside).

In November 1985 I tested positive for the human immune deficiency virus (HIV) and was diagnosed with AIDS-related complex (ARC). I had been infected by my lover Nado, who was unaware that he was carrying the virus. In reaction to my diagnosis I vacillated between deep numbness and extreme rage. Ultimately I surrendered and accepted the unacceptable: death. In that instant, I recognized that I could no longer pretend that I was not personally accountable for my physical condition. I will always be grateful to my doctor for admitting that there was nothing he could do, because his honesty forced me to take responsibility for my own life.

I could no longer pretend that I was not personally accountable for my physical condition.

I realized that I had a finite number of days to live — approximately 500 if I was lucky. Each day was very precious, so I rearranged my priorities and put myself on the top of the list.

Up until that point in my life, I had always denied my needs, playing the role of the caretaker to my parents, my husband, my children, and even my spiritual master. Having nothing left to lose, I decided to use my disease as a final opportunity for learning and growth, instead of being victimized by it. I embarked on a journey to discover who I was, not in relation to the world outside, but in terms of my true essence within. It was the beginning of the most important journey of my life.

Back in 1985, due to the hysteria of the media and the medical community, an AIDS-related diagnosis was virtually a death sentence. It is my belief that it is because I totally accepted that I would die, and began living in the moment, that I am still alive today. By May 1986 I was symptomless and in full remission from ARC. To my surprise, I even tested HIV-antibody negative and have remained so ever since.

Here are some of the specific ways I allowed my body to heal itself:

- I learned to live in the moment.
- I reprioritized my life, putting myself at the top of the list.
- I learned how to be committed to myself and created healthy boundaries in my life.
- I slowed down my pace and learned to say yes to the precious gift of life as it was offered to me moment by moment.
- I became a disciple of life rather than of my neurosis.
- I meditated daily for a minimum of one hour, and sometimes for up to three hours.
- I developed a dialog with my inner child and learned to embrace all of her.
- I trusted my healer within.
- I used visualizations and affirmations.
- I exercised daily.
- I changed both my physical and my mental diet, consciously choosing what I would eat, what I would read, and what I would watch at the movies or on TV.
- I carefully chose whom I wanted to spend time with.
- I created an honest and supportive relationship with my doctor and trusted my intuition to abstain from any medication. (That was my personal choice; I don't necessarily advocate it for anyone else.)
- I made sure everything around me, including the day-to-day details of life, measured up to my own personal standards.

AIDS has detonated a bomb under the surface of society with all of its collective fears and judgments. I have not met anyone who has remained indifferent to AIDS. Some may be judgmental, terrified, or even self-righteous about it, while others may be open, compassionate, and sincerely supportive. Either way, everyone has a reaction to it. AIDS has created a healing momentum on our planet. Virtually every level of our society is affected by it. It is the beginning of the drastic change that needs to happen on our planet.

Mother Earth's breath, blood, and flesh have been polluted by parasites called human beings

---

Our planet, Mother Earth, is suffering from AIDS herself. Her breath (our air), her blood (our water), and her flesh (our land) have been polluted by little parasites called human beings. The immune system of our planet has severely deteriorated through years of abuse, neglect, and exploitation. The time bomb is ticking — it is literally our wake-up call.

I believe that AIDS is the most powerful transformational tool that has ever been available to us on a mass level. It is forcing us to reevaluate the entire foundation of life as we know it. It is shaking the medical community and its related industries; it is affecting the educational and judicial systems. It is forcing us to question our values, our morals, and our identities. It is challenging us to treat our fellow human beings with compassion and understanding. This is the message of AIDS.

Allotments for the unemployed

DEDA FRANCIS

IN THE GOOD OLD DAYS IN THE UK, citizens had to go on a waiting list to get an allotment, their small piece of land for growing vegetables. Not anymore. Now frozen vegetables have come into their own, with the result that there are many vacant allotments. Some of these are threatened with development. These green oases are lungs in our cities and we must keep them.

Frozen vegetables have come into their own, with the result that there are many vacant allotments.

With the help of a friend (we each put in £50 at the outset), I started Allotments for the Unemployed. We helped with rents, tools, and seeds. The latter I bought at a discount from a friendly garden center. Tools came from army surplus, sales, and friends. All the project needed was a little spare cash and a contact with the unemployed. The local press and Friends of the Earth helped with publicity.

A productive allotment can greatly reduce a family's food bill.

How it works is this: an unemployed person calls at the Norwich Claimants Union and sees our poster. I send him to the appropriate City Hall department to get an allotment near his home. Then he sends me the bill, which I pay to City Hall. In the first season two allotments were rented, and in the second season, four allotments.

A productive allotment can greatly reduce a family's food bill and provides fresh organically grown vegetables. It can also be the source of much pleasure and social life (allotments are friendly places). In addition to all that, allotments make excellent picnic sites. In fact, every urban family needs one.

So let's save our allotments and at the same time help the unemployed.

→ *Deda Francis, 11 Mill Road, Reedham, Norwich NR13 3TL, UK.*

Ambulance run by teenagers

From items in the *National Enquirer, Parade Magazine,* and the *Darien News Review,* all monitored by Roger Knights.

SINCE THE 1970S THE SECONDARY SCHOOL KIDS in Darien, Connecticut, have run Boy Scout Explorer Post 53, with three 24-hour ambulances for the population of 20,000. The squad has about 30 boys and 30 girls and accepts only about one out of ten of those who apply to join. The students work in the radio room from age 14, and at 15 they are promoted to rider on the ambulance. During these first two years, a student is also putting in 150 hours of training to become an Emergency Medical Technician who can drive the ambulance and perform a variety of lifesaving techniques, from applying splints to broken bones to handling severe wounds and burns.

Post 53 is the brainchild of John "Bud" Doble, a former advertising executive, and his then-teenage son, who thought a rescue-oriented Explorer Scout project could teach young people about the dangers of drugs and alcohol by helping those injured in drug-related accidents. Several other fathers with teenage sons joined in. In the beginning, the fledgling emergency service had to prove itself to the community. "When I came in, police used to run the ambulance," recalls Lt. James Winn, a veteran of the police department and a former Post 53 advisor. "At first there was reluctance, but it didn't take long for the men to realize that the kids and advisors really know what they're doing."

The service handles about a thousand calls a year, referred to them by the Darien Police Department. An adult supervisor is always on hand, but the teenagers take charge.

"I've been on calls where it looked like we had lost the victim," said Jamie Green, 17. "On one occasion an older man had stopped breathing and we couldn't detect a pulse. We started CPR immediately, and within two minutes we had him breathing on his own. Knowing you actually saved a life is the greatest satisfaction in the world."

The students wear pagers that go off in an emergency, calling them from their homes at night or out of class during the day.

When not at headquarters, the students wear pagers that go off in an emergency, calling them from their homes at night or out of class during the day. The student driver on duty drives the ambulance wherever he goes so that he can respond immediately and meet up with the others at the accident.

The group's $120,000 annual budget comes from donations. The service is praised by the medical professionals. Dr. Dorothy Turnbull, Stamford Hospital's director of emergency services, says: "They're as good as any professional operation in the state."

Twenty-eight graduates of the program are now practicing medicine, including Doble's daughter Lisa, an anesthesiologist in Boston.

Appreciation lists enhance self-esteem

Summarized from a letter to the *Seattle Times* "Dear Abby" column by Sister H.P.M., St. Paul, Minnesota, entitled "List that everyone saved teaches a valuable lesson," monitored by Roger Knights.

WHEN EACH PERSON IN A GROUP is given a list of the positive things said about them by the others, it can have immense long-term value in enhancing feelings of self-esteem.

A young math teacher in a junior high school was dealing with a stressed and frustrated group of students who were carping at each other.

She told them to write down the nicest thing they could say about each other.

She asked the students to take some blank paper and to list the names of the other pupils, leaving a space after each name. Then she told them to write down the nicest thing they could say about each of their classmates. The teacher then wrote the name of each student on a separate sheet of paper and listed what the others had said about that individual.

The exercise was never mentioned again, but it had accomplished its purpose. The students felt better about themselves and each other and realized that their qualities were appreciated.

Years later, at the funeral of one of her ex-students who died in Vietnam, the teacher was told by the parents that the young man had been carrying in his wallet the list of all the good things his classmates had said about him. It transpired that the other ex-students at the funeral had also saved and treasured their lists.

"That's when I finally sat down and cried," writes the teacher. "The lesson my former students taught me that day became a standard in every class I taught for the rest of my teaching career."

ApprenticeMaster Alliance

THE APPRENTICEMASTER ALLIANCE, which was launched in the UK in 1994 (following a since-defunct San Francisco model), links apprentices — those wishing either to learn a new skill or trade or to supplement an existing one — with "masters" who wish to train an apprentice in their field of expertise. The masters are usually small businesses, but they may also be independent artisans whose output can be significantly increased by the engagement of an apprentice.

Apprentices may be school leavers or graduates, unemployed persons or those seeking a career change. Either way, the scheme fulfills a vital function by facilitating the possibility of "hands-on" learning without the risk and expense of courses, though some apprentices manage to work around a course or part-time employment. In a competitive job market, where work experience is frequently necessary but invariably difficult to acquire, the apprentice can expect to learn valuable skills firsthand, which may lead to full-time, salaried employment with the master or elsewhere within the trade.

Masters are able to choose the apprentice who fits the specifications from as far away as Australia.

In return, masters benefit from the help and commitment of their apprentices and any prior experience they may be able to contribute, where paid assistants may be untenable. Further, the accessibility of the information on the website, and the consequent level of interest generated by a number of apprentice positions, means that masters are frequently able to choose the apprentice who fits the precise specifications from a group of candidates, some from as far away as Australia. As one master put it, "It's great to have all these people interested and contacting me without me having to go out and find them."

The ApprenticeMaster Alliance maintains a Directory of Masters listing 124 masters with skills as varied as architecture, woodland management, fine art silk painting, and puppet making. Each entry on the website, which can be accessed directly by the would-be apprentice, provides details of the position. The masters give profiles of their businesses, the aptitudes and experience they're looking for in an apprentice, and the terms they are offering.

When you match up someone who really wants to teach with someone who really wants to learn, it is one of the finest one-to-one relationships.

No charge is made to either the master or the apprentice. ApprenticeMaster Alliance is administered by the Institute for Social Inventions and is a project of the registered charity Fourth World Educational and Research Association Trust.

Although based in the UK, it is beginning to take on masters from all over the world. John Beasley is a professional sculptor working from his home in the rainforest near Kuranda, North Queensland, Australia. "The scheme has operated extremely successfully for me," he writes. "I have had approximately 30 applications, mostly from the UK but a few from the USA and Canada and from Europe. I am currently working with my third apprentice."

Rachel, his first apprentice, reports: "I started with sanding and was gradually introduced to more and more power tools, culminating in chain saws. I worked on a large number of his sculptures (apparently helping him to double his output) and also produced a sculpture of my own, of which I am very proud. Since returning I have turned my greenhouse into a small, but adequate, workshop."

These successful matchings are a vindication of the ApprenticeMaster Alliance's belief that when you match up someone who really wants to teach with someone who really wants to learn, it is one of the finest one-to-one relationships.

→ *ApprenticeMaster Alliance, 20 Heber Road, London NW2 6AA, UK (Phone: Int.+44 [0]20 8208 2853; Fax: Int.+44 [0]20 8452 6434; E-mail: rhino@dial.pipex.com; Web: www.apprentice.org.uk).*

A to Z avenue of trees to aid in learning tree names

NICHOLAS ALBERY

MANY CHILDREN AND ADULTS living in cities are remarkably ignorant about trees. A suitable project to counter this ignorance would be an "A to Z"

avenue of the most common trees, located in an urban park or on a site readily accessible from a city, with each tree along the avenue in the alphabetical
order of its common name (with variants going off sideways). Trees would be
labeled with their common and Latin names.

**At the start would be acacia, alder, almond, apple, and ash,
and at the end would be walnut, wellingtonia,
whitebeam, willow, and yew.**

Visitors would find it easier identifying and remembering trees from
knowing their position in the avenue — for instance, at the start would be
acacia, alder, almond, apple, and ash, and at the end would be walnut,
wellingtonia, whitebeam, willow, and yew.

Depending on the space available and the ground conditions, there
could be between 35 trees (for instance, just native trees) and 500 trees
(including the more exotic ones from around the world). If the trees were
spaced at least 50 feet (15 meters) apart, the avenue would need to be
between about 790 feet (240 meters) and 3,950 feet (1,200 meters) long and
stretching out 215 feet (65 meters) to each side (a total width for the project
of about 460 feet [140 meters]).

Ideally, the avenue would lead to a striking building of some kind, like
the Pagoda avenue at Kew Gardens (in London, UK), that would incorporate
a cafe and multimedia tree study center. Such a project would take 50 to 100
years to reach maturity, but would become a site that every school would
want to visit.

→ *Please send feedback to The Institute for Social Inventions, 20 Heber Road,
London NW2 6AA, UK (Phone: Int.+44 [0]20 8208 2853; Fax: Int.+44 [0]20
8452 6434; E-mail: rhino@dial.pipex.com; Web: www.globalideasbank.org).*

Attitude Factor —
Extend your life by changing the way you think

The Attitude Factor: Extend Your Life by Changing the Way you Think is an innovative book by Thomas Blakeslee (published by Thorsons, an imprint of
Harper Collins). It introduces a radical internet experiment to replicate longevi-
ty research from Germany — research which demonstrated that a healthy
mental attitude is a far better predictor of long life than a healthy lifestyle.

The book's associated website <www.attitudefactor.com> provides people with tests to measure their well-being, sense of pleasure, and self-regulation. It also provides a tailor-made set of exercises to help people improve
their attitudes in these departments.

And by following up those tested, in future years, to see who is still alive and well, Blakeslee hopes to be able to test the wider applicability of the German findings.

Blakeslee's work could revolutionize the way society approaches education, health promotion, and the treatment of the elderly, while greatly increasing people's sense of well-being.

By extending, internationalizing, and popularizing this Heidelberg research, Blakeslee's work could revolutionize the way society approaches education, health promotion, and the treatment of the elderly, while greatly increasing people's sense of happiness and well-being. There are very few other individuals in history for whom the same claim could be made.

These people smoked 20 or more cigarettes a day and outlived a group with healthy lifestyles but poor self-regulation by 8.5 years.

About 300 of the people in self-regulation experiments organized by Dr. Ronald Grossarth-Maticek in Heidelberg had good scores on self-regulation but very unhealthy lifestyles, as Blakeslee illustrates: "For at least ten years these people smoked 20 or more cigarettes a day and drank over two ounces of alcohol a day. They also had an unhealthy diet and did little exercise. In spite of their unhealthy lifestyles, this group outlived a group with healthy lifestyles but poor self-regulation by 8.5 years. Clearly self-regulation has a health impact that is stronger than — and goes much deeper than — healthy habits alone. Healthy lifestyle was defined in this experiment as no smoking or drinking, good diet, and at least 1.5 hours of exercise a day."

"Feelings of pleasure and well-being are vital to good health," argues Blakeslee. "These feelings originate in the ancient, non-verbal parts of the brain that we share with lower animals through our common evolutionary past. This part of the brain also interacts with body systems which control blood pressure and immune responses. When your basic needs are met, your body's systems work at peak efficiency.

Feelings of well-being originate in the non-verbal parts of the brain that interact with body immune responses.

"When these same needs are frustrated," says Blakeslee, "you may have chronic feelings of hopelessness, which drive your body's systems into a kind of 'self-destruct mode' where diseases and cancer can easily get a foothold, and heart disease, strokes, and accidents become more likely. Your ability to think logically in words is a powerful ability which also has the power to ruin your health if it is directed at goals which are actually at odds with your basic needs."

Self-regulation, as defined by Blakeslee, describes our ability to regulate behavior to maximize long-term pleasure and well-being. It means that you pay attention to the results of your behavior and make corrective adjustments as required. Blakeslee's thermostat analogy is helpful, for just as a thermostat regulates the temperature in a building and, when broken, causes a rise in room temperature, habitual behaviors which produce poor results are repeated endlessly when a breakdown in self-regulation occurs.

Self-regulation means that you regulate your behavior to maximize well-being, making corrective adjustments as needed.

The result of such a behavioral rut is disastrous. Repeated failure to adjust response to outcome results in an increasingly frangible state of health, both mental and physical. Blakeslee believes the self-regulation test scores represent an accurate predictor of future health because those able to self-regulate effectively will be better able to optimize their long-term well-being.

"Evolution works by culling the weak and preserving the strong," he says. "Mating battles in some species allow only the strongest to reproduce. Predators cull the weak in others. Perhaps the weakening of the human immune system by feelings of helplessness is nature's way of culling the outcasts and the unsuccessful to improve the breed."

Their probability of dying actually
doubled in the week after they had lost their mate.

Blakeslee cites a Finnish study which examined the health records of 96,000 widowed people and found that their probability of dying actually doubled in the week after they had lost their mate. "Feelings of pleasure and well-being are messages from the ancient parts of your brain and limbic system that you are thriving and your immune system is running at peak efficiency," he says, "while feelings of hopelessness indicate the opposite."

Risk taking

According to Blakeslee, each time you confront a minor risk with boldness, you boost your confidence and sense of control and effectively add days to you life; conversely, fearful attitudes have the power to substantially limit your life span. As the insurance industry and safety engineers have developed extensive tables of the actual risks involved in living, your calculated life expectancy can be determined by subtracting Loss of Life Expectancy numbers (expressed in days) from your basic life expectancy as determined by age and sex. For example, spending one year pursuing a hang-gliding hobby takes 25 days off your life expectancy.

"Attitude jogging," as prescribed by Blakeslee, is clearly a fruitful way of redirecting your efforts to achieve a prolonged, healthier life. His study indicates that your attitude factor, as determined by your scores on the tests, has the greatest capacity for adding years of good health and happiness to your life and is far more beneficial than avoiding, and potentially worrying about, small risks.

Good social connections can make a nine-year gain in your life expectancy.

Good social connections have been found to make a 3,285-day (nine-year) gain in life expectancy, according to Blakeslee, with marriage adding an average five years. "If avoiding second-hand smoke (50 days loss of life expectancy) is limiting your social life," he says, "you are certainly shortening your life by trying to lengthen it."

Attitude jogging

Here is a sample selection from the hundreds of exercises that Blakeslee suggests for improving your attitude factor:

- Make a list of things you used to enjoy in your youth.

- Make a commitment pact with a close friend or lover to help each other work on attitudes.

- Try foods at an ethnic restaurant that you have previously avoided because you consider the food "creepy."

- Count your laughs for a whole day. A researcher found that small children laugh an average of 450 times a day, while adults average only 50.

- Watch the video *Two for the Road*, with Audrey Hepburn and Albert Finney. The contrast between their joyfully living as backpackers in their youth and their present fussing about luxury hotel conditions vividly demonstrates what attitude jogging is all about.

Next time a friend invites you to do something challenging, say yes and then push through any temptations to find excuses to cancel.

- Next time a friend invites you to do something challenging, say yes and then push through any temptations to find excuses to cancel or drop out.

- Does drinking alcohol give you pleasure and improve your ability to communicate your feelings? If the answer is yes, pour yourself a drink and enjoy!

If you are currently living alone, think how you could share your accommodation with a good friend.

- People are social animals. If you are currently living alone, think how you could share your accommodation with a good friend or relative.

- Volunteer to work on some kind of useful cause where you can directly help others.

- Dance to music with no thought of how you look. Let your body naturally express its response to the music.

→ *Thomas Blakeslee lives in California (E-mail: TBlakeslee@attitudefactor.com; Web: www.attitudefactor.com).*

Audience discussion period after films

Nicholas Albery

I PROPOSE THAT MOVIE THEATERS HAVE a 15-minute period at the end of a film, where the audience is encouraged to remain and to discuss the film it has just seen, perhaps with the discussion moderated by a member of the theater's staff. A stimulating discussion could be had while the film was still fresh in the mind, and new friendships might be formed, which could be continued afterwards in a nearby cafe or bar. This might also make the job of working at the theater more interesting and could help some of those living in a city to feel less lonely or alienated.

I often find myself listening to other people's comments as I am leaving the theater.

I often find myself listening, fascinated, to other people's comments as I am leaving the theater. But the discussion of a film tends to die out quickly when you are part of a couple or in a small group, as there are not enough comments generated or the focus is not sufficiently agreed upon to sustain that particular topic of conversation. A big audience could have a much more lively and intense dynamic, with many diverse perspectives.

At the very least, the theater could put up a notice or flash up a screen just before the film starts, saying that those who wish to discuss the film afterwards can go to such-and-such cafe nearby and make themselves known to the staff, who will be happy to sit would-be debaters together. Or the viewers could be identified by lapel badges made available by the theater (further free publicity for the film and the theater).

Everyone would gain: the theater would become known as a trigger for lively meetings, the audience would be able to interact more, and the nearby cafe would gain business.

In the meantime, I have helped to create the website <www.DoBe.org> which will eventually have sections for every city in the world, where people can advertise for others to join them on outings to films, and in a discussion of the film over a meal or drink afterwards.

→ *Please send feedback to The Institute for Social Inventions, 20 Heber Road, London NW2 6AA, UK (Phone: Int.+44 [0]20 8208 2853; Fax: Int.+44 [0]20 8452 6434; E-mail: rhino@dial.pipex.com).*

B

Benefits of a compulsory switch from cash to e-cash

Summarized from an article by Dave Birch, in *New European* entitled "Do you take cash? The technology of money isn't neutral".

THE TECHNOLOGY OF ELECTRONIC MONEY ("E-CASH"), spurred on by the internet, is developing rapidly – there is now Mondex, VisaCash, Geld Karten (in Germany), Proton (in Belgium), DigiCash, and CyberCash (on the internet).

If everyone used e-cash, transaction costs for society as a whole would be lowered, simply because e-cash is cheaper to handle than notes and coins.

What about those who cannot or will not move to e-cash? There are, essentially, three options:

1. People should be allowed to continue to use notes and coins at their own expense; or
2. People should be allowed to continue to do so but at someone else's expense; or

3. People should not be allowed to continue to use physical cash.

People should not be allowed to continue to use physical cash.

While options 1 or 2 might seem to be immediately compatible with the conservatism of prevailing attitudes and while certain lobby groups (representing the aged, the poor, and so forth) might prefer option 2 over option 1, it might well be the case that relinquishing notes and coins altogether — extreme though that may seem — is the only realistic future.

Financial institutions could be obliged to provide a new form of service to everyone over 16.

Universal service in the e-cash context might mean that certain financial institutions could, for example, be obliged to provide a new form of service to everyone over 16, comprising an interest-bearing account and an e-purse: no statements, no checkbook, no debit card — nothing but a place to pay e-cash in and draw e-cash out.

This basic account could be provided free of charge, paid for with the money saved by turning bank branches into video game arcades and melting down ATMs for scrap metal.

Since every telephone and TV set might become a bank branch, people in depressed or remote areas would actually have better access to banking services than they do now.

✦ *David Birch (E-mail: daveb@hypenon.co.uk) is director of Consult Hyperion, an information technology management consultancy company, editorial board member of the* **Financial Times Virtual Conference Report** *and a correspondent for the* **Online Journal of Internet Banking and Commerce.**

✦ **New European,** *14-16 Carround Road, London SW8 1JT, UK.*

Bidding for the right to watch TV programs

ROBIN HANSON
The following is summarized from an e-mail message to the Alternative Institutions discussion group on the internet. (To subscribe to this online discussion group, send a request to <AltInst-request@cco.caltech.edu>; the response may take up to two business days.)

WHEN I WAS A KID THERE WAS ONLY ONE TV IN THE HOUSE, and my two brothers and I had differing opinions on what programs to watch and when. My parents got tired of trying to arbitrate every dispute, so my father implemented a succession of various systems to deal with the problem. We tried voting on it, giving each person standard times, and I forget what else.

TV time is a nice laboratory to teach children about the possibility of alternative institutions.

The alternative I enjoyed most consisted of handing out so many points to each child every week and having us bid for the right to choose each half hour.

I can't really tell you this is the best system — I remember so little. But I can tell you that TV time is a nice laboratory to teach children about the possibility of alternative institutions and to let them try out different ones. I think that experience was formative for me in leading to my current interest in alternative institutions.

➔ *Robin Hanson, assistant professor of Economics, George Mason University, MS• 1D3, Carow Hall, Fairfax VA 22030-4444 (Phone: 703 993 2326; Fax: 703 993 2323; E-mail: rhanson@gmu.edu; Web: http://hanson.gmu. edu/home.html).*

Bikes needing repair donated to developing countries

Summarized from the Re-Cycle website <www.re-cycle.org>.

WHILE MERLIN MATTHEWS WAS STUDYING at the London School of Economics, he acquired the nickname Dr Bike, fixing bikes and running bike repair workshops in exchange for beers on Friday evenings.

In due course he was approached for advice about starting up a bike factory in Haiti that aimed to provide cheap, pollution-free transport for the masses. Merlin was eager to get involved, as he knew that in the UK there were large numbers of bikes being thrown away that could be fixed.

He aimed to set up a project on his own and envisaged establishing a source of bikes in the UK, then spending most of his time in Haiti, running the workshop. Over time, he realized that he would be of more use to the Haitians and people in other countries if he spent most of the time in the UK, fundraising and facilitating the collection and shipping of bikes.

Since then, Re-Cycle has linked up with three US groups — ITDP, Bikes Not Bombs, and the International Bicycle Fund — to teach local people how to repair and maintain bikes to improve their lives in a sustainable manner.

Re-Cycle celebrated having shipped over 3,000 bicycles to five countries.

This year Re-Cycle celebrated having shipped over 3,000 bicycles to five countries, among them Sierra Leone, Zambia, and Nigeria. Its efforts will be assisted in the future by Royal Mail's agreement to donate some 4,500 old bikes a year.

→ *Re-Cycle, 60 High St, West Mersea, Essex CO5 8JE, UK (Phone: Int.+44 [0]1206 382207; Cell: 0797 073 1530; E-mail: info@re-cycle.org).*

→ *For details of other organizations doing similar work, see <www.re-cycle.org/ Links/Our_Partners/our_partners.html>.*

Book pals

STEPHEN ROGERS

HAVE YOU GOT FAVORITE BOOKS that you would love to discuss in depth with other enthusiasts? Selected library books could have a contact sheet pasted in the back. People wanting to meet those drawn to the same work could enter their names and contact information (phone number, e-mail).

Selected library books could have a contact sheet pasted in the back. People wanting to meet those drawn to the same work could enter their names and contact information.

I have often felt the urge to get in touch with those who have underlined and dog-eared the very pages I found significant. My proposal would be the next best thing — it would certainly provide a new means by which people could relate to each other.

Editorial comment

This idea would add interest and value to amazon.com and other web bookshops. People could go to their favorite book in the web shop and sign up to join or form an online club with others who are likewise passionate about the book.

→ *Stephen Rogers, 7 Avenue des Eglantines 24, 1970 Wezembeek-Oppern, Belgium.*

Boyfriend pays $20 deposit for date

Extracted from an item by Scott Martin in *Reader's Digest,* monitored by Roger Knights.

MY CO-WORKER, whose daughters are now of dating age, is determined to keep a rein on their boyfriends. So he requires a $20 deposit as a prerequisite for a date with one of his daughters. If the girl is not back by midnight, the money is his.

The Brain Exchange

Summarized in part from the website <www.thebrainexchange.com>.

JOY-LILY, CO-FOUNDER WITH LEE GLICKSTEIN of the San Francisco Brain Exchange, writes: "I define creativity as 'the artful and innovative solving of problems in all spheres of life.' There are several ways to solve problems creatively. My personal favorite is to get help from other people. Why struggle alone? The most enjoyable and dynamic form of group problem-solving I have found is brainstorming — the process where quantities of ideas are offered with no criticism. Only later are the ideas analyzed to find realistic solutions."

A monthly, open-ended brainstorming group for women meeting to deal with any issue

---

There are currently a number of Brain Exchange groups meeting in California, discussing whatever problems people care to bring with them. For instance, Joy-Lily facilitates brainstorming meetings for men and women once a fortnight in San Francisco; in East Bay, Susan Goldstein and Anita Goldstein facilitate a monthly, open-ended brainstorming group for women meeting to deal with issues such as retirement, a new job or relationship, or even the practicalities of finding a new house or baby-sitter.

To others trying to set up a brainstorming group in their own localities, Joy-Lily has this advice to offer:

- Introduce it to friends as a game.

- Advertise in newspapers and local business publications.

- Speak with the Chamber of Commerce and other business organizations.

- Stick with a regular meeting schedule no matter how small you start, and you will attract the right people.

- Invite journalists. It's a good story for them.

- Call a meeting to discuss a particular local problem.

- Make it a big event by flying in famous brainstormers to lead a meeting.

Throw a potluck where people can bring their favorite food and favorite problem.

- Throw a potluck where people can bring their favorite food and favorite problem.
- Have a meeting on the subject of how to meet romantic partners.
- Brainstorm on a radio call-in show.

Joy-Lily suggests you try brainstorming with your friends, family, or co-workers. Here are her guidelines:

1. Keep ideas brief; don't tell stories.
2. Give only one idea per turn.
3. Speak in the imperative ("do this, try that" instead of "have you considered ... ?").
4. Make it safe by not criticizing or "yes butting" anybody's idea (including your own before you speak).
5. Make your thinking as funny or as silly as possible.
6. Piggyback (build) on previous ideas freely.
7. When it's your question, write down all ideas without evaluating them, and don't speak during the brainstorm.

(Editors' Note: Many perfectly successful brainstorming groups do not follow guidelines 2, 3, or 7.)

We notice that some people habitually critique ideas thrown their way. Whether with frowns or "I've-tried-that-already," these prejudgers cast a stifling gloom over the room. But anyone who accepts all suggestions as gifts (you wouldn't say "I have one of those already, yuck") has already solved the bulk of the problem.

Lee follows up the brainstorming with an evaluation process in which the following four questions are asked, with ideas offered, brainstorm-style:

1. What's good about this idea?
2. What's wrong with this idea?
3. How can these problems be overcome?
4. What new ideas are suggested by this evaluation process?

→ *For more information on the Brain Exchange, e-mail Joy-Lily at <sfbrainexchange@yahoo.com> or Anita at <brainexchange@aol.com>, or see <www.thebrainexchange.com/links.html> for details of the other groups.*

B

Brazilian city where neighborhood groups allocate budget

Summarized from an e-mail Tom Atlee sent to the Institute and from an article entitled "The Experience of the Participative Budget in Porto Alegre, Brazil" on the UNESCO website <www.unesco.org/most/southa13.htm>.

IN 1989 THE CITY OF PORTO ALEGRE CAME UP WITH A RADICAL SOLUTION to its major problems of unaccountability and extreme poverty: a participative budget. For the last decade, the people of the city have been deciding how the budget for public works should be allocated. Neighborhood groups propose projects, and people from community groups and non-profit organizations, who have been elected by their neighbors, decide which projects will go ahead. In some cases the community delegates also oversee implementation of the final projects. This has had the triple result of avoiding corruption and the mismanagement of funds, improving concrete matters on the ground, and drastically increasing democratic participation in the process.

The percentage of the population served by the sewerage system has leapt from 46 percent to 85 percent, and 65,000 more homes now have a basic water supply.

Since this budget system came into force, there have been some startling results. The percentage of the population served by the sewerage system has leapt from 46 percent to 85 percent, and 65,000 more homes now have a basic water supply. In the poorest sections of the city, 15 to 20 miles (25 to 30 kilometers) of street are paved each year, while drainage and public lighting have both risen to the head of the priority list. The participative budget has had a massive impact in education, too, with new focused funding resulting in a doubling of the total number of enrollments between 1988 and 1995 alone. Perhaps the most dramatic effect of all, though, has been on the number of people involved in the whole process. Tens of thousands of people regularly attend the two public assemblies each year, where they elect the delegates and check up on last year's achievements, and there are a huge number of local associations and popular organizations that have received overdue representation.

The system is viewed as a success not only by the citizens of Porto Alegre (who recently gave it an 85 percent approval rating in a poll), but also by other cities in South America. Fifty other cities in Brazil, Argentina, and Uruguay are putting the same budget system into place, and the practice seems destined to spread. Porto Alegre should be an example to everyone of what can be achieved when the people whom policies affect are allowed to be truly involved in the making, funding, and effecting of those policies.

→ *Porto Alegre Council can be contacted at Porto Alegre City Hall, Praca Montevideo 10-11/4 andar, Porto Alegre, Rio Grande do Sul, Brazil 90010-170 (Phone: Int.+55 [0]51 224 4400; Fax: Int.+55 [0]51 228 8725; E-mail: zanotta@procempa.tche.br).*

→ *Tom Atlee is at the Co-Intelligence Institute, PO Box 493, Eugene, OR 97440 (E-mail: cii@igc.org; Web: www.co-intelligence.org).*

Building a retreat to refresh the spirit

G. LAWSON DRINKARD III

Summarized from an article in *New Age* journal, monitored by Roger Knights, and from *Retreats: Handmade Hideaways to Refresh the Spirit* (published by Gibbs Smith).

WHETHER IT IS a cottage in your backyard, a cabin in the mountains, or simply an attic room, any solitary space can become a soothing retreat for your soul.

I can just barely conjure up an image of the first retreat I remember, which I built when I was around eight years old with my then best friend, Pete Obenschain, and his pesky little brother, Tommy. From somewhere in our Virginia small-town neighborhood we salvaged enough barely rotting planks to build a wooden box that was just big enough to hold three or four small boys squeezed tightly together, dressed in whatever costumes represented our dreams on that particular day. In our fantasy world, this rickety wooden box was a sacred place, a place where pacts were made, plans were hatched, and neighborhood assaults were launched. It was a private place, a hands-off place, a place off-limits to moms, where girls didn't dare to enter.

Where do people go and what do they do when they want to refresh their spirits?

My childhood was filled with adventures in small spaces, and those moments have stuck like pine pitch to the deep recesses of my psyche. So after a formal education in architecture at the University of Virginia, I found myself part owner of a start-up architecture firm in Charlottesville, Virginia. I set out on a quest to discover the answers to the following question:Where do people go and what do they do when they want to get away from it all, to reflect, to question, to rest their minds and refresh their spirits, to lose themselves in order to find themselves again?

At first my investigations were mostly about the physical places of retreat — about the rooms, spaces, buildings, or shelters set aside to afford people seclusion, privacy, peace, and quiet. These retreats could be described with such words as "refuge," "haven," "hideout," and "sanctuary." They could take the form of cabins, cottages, caves, trailers, tents, or shacks. But while on this voyage of discovery, I learned that people and place are inextricably linked together. For me, a retreat is not a location; it is a state of mind. It is not a destination, but rather a journey. If you decide to make a place for your body's relaxation and your spirit's refreshment, you have in store many moments of inspiration, rest, creativity, and joy.

A retreat is not a location; it is a state of mind.

Where does one begin when setting out to create a personal retreat space? With a dream? With a site? With a budget? With a set of drawings? With an existing structure or a pile of old materials? I'd say, start wherever your spirit moves you. No matter where you choose to begin, there are two aspects that will eventually need to be confronted. They are purpose or potential use, and place.

The purpose of a retreat seems obvious. "I just need a place to get away!" people say. For many there is a component of the spirit that demands just that — a place of their own to relax, rest, recharge, and center. Yet it may be helpful to take some time to examine the specific purpose of your own personal retreat. Will it be activity-related, vocation-related, or avocation-related? Will it include skiing, painting, potting, or writing? Should it be solitary or inclusive of others? For some, examining questions like these is just too much work and may inhibit getting started.

One of the key ingredients of the retreat: the chance to question one's self and to evaluate the essence of one's life

---

For others, this kind of probing leads to a deeper understanding of the self and thus begins to capture one of the key ingredients of the retreat: the chance to question one's self and to evaluate the essence of one's life.

Write some lists of aspects of a retreat, or of retreating, that are meaningful to you. Large easel pads work well for this activity because the pages can be hung on the wall for reference as you go along. Consider questions like these:

- For you, what is important about the idea of a retreat?
- What are your special dreams and aspirations for this place?
- What will this retreat make possible for you?
- What will make it possible to have your retreat?
- How will you use your retreat?

- When will you use this place?
- Why will you use your retreat?
- Who will use this place?
- What might you need, or what are you willing to give up, to have a physical place for a retreat?
- What might you need to give up to have time to retreat?
- For you, what is essential about this retreat?
- For you, what is not essential about this retreat?

These questions will probably lead to more. Keep good notes or start a journal. Making sure your retreat meets the criteria you have defined will insure your greater enjoyment of it.

The choice of place for a retreat may be the most important and difficult task for the aspiring retreat builder. Issues to be considered when choosing a place include cost of land, zoning, natural characteristics, and distance from your permanent residence. All of these issues affect other practical questions, such as:

- How long might it take to build?
- How easy or expensive will it be to build?
- How often can the retreat be used?
- What is the hassle factor in getting it built?

Some yearn for the mountains, some for the desert, and some for the sea.

For some, place doesn't seem to matter at all. One place is as good as another. For others, place is everything. The deliberation about where to create your retreat will draw out many clues as to what is meaningful to you about being there. Some yearn for the mountains, some for the desert, and some for the sea. Some want total seclusion and some want a sense of community. Some want snow and some want eternal spring. Many people have fond childhood memories of riverside camps, of summers on grandma and grandpa's farm, or of primitive mountain cabins. These deep impressions have shaped, or will shape, the place and style of their retreat.

Your place can be as close as your backyard, a corner of your pasture, or even the end of your attic or basement. It can be as far away as you are willing to travel to get away and cleanse your spirit.

The following questions may serve as a helpful reference for you as you plan your retreat. By no means should they be considered a definitive list. Rather, they should get you started on your journey.

B

Natural characteristics

- What is the direction of the prevailing winds or breezes?
- What are the views from your retreat — long-range, mid-range, and short-range?
- What are the views of your retreat from adjacent properties?
- How does the sunlight move across the property in each season?
- What is the topography and slope of the property?
- Are there trees and natural formations that need to be considered?
- Is there a potable water source?
- What is the local success rate for drilling, digging, or boring a well?

Utilities

- Is electricity available?
- Is telephone service available? Do you want it?
- Is natural or bottled gas available?
- Is city water available?
- Is there a handy source for firewood?
- Is sewage disposal available?

How close are the nearest neighbors?
How close do you want them to be?

Location

- How far away is your permanent home?
- How far away from the site are the various services you deem necessary (grocery store, medical facility, library, post office, bank, church)?
- How far away are the various building trades and suppliers you will need (concrete, lumber, plumbing, electrical, road grading, septic system)?
- How far away is the nearest fire department (this will affect your property insurance rates)?
- How close are the nearest neighbors? How close do you want them to be?

Bureaucracy Encounter Forms
— Giving bureaucrats a dose of their own paperwork

Summarized from Number 89 in "101 Things to Do 'till the Revolution" by Claire Wolfe, (Loompanics, 1996). <www.loompanics.com>. Monitored by Roger Knights.

IN RESPONSE TO bureaucrats' arrogant requests for personal information, Claire Wolfe and Charles Curley suggest you hand them a copy of a Bureaucracy Encounter Form to give them a taste of their own paperwork. The form should request certain information from personal records. Ask that it be filled out in triplicate and request that the bureaucrats in question fill out a separate form for each request that they themselves have made. A note to the effect that this is all in order to better facilitate the bureaucrat's request is also advised. And, in the true spirit of bureaucratic red tape, there should be no limit on the number of times you use the form.

A sample form could include the following points:

Date: *Location:*

Your name: *Agency(ies) you represent:*

Your business address:

City and county: *Zip code:*

Telephone number: *Your annual salary:*

Your supervisor's name: *Supervisor's telephone number:*

Describe your request in detail: (leave two lines at least here)

Are you required to make this request?

If so, what person or agency required it of you?

Please state what statute, and what section and/or subsection of that statute, authorizes you to make this request:

Please state what law or part of the Constitution authorizes you to make this request:

Have you filled out a form like this for me in the past?

When? Exact date(s):

What will be done with the information you receive from me?

Is this part of a criminal investigation?

Will this become part of a criminal investigation?

I swear (or affirm) under penalty of perjury that the foregoing is true and correct.

Signature

This is just an example. We encourage you to use imagination and creativity to give the Bureaucracy Encounter Form your own personal touch. It's not so much fighting fire with fire as tying the bureaucrats up in their own particular brand of red tape.

B

Burning Man — A festival with no spectators

NICHOLAS ALBERY

The following makes use of information in e-mails from Milena Petrova, on the website <burningman.com>, and from "Burning Man grows up," an article by Brian Doherty in *Reason*. This last was monitored by Roger Knights.

WHAT CAN FESTIVALS elsewhere learn from the annual Burning Man festival in Nevada's Black Rock Desert?

First and foremost, keep the festival small. If it becomes bigger year by year, it inevitably has to transform from being a "temporary autonomous zone," an anarchic free space, into a mob, with all the attendant dangers, such as the eight men crushed to death at the Danish Roskilde festival in 2000.

In the case of Burning Man, the sadly necessary and no doubt sensible rules that have now evolved include no open campfires, no tiki torches, no guns, and no fireworks.

But the interesting rules, which other festivals could with advantage copy, include the following:

- No vending (except for ice sold by kids from the local school) — you bring your own food, water, and shelter for a week. It's a barter economy; people give each other stuff, and no one sells anything. It's a form of self-reliance; you are supposed to be prepared.
- No driving (unless your car is an artwork in itself).
- No unregistered video cameras.

Everyone is supposed to be an active participant rather than a mindless consumer.

- No spectators (everyone is supposed to be an active participant, adding creativity to the event, rather than a mindless consumer). Milena Petrova describes, for instance, how "our mobile bar Barzilla was fantastic, we were in the middle of Gigsville one afternoon drinking, and as people approached and took pictures without permission we'd shout: 'Spectator! Spectator! Approach the bar!' Then Weasel boy, attorney of Gigsville and Magistrate of Fashion, chair of the committee for girls who like boys who dress like girls and senior Barzilla bartender, would read from a bound copy of the Gigsville code of conduct that spectating is not allowed, but the person could become a participant if he (all shout): 'Sing, Dance or Drop Your Pants.' It was funny how many people chose the third option."

Darryl Van Rhey, one of the organizers, has a word of caution to add: "Sometimes I wish we'd never promoted the phrase 'no spectators.' In 1999 there was a fellow who invested hundreds of hours creating a theme camp, but he dressed conventionally. When he walked down his street he was harassed by some people at another camp for not 'participating.' Apparently they thought he should be wearing a costume. Radical self-expression concentrates on giving gifts and inviting others to play, not on some intolerant form of censorship."

The policing of Burning Man festival also offers lessons for other festivals. Real police patrol the site only alongside the festival's own 160 rangers and rarely act without consulting the rangers. The volunteer rangers all yell "We are not cops!" as part of their training, and they are there mainly to be helpful.

Nine days in the desert
To capture something of the atmosphere of the Burning Man festival, here is Milena Petrova's description of her experience of it (from the Institute for Social Inventions' forthcoming book *Seize the Day*, October 2001.).

This haiku (from the BORG-produced video on Burning Man 1998) brings tears to my eyes:

> *Hey, your hair's on fire*
> *Is that some performance art*
> *Or should I get help?*

Came back this morning, after nine days in the desert. I had a great time, a healing experience and initiation into more of life's magic.... The first three days we were entertained by the weather jackassery: tents and shade structures were collapsing in the 100 mph winds, people ran across the playa chasing trash, dust penetrated every fiber of my body, it was cold. My ticket said that I voluntarily assumed the risk of serious injury or death by attending. This was not the fun I was prepared for, but fun anyway, it made me feel strong and confident. I had arrived in Black Rock City, my home.

My most beautiful evening started with a 4 p.m. communion in the church of Holy Fuckin' Shit, and as dusk fell we wandered around, admiring the culture that had emerged out of nothing. Illuminated towers, domes, art, fires, dust storm, there was so much mystique and magic in the air, Black Rock City was amazing. I was wearing my Desert Queen costume and hiding under the veil, feeling small amidst all that beauty, realizing how quickly it becomes obvious in the desert what is good and what is bad, how used I had been to buying stuff and how much I really wanted to make art now, how much creation matters for our civilization. Yes, out in the desert, away from all the cushions that the city life and the mass market had provided for me, there was nothing to take for granted, no existing culture except the one we had brought with us and were prepared to work on during the next seven days.

I felt a strong urge to create something tangible.

Pursuing intellectual goals and living inside my head for most of my life, I didn't have much time, or let's say confidence, for artistic creation. In the environment of Burning Man, however, where there are no definitions, no boundaries, and no judgment, I felt a strong urge to create something tangible, something which does not have to be processed in the context of history or intellectual theorizing.

That's what the art of Burning Man is — direct and immediate. Yield to change, yield to temptation; that's what the entrance signs said and I certainly followed. I also became more aware and involved in the creation of the community. With Gigsville, everyone had a number of unique, handmade costumes, art installations, and events. I loved the organic entertainment, fire, fireworks, drumming, making stuff, acting, going away into the open and shouting and screaming, communing with the desert. Time for decompression....

Some more ideas

I have two further suggestions for improving the average festival, although these may not be applicable to Burning Man itself.

- When participants arrive, those controlling the entrance could let them choose a blank badge or label from one of 12 colors, one for each of the astrological birth signs. People could write their actual birthday on this badge. The idea is that you look out for others with the same birthdate (or sign) as you, and you are then part of their tribe or "karass," as Kurt Vonnegut put it, and have responsibilities towards them. The responsibilities could vary, depending on the size of the festival — maybe to have a chat and a drink together; or if there turns out to be a group of you with the same birthday, to go in the sweat lodge together. There always seem to be quite a few disconnected people milling around, and this could help them.

- A talk tent would help too. The playwright Neil Oram used to run what he called a Rap Tent at the green festivals. You could go in and talk with him on a non-trivial level. I'd like to see a quiet area at a festival site with advertised chats for particular times and maybe somebody as master or mistress of ceremonies.

→ *Please send feedback to The Institute for Social Inventions, 20 Heber Road, London NW2 6AA, UK (Phone: Int.+44 [0]20 8208 2853; Fax: Int.+44 [0]20 8452 6434; E-mail: rhino@dial.pipex.com; Web: www.globalideasbank.org).*

→ *For more ideas on improving festivals, see "From mass festivals to human-scale fairs" by the late Nicholas Saunders, on the web at <www.globalideasbank.org/BOV/BV-481.HTML>.*

C

Camping together before marriage

Summarized from an article by Betsy Wade in an unidentified American clipping, monitored by Roger Knights.

HERE'S A PIECE OF ADVICE I FEEL WOULD KEEP MY FRIENDS from contracting any more doomed marriages: Never marry anyone until you have taken an eight-hour train ride together, learned his/her temper in the morning, and gone camping together for a week. I feel that this rule covers all possibilities, including covert alcoholism, deviationist toothpaste-squeezing, and mismatched politics.

Cantonizing the United States of America

GORE VIDAL

Summarized from an interview with Gore Vidal in *Modern Maturity*, monitored by Roger Knights.

Interviewer: You've said that probably the best system of government is Switzerland's cantonal system, in which political powers are divided between the central government and the 26 cantons and half-cantons (states). How might that work in the USA?

> In Switzerland no one likes anybody — and they make it work superbly. They've done it by avoiding federalism.

Vidal: I spent a lot of time in the town of Klosters and observed up close how Switzerland works. You have about 6 million people crammed together in a small place. You have four different tribes: German, French, Italian, and Romansch. You have Catholicism and Protestantism. No one likes anybody — and they make it work superbly. They've done it by carefully avoiding federalism. They have a rotating presidency and nobody ever remembers the president's name. He's in place to go down to the railroad station to meet dignitaries, and that's it. The people have 90 days to call for a referendum to accept or veto any law the government makes.

Interviewer: But Switzerland is so much smaller than the United States. Is there really any comparison?

Vidal: There's a strong movement to split California into three parts. There might be other regional groupings where people would be more at home.

Interviewer: Are you advocating we break up America into separate and autonomous regions? If so, would citizens still be taxed?

There wouldn't be an income tax because there wouldn't be much of a federal government.

Vidal: There wouldn't be an income tax because there wouldn't be much of a federal government. Each regional government would decide how much to send to Washington. They'd say, "We'll pay so much to keep the post office going and so much for printing the money, keeping up the White House, and having a ceremonial President."

Chanting in pregnancy and childbirth

FREDERICK LEBOYER, AUTHOR OF *BIRTH WITHOUT VIOLENCE* (published by Healing Arts Press), which showed childbirth for the first time through the eyes of the newborn, has attempted to launch a second revolution in the way childbirth is envisaged — this time by encouraging the mother to take up Indian chanting and thus to transform pregnancy and childbirth into a spiritual experience.

In essence, Leboyer is suggesting that the mother breathe in deeply and slowly from the belly, chanting a loud pure sound on the outbreath and with the contraction, then waiting at the end of the outbreath for the contraction to be over before breathing in again. Leboyer learned the chanting from the Indian teacher Savitry Nayr.

Nicholas Albery interviewed Leboyer about this approach.

Albery: Is there any culture or society on earth that you know of where chanting has been used by the mothers in pregnancy or birth?

This new connection of pure sound with birth is opening the gate for women into a totally unknown experience.

Leboyer: No. This new connection of pure sound with birth is opening the gate for women into a totally unknown experience.

When a woman is giving birth, she is reborn herself. She goes back to her own birth and can go beyond herself. Her little self merges with the real self, the totality, the one and all. Going through this frightening experience, she comes to the limitations of the small "I;" the ego collapses. She's both herself and the totality.

Albery: Are there signs that the unborn child in pregnancy appreciates the chanting of the mother?

Leboyer: Yes. Very often when the woman has a restless child in the womb, it signifies that the child is unhappy. With the chanting, the mother knows, "My child is different now." She knows because the child moves around less.

Albery: Can you imagine groups of pregnant women getting together to practice chanting?

Leboyer: No. It needs to be a one-to-one relationship, almost like psychoanalysis, it is so intimate. Some women believe you can take six quick lessons before birth, like before taking a car for a drive. But there are things which cannot be taught. All inner experiences are a matter of getting attuned. Little by little you awaken. The disciple is trying to understand and, reading about it, may say "Ah yes," but the teaching can only be the confirmation of personal understanding; it has only this value.

Albery: Does it need to be the specific type of Indian chanting you are describing?

Leboyer: Some people say, "It is very nice to have music in labor, what would you like, Vivaldi or what?" But listening to pure sound is different: a perfect sound includes all its harmonies, it is all sounds put together, just as the rainbow includes all colors. With pure sound you can touch absolute perfection. You need to let the sounds open and awaken within yourself. If women can connect with this level of themselves, the experience of childbirth has another dimension.

**This kind of childbirth cannot happen in hospitals;
the doctor stops the woman from going on her journey.**

This kind of childbirth cannot happen in hospitals. It is only for a few. The doctor stops the woman from going on her journey. He is so afraid. I would never advise women to have a home birth. That is not my business. However, if the woman says, "This is what I want," I would encourage her. There is no right way of giving birth. Everything is itself.

Birth is not something sweet. It is the most intense experience a person can go through. But as long as you fight it, you're finished. Just as the mystics tell of the joy of getting drunkenly flooded with excessive energy, so for the woman it is possible to go through the storm of labor like this, instead of containing the contractions or bearing the pains.

In childbirth, breath is the ultimate. The breathing and contraction become completely attuned. It is a matter of becoming aware that breath and contraction are one and the same movement, in time with the cosmic breath, the breath of the universe. The breath is breathing you; it is a holographic concept of one in the whole, each part a reproduction of the whole.

And during the months of pregnancy, the woman who is so-called expecting is not expecting anymore. She is beyond time. It is a state of grace. There is a field energy around the body. But once pregnancy is institutionalized, the magic is gone; it becomes like a supermarket. It is no longer sacred.

→ *See* **The Art of Breathing** *by Frederick Leboyer (published by Element Books). Leboyer also has a film on this subject,* **The Rite of Birth.**

Citizen juries for considering policy options

Summary of a report entitled "Citizens' Juries: Theory into Practice," published by the Institute for Public Policy Research.

CITIZEN JURIES USE A REPRESENTATIVE SAMPLE OF VOTERS from different constituencies. The participants are briefed in detail on all background and current thinking relating to a particular issue (such as healthcare) and asked to discuss possible solutions, sometimes in a televised group.

Citizen juries use a representative sample of voters
briefed on the background and current thinking
relating to a particular issue.

The system is effective because it involves all citizens in real decision-making with access to all available facts. Views expressed by such a jury can attract the attention of the legislative body since they tend to be representative.

One of the problems with democracy at present is that it does not facilitate this acquisition of information by ordinary people. They are manipulated by politicians and the media alike, and with only one vote in several million feel unable to exercise influence.

The commissioning body must publicize the jury's findings
and must undertake to respond to them.

The Institute of Public Policy Research has test-run a series of five small citizen juries along the lines of similar projects set up in the USA and Germany (in Germany the juries are called "planning cells"). Between 12 and 16 jurors are recruited randomly from various sectors of the community. They are fully briefed with relevant background information and meet key witnesses. The jury then studies the information in small groups, cross-examines the witnesses, and discusses various aspects of an issue. The smaller groups' findings are presented to the whole jury, and the jury's conclusions are presented to the body that commissioned the jury in the first place. The jury's verdict need not be unanimous, nor its proposals binding. However, the commissioning body must publicize the jury's findings and must undertake to respond to them within a given time frame, either by following the recommendations or by setting out publicly its reasons for not doing so.

The studies showed that members of the public were willing to take part in decision-making and were capable of grasping complex issues. The jury format appeared to help the participants achieve a wider, more objective perspective and see issues from others' points of view. Many jurors expressed interest in further involvement at the end of their session.

Juries seemed better for the formulation of guidelines than for concrete, detailed plans.

The juries appeared to work better with newer issues, where views had not become entrenched. They also seemed better for the formulation of guidelines than for concrete, detailed plans. The jury model proved to be a powerful tool for consensus building and for creating a better understanding between members of the public and decision-makers. Further, citizen juries can be used not only by local or national governments, but also by organizations on a smaller scale.

→ *The Institute for Public Policy Research can be contacted at 30-32 Southampton Street, London WC2E 7RA, UK (Phone: Int.+44 [0]20 7 470 6100; E-mail: ippr@easynet.co.uk).*

Clan work parties to do up relatives' homes

Summarized from an article by Elizabeth Rhodes entitled "The family that works together," published in the *Seattle Times*, monitored by Roger Knights.

THE WIDESPREAD HAUGEN CLAN IN THE SEATTLE AREA takes it in turns to host family weekend work parties once every other month; they fulfill both a social and practical purpose. Various members of the clan are, or have been, electricians, carpenters, painters, and wallpaper hangers, and others learn by working together.

They have repainted houses, built patios, done reroofing, and saved themselves many thousands of dollars.

On their various working parties they have repainted houses inside and out, built patios, done reroofing, replaced gutters and windows, remodeled a kitchen — and saved themselves many thousands of dollars in the process.

They recommend the concept to other families or groups with close-knit members: "It's not just getting the family together, but it's getting them together in a productive endeavor."

The rules that they have evolved and that they recommend to other groups are as follows:

- When a member cannot attend a work party for some reason, it is expected that he or she will make up that time.

The family hosting the work party must have all the materials ready, including a large breakfast and dinner.

- The family hosting the work party must have all the work planned and the materials and supplies ready, including a large breakfast and dinner and plenty of snacks and beer.
- Each family pays $10 per month towards amassing a group-owned tool chest of expensive equipment, such as a pressure washer. For smaller tools, all members bring their own, color-coded with spray paint so they can tell who owns what.
- At dinner, each family member — especially the children — is recognized and praised for his or her cooperation that day.

During the work day, the less competent adults may be left to do painting jobs, and younger children may be assigned tasks such as baby-sitting, weeding, general outdoor cleanup, or manhandling wheelbarrows. But even five-year-olds may be given their own tool belts.

As Dustin, aged 13, put it: "At work parties you don't have to do all the hard work yourself, and it's fun to see the whole family and mess around."

Community administration of Brazilian prisons to break the cycle of criminality

Summarized from information sent by Roberto da Silva, founder of Citizenship in Jail.

A PROJECT IN BRAZIL THAT PUTS THE COMMUNITY IN CHARGE of its local prison is hoping to transform the way criminals are treated in the country and to radically alter its flawed prison system. The idea is based on communities running their local prisons and taking responsibility for each prisoner's rehabilitation and care. In this way, the state prison system can be circumvented, riddled as it is with maltreatment and corruption.

The Citizenship in Jail project consists of an architectural plan for 30 prisons, each designed to house 210 prisoners and to be called a Center of Resocialization. In all the cities where the prisons are being built, an association made up of people from the local community has been formed to administer their prison. Each local association has signed an agreement with the government, under which the locals are responsible for the administration of the prison, with the government providing the budget for each prisoner. The community association is then fully responsible for running the prison, including the provision of security, healthcare, education, work, food, and even a chaplain. The prisons in the state of Sao Paulo experimented with this model in 1995, and the success of the scheme should lead to the construction of 15 prisons in 2001 and 15 more in 2002 if all goes as planned.

The scheme is the brainchild of Roberto da Silva, who is also an advisory expery with the United Nations (Latin America Section) on the prevention of crime and the treatment of the criminal. He has become a human rights scholar and expert despite having spent twelve years of his life in care and a further six years in jail. While in prison he met many other adolescents from the care system who had had experiences similar to his own. Da Silva gradually came to believe that the internment of such young children in the draconian care system directly leads to criminal behavior, and on his release he set out to prove this.

Of 370 children in the state care system, 36 percent had become criminals.

He studied a sample of 370 children who were his contemporaries in the state care system, and he found that 36 percent of them had become criminals, committing over 400 crimes (including 40 murders) between them. At the root of their criminal behavior was the government's system, which interned children under the legal condition of "moral abandonment," but only provided them with food and a place to live. Furthermore, the levels of education in the system were very poor, and children often found themselves arbitrarily sent away for little more than minor mischiefs, which only unsettled the child further. The government also never informed many of the children of their brothers and sisters who lived elsewhere in Brazil. Da Silva himself found two of his brothers through his own research, but they knew nothing of him nor of a long-since disappeared elder brother. As well as being kept in prison-like homes, the children were (and are) denied any sort of familial support.

Da Silva went on to take legal proceedings against the government and published a thesis entitled "The Formation of Criminal Identity in Orphan Children," arguing that the treatment of teenagers and children needs to be a priority if the level of crime in Brazil is to fall. This belief engendered the prison project, which places an emphasis on education and human rights for prisoners rather than just focusing on suspicion and punishment. The idea has won a Social Enterprise award from the Ashoka-McKinsey Centre for Social Entrepreneurship, and with an agreement with the state government of Sao Paulo already signed, a full implementation seems to be imminent.

➔ *For more information on the project, see Roberto da Silva's website <www.webtrade.com.br/histpresente> (in Portuguese) or contact him at Rua Tapes 57, Apt. 182 Liberdade, Sao Paulo, Brazil, Cep 01527-050.*

➔ *Details of the Ashoka-McKinsey Social Entrepreneurship Centre can be found at <www.ashoka.org/fellows/global_net_center.cfm>.*

Community grants from young people to young people

MICHAEL NORTON

THE CHANGEMAKERS GRANTS FUND IN THE UK allows young people to act as grantmakers to support community projects developed by young people.

There is growing interest in the idea of youth-led community projects, where young people are invited to respond to issues and needs that concern them by developing their own ideas for a community project, planning the project, resourcing and undertaking it, seeing it through to completion, and then reviewing their experience and learning from it.

What young people do is up to them and can range from the conventional (visiting schemes for the elderly, helping out at a local childcare center) to the highly imaginative (a five-minute play on landmines that a group of 13-year-old boys present at assemblies at local primary schools, the renovation of a piece of wasteland as a BMX track, or a sponsored night in a prison).

Changemakers has been developing this concept and now works in over 80 schools and youth organizations across Britain. There is growing recognition of the value of this approach in developing a sense of engagement among the young people involved, in enhancing their skills of employability as well as in promoting active citizenship.

A fund where young people can go to get their project costs funded

---

To respond to this growing interest and to help promote further community involvement by young people, Changemakers has teamed up with the Prince's Trust, the National Youth Agency, and the Association of Community Trusts and Foundations to create a fund where young people can go to get their project costs funded. This fund, launched in 1999, began on a pilot basis in six or seven areas of the UK and is being extended nationwide.

→ *Michael Norton, executive chair, Changemakers, 9 Mansfield Place, London NW3 1HS, UK (E-mail: norton@civa.prestel.co.uk).*

Compost toilets — A council's incentives

The following is adapted from an item entitled "Tanum declares war on WCs," which appeared in the Norwegian Ideas Bank.

THE MUNICIPAL COUNCIL OF TANUM (population 12,000), on the west coast of Sweden, has used financial incentives to reduce the number of mains toilets in the community.

Tanum is a sparsely populated community with several thousand holiday homes. To connect all the permanent residents, not to mention the summer guests, to sewerage and install modern cleaning plants would have been extremely expensive.

The council was also convinced that the WC was an ecological blunder — instead of returning nutrients to the soil, the toilet uses clean water to wash them out to sea, where they become pollutants (even after partial cleaning). Farmers have to use chemical fertilizers to replace the lost nutrients.

For new homes, they would give ready permission only for composting or urine-separating toilets.

To close the nutrient cycle, politicians in Tanum decided that for new homes they would give ready permission only for composting or urine-separating toilets (meaning toilets where the urine, which contains most of the nutrients, goes into a storage tank). They also decided that people who already had WCs should be encouraged to replace them.

The municipality did not have the power to ban WCs outright, but permission to install one was made dependent on an environmental assessment in each case — and even if one got the permission, there was a strong disincentive as the charge for hooking up to a sewer was 60,000 SEK (about $2,400). As a result, only two or three out of the 40 to 50 new houses being built each year come with WCs.

Those who opt for other solutions can avoid outgoing mains connections altogether and can, in most cases, allow the gray water to infiltrate into the ground. Those already connected to sewers have their annual service fee cut by 50 percent if they convert to composting or separating toilets. In particular, a number of farmers in Tanum now use urine or composted toilet wastes on their land.

Tanum's example has inspired other Swedish communities to include goals for human waste recycling in their city plans.

➔ *Birgitta Jonsson, Environment Department, Tanum municipality, S-457 81 Tanumshede, Sweden (Phone: Int.+46 [0]525 182 82; Fax: Int.+46 [0]525 183 00).*

➔ *See also Stiftelsen Idebanken, PO Box 2126, Grünnerlokka, Norway (Phone: Int.+47 [0]2203 4010; Fax: Int.+47 [0]2236 4060; E-mail: idebanken@online.no; Web: www.idebanken.no).*

Conflict resolution journalism

DUDLEY WEEKS

From an article entitled "Perpetuating Peace" in NPC Research Prospect in Peace Journalism (media bulletin No. 3). A version of this article first appeared in EJN News, (Paris). Dudley Weeks is one of the world's leading facilitators in conflict resolution. He has worked with conflict parties in over 60 countries and has counseled thousands of families, businesses, and communities in the US. He writes regularly on the subject for the international press.

AS SOMEONE WHO HAS SPENT MOST OF HIS LIFE working as a practitioner in conflict resolution and peace building, I have been intrigued by the emergence of what some are calling "conflict resolution journalism." Exploration among the media and conflict resolution professionals seems to indicate that no one quite knows what the term means, not that there needs to be one clear definition, of course. Yet a search for a few basic parameters might be helpful.

To me, responsible media commit themselves to "telling the complete story." The complete story involves what has happened, what is happening, and what might happen. Every "complete" story involving a conflict situation should include whatever conflict resolution possibilities are operating. The journalist should not seek to focus solely on the causes of the conflict and the behavior that is perpetuating it.

It has been my experience that media have often become fixated on the more sensationalistic divisions among conflict parties and ignored what I call the "connections" that exist even in the midst of what divides the parties.

It is these connections, often involving "shared needs," that build the foundations for effective conflict resolution. To ignore them is to tell an incomplete story.

Take the way a journalist conducts an interview, for example. Often the questions asked are aimed at extracting information about the demands and positions of a particular person or group. They also tend to be angled toward the depths of negative feelings directed at the other party in the conflict.

Such information is certainly part of the story. However, so is what I term the "broader picture." This includes possibilities for dealing effectively with a conflict and improving the relationship, taking into account both past and present animosities and limitations. Asking questions that help broaden the picture should not, I suggest, be limited to "conflict resolution" or "peace journalism." Asking questions that enlarge the picture and help audiences understand what is happening is an essential part of getting and telling the complete story.

I work in conflicts around the globe as a "conflict partnership facilitator." This is based on the Conflict Partnership Process for conflict resolution and relationship building that I have developed through 25 years of experience. I use the term "facilitator" rather than "mediator" because it promotes the notion of serving as a catalyst to help empower conflict parties. I can provide them with a process and effective skills to work with each other in improving a situation, rather than serving as a "middle person" between parties and managing the traditional bargaining approach of adversarial competition. I do not advocate that journalists attempt to serve as conflict resolution facilitators or mediators.

However, I do believe that some of the questions I ask conflict parties in my individual meetings with them and when I eventually get them together do have a role to play in obtaining the complete story. A few examples of the "broadening the picture" questions include the following:

- When one party in an interview is expressing only the negative aspects of its relationship with the opposing group, I ask: "Have you had any cooperative dealings (with the other party)?"

- If a party is seeing only the potentially disastrous possibilities of a particular event, such as the return of refugees of a different ethnic group, I ask: "Are there any positive benefits to your community the return of the refugees might bring?"

- When one party persists in telling me its demands and what it wants, I ask questions about needs and then ask if the party thinks there are any needs it shares with the other party.

What kind of overall relationship would be most mutually beneficial?

- When the parties are focusing only on the immediate conflict, almost defining the other party or the entire relationship by the most negative aspects of the current situation, I ask questions such as: "What kind of overall relationship would be most mutually beneficial?"

- When the parties are assuming that a conflict can only be dealt with through adversarial competition, I ask: "What among the things you've told me you need can be accomplished by working with each other rather than against other?"

Are these legitimate questions for a journalist to ask? I believe they are. I ask such questions as part of a process that empowers conflict parties to discover together additional action steps for dealing effectively and in a sustainable manner with a conflict and improving the overall relationship. A journalist, I suggest, asks such questions as part of uncovering the complete story, as a basis for telling the complete story. To me, that is *responsible* journalism, not conflict resolution journalism.

➔ *NPC Media, 162 Holloway Road, London N7 8DD, UK*
(Phone: Int.+44 [0]20 7609 9666; Fax: Int.+44 [0]20 7609 9777;
E-mail: npcmedia@gn.apc.org)

Co-parents

ANGELA MURPHY
From a letter to the *Independent* newspaper.

MY HUSBAND AND I WANT A NUMBER OF CLOSE FRIENDS to take a long-term interest in our child — in other words, to take on all the responsibilities of a godparent, except for religious education.

The tradition of asking close friends or family to take a
special interest in children goes back to the fourth century.

Our choice of a name for our son's "sponsors" was the term "co-parent." It seemed to contain the right degree of warmth and also has a historical precedent. The tradition of asking close friends or family to take a special interest in children goes back to the fourth century, and the terms "commater" and "compater" (they also carried the meaning of "intimate friend") first occurred at the end of the sixth century.

Christenings and spiritual kinship were primarily seen as a means of extending and intensifying natural kinship relations in an uncertain world when wider social and family ties were threatened. The religious education of the child was, in those days, its least significant aspect.

Parents would choose people with whom they wished to create a formal state of friendship (just as in rites of blood-brotherhood). Now that the extended family is stretched and scattered, it is even more important to confirm the bonds of friendship. We believe that our celebration has helped us to do this.

➔ *Angela Murphy, 21 Leamington Road Villas, London W11 1HS, UK.*

The Council for Posterity

PROFESSOR RICHARD SCORER

THE FUTURE IS ESSENTIALLY UNPREDICTABLE. Unforeseen discoveries, declarations of new objectives, boredom with old promises, and the emergence of new genius sway the unstable surges of history with alarming irregularity.

Yet some trends are clear. The rate of change appears to have increased throughout the world's existence. While at least several hundred million years seems a safe bet for the possibility of life on earth, we nevertheless find ourselves

- using up in a very few centuries, at most, the world's store of mineral fuel, for the purpose of daily living;
- destroying large capital reserves of forest, fish, and genetic variety, and seriously damaging the habitat of most other life forms;
- multiplying our own species beyond all reasonable bounds, making the sustenance of this excess possible only by the destruction of anything in the biosphere that does not contribute to that greedy process, and consuming anything that does.

This makes us a plague on earth, lacking the dignity of the lion and without the tolerance of the fauna of the field.

This makes us a plague on earth, lacking the dignity of the lion and without the tolerance of the fauna of the field.

We have become like this because we fostered images of ourselves that are not only disastrously arrogant, but also fundamentally erroneous.

We are escaping slowly from the fear that we may destroy ourselves collectively by unrestrained war or individually by the depressing limitations of our psyche. The pessimism of the recent past is demonstrably curable, but it requires the widespread acceptance of a more loving picture of ourselves, of our environment, and of human purposes. The acceleration of change has so reduced our perspectives in our worries about our own persons and the uncontrollability of human conflict that we have forgotten the world, as if its state were of secondary importance to ourselves. The evident power of today has made us lose sight of the billion years ahead.

To extend our feeling of community with all of life, which has been lost from those human societies that wondered at the incomprehensibility of space and time and the mystery of life; to extend the sense of responsibility that we undoubtedly feel towards our own young children and to the multitude of generations ahead; and to keep their environment beautiful, we need a new priesthood that will tell us the story of humanity as we have only recently (in the last 200 years) come to know it through science. I would call this a Council for Posterity.

To establish this, we would naturally draw on our experience of setting up learned bodies to inform and guide us into truer perceptions of our own reality. But we may prefer to make it more personally anonymous than assembling a collection of gray eminences. We cannot presume at first to specify any limiting terms of reference, but we can require it to teach us to love the world we scarcely yet know. It will be necessary to specify new concepts of greatness beyond the individual. At the moment of history when we have at last learned about our own evolution, we have to halt our destruction of the very foundation of that marvelously creative process.

Above all, we have to learn that the greatest benefit and opportunity we can give our descendants is that there be fewer of them. Even if we can divert our impatient energies into games, philosophies, and space "toys," we still need to understand individually the exciting and absorbing story of life, of which we are but one manifested form among many whose silent genetic wisdom surrounds us.

We are one of the atmosphere's children.

The story of the ocean has still to be explored. What is already known about its origin, its evolution, and its wealth is enough to indicate that it will be framed in allegories that will humble us. Already the story of the atmosphere glows with drama that can be Part One of the story in which we will tell our children how they came to be what they are.

We are one of the atmosphere's children, and if we may call ourselves the most glowing of the brood, we must remember that it participated in the evolution of all mammals and was not designed or made for us, but that we evolved in it. It may yet produce in the eras stretching a million times a human generation forward a species which, when telling its offspring of their origins, will speak of us with admiration or contempt. Which shall it be?

The Council for Posterity must also take on the role of Counsel for Posterity. It must consist of people who can devote their deepest thoughts to the theme and muster all the arguments to call the present generation away from its myopic trends. It will need

- scientists who can speak with authority about the believed facts of global evolution;
- ecologists, in particular, who can gather together a responsible statement of the danger in the present trends;
- people with experience in politics, economics, and historical interpretation who can imagine the themes that will make people want

to act in a way so that when future generations describe us, we
would be proud to hear what they say;

- writers who can present a picture of humanity that young people
  will absorb and will be stimulated to want more of, and that will
  help them develop a hope that they can be part of the road into
  the future — rather than become the refuse of the present.

The Council will need young and old, people from various traditions,
but none who believe their own tradition (e.g., Islam or Christianity) has
authority of a superior kind not possessed by others. Each is merely one of
the experimental traditions of history (which itself is a very new thing in the
world). The Council must merge science with morality. It must destroy the
dichotomy that sets the individual on a pedestal while sending conscripts to
death in defense of individualism. It must recognize the limitations of all
human issues, for time dissolves them. Thus human rights, animal rights,
sacredness of human life, sacredness of all life, territorial property and ownership concepts, limits to personal wealth and poverty, legitimacy of political
authority — all these require new definition in the light of scientific knowledge and the ecology of nature.

A force in formulating visions of the community of life on earth

If the Council is sponsored by government, it must be free from any threat
or pressure and must have no national or racial commitment. Thus it needs a
promise of about a decade of support, which would give it time to demonstrate its value as a force in formulating human self-images, and visions of the
community of life on earth, which are intelligible to ordinary schoolchildren.
It must generate a humility together with a sturdy commitment among the
young. This means understanding the motivations of the present self-oriented
generation and, by capturing its imagination, drawing it into new objectives
without overtly criticizing the viewpoints from which they are to be weaned.

In order not to be invidious, a list of people from the past who are not
available but who typify the qualities required could include: H.G. Wells,
Julian Huxley, John Boyd Orr, Tom Paine, Francis of Assisi, Peter Medawar,
Isambard Brunel, Albert Schweitzer, Albert Einstein, Mahatma Gandhi,
Erasmus, Chief Seattle, Martin Luther King, Aesop.

To gather the nucleus requires about £1 million capital (about $1.5 mil-
lion) or £100,000 (about $150,000) a year, or a rich publisher's or industrial-
ist's foundation to sponsor the experimental stage. I do not favor a UN or
European Economic Community base because much would be wasted in
bureaucracy and in generating political acceptance.

There already exist many texts that will provide the basis for most of
the educational documents required. In an era of less urgent change and

growth it would probably suffice to have these texts gradually permeate the educational systems. But that progress is slow, and the recrudescence of dogmatic religious and political beliefs requires a counterforce.

The Council must be competent continually to examine the behavior of governments and to reexamine the assumptions on which their policies are based. For this reason, a broader than scientific authority is required, and verbal power will be useful.

The Council would formulate political and social objectives consonant with Earth System Science. It would not concern itself with the promotion of scientific research, but with its political and economic impact and the legitimacy of technological exploitation. It must concern itself with the prospect of a widespread dearth of resources, starvation, and the present uncontrollable growth of human numbers and its incompatibility with the hope of future freedom.

And it must inspire with words of pride the objectives of the young.

The following are some of the people and institutions that have provided thematic texts on which some of the Council's work could be based: David Attenborough, David Bellamy, Jean Medawar, Richard Dawkins, Paul Ehrlich, Donald Mann (Negative Population Growth), the Chinese government's one child policy, Eric Deakins, James Lovelock, NASA — Earth System Science. A much fuller bibliography is possible.

→ *Professor Richard Scorer of the Department of Mathematics, Imperial College (London) can be contacted at home, 2 Stanton Road, London SW20 8RL, UK (Phone: Int.+44 [0]20 8946 1313 at home; Int.+44 [0]20 7589 5111 at work). This scheme won a main Social Inventions Award.*

Council for Posterity's progress

A UK Council for Posterity, based on a scaled-down version of Professor Scorer's ideas, was launched in 1990. The initial core group included Scorer himself, Herbie Girardet, Fern Morgan-Grenville, Professor Meredith Thring, Tanya Schwarz, Guy Dauncey, Liz Hosken, Brian Aldiss, Lord Young of Dartington, Doris Lessing, Sir William Golding, Anita Roddick, Maxwell Bruce QC, John Seymour, Dr Alice Coleman, Teddy Goldsmith, and Diana Schumacher, with Nicholas Albery of the Institute for Social Inventions as General Secretary. The Council is the UK National Liaison Unit for the UNESCO-related Global Network on Responsibilities Towards Future Generations (in Malta), and the Council's plans include

- providing legal representation for the interests of future generations at any inquiry or assembly looking into developments with potentially very harmful long-term effects;

- stimulating the development of Declarations of the Rights of Posterity and publicizing their contents (see the Council's own draft in the box below);

- involving young people through a £1,000 Adopt-a-Planet competition in schools (see the "Adopt-a-Planet" entry for more details on this);

- presenting awards for the best published articles or books about future generations (The authors will be invited to present their themes at dinner-discussion award ceremonies);

- encouraging the formation of similar councils in other countries.

**Posterity offers you an altruistic aim,
a life with added meaning.**

To those whose first scornful reaction is "What has posterity ever done for me?" the Council answers: "It offers you an altruistic aim independent of age, sex, family, creed, or nationality; that is, a life with added meaning."

A DECLARATION OF THE RIGHTS OF POSTERITY
Those who live after us have no voice amongst us
We therefore declare and determine their right to inherit

a planet   that has been treated by us with respect
            for its richness, its beauty, and its diversity
a planet   whose atmosphere is life-giving and good
            and can remain so for eons to come
a planet   whose resources have been carefully maintained
            and whose forms of life retain their diversity
a planet   whose soil has been preserved from erosion with
            both soil and water unpoisoned by the waste of our living
a planet   whose people apply their technologies cautiously
            with consideration for the long-term consequences
a planet   whose people live in human-scale societies
            unravaged by population excess
a planet   whose future generations have interests that are
            represented and protected in the decision-making
            councils of those alive today.

→ *This Declaration is published by the Council for Posterity, 20 Heber Road, London NW2 6AA, UK (Phone: Int.+44 [0]208 2853; Fax: Int.+44 [0]20 8452*

6434; E-mail: rhino@dial.pipex.com). Please send in your suggested improvements or alternative versions.

➔ *Hilary Caruana, International Liaison, Global Network on Responsibilities Towards Future Generations, International Environment Institute, c/o Foundation for International Studies, University of Malta, Valletta, Malta (Phone: Int.+356 224067 / 234121 / 234122; Fax: Int.+356 230551).*

➔ *For a similar iniative, see also <www.descendantsday.org>.*

Court finds nuclear weapons to be illegal

IN 1988 THREE JUDGES, Alfred P. Rubin, Francis A. Boyle, and Burns H. Weston, at the end of the first judicial tribunal ever to address the issue of the legality of nuclear weapons, declared, in Judge Rubin's words, "that the international rules of war apply to nuclear weapons and their use in warfare and that in all cases the threat or use of those weapons in ways forbidden by the international humanitarian rules of warfare is of sufficient interest to the general international community to justify that community in taking legal measures to prevent it. I therefore grant to the Plaintiffs an injunction forbidding the threat or use of nuclear weapons in any way violative of international law." Concurring with Judge Rubin, Judge Weston delineated six "core rules" of international law regarding nuclear weapons:

- First, that it is prohibited to use weapons or tactics that cause unnecessary and/or aggravated devastation and suffering.

It is prohibited to use weapons that cause indiscriminate harm as between combatants and civilian personnel.

- Second, that it is prohibited to use weapons or tactics that cause indiscriminate harm as between combatants and non-combatant military and civilian personnel.
- Third, that it is prohibited to effect reprisals that are disproportionate to their antecedent provocation or to legitimate military objectives, or that are disrespectful of persons, institutions, and resources otherwise protected by the laws of war.
- Fourth, that it is prohibited to use weapons or tactics that cause widespread, long-term, and severe damage to the natural environment.
- Fifth, that it is prohibited to use weapons or tactics that violate the jurisdiction of non-participating states.

- Sixth, that it is prohibited to use asphyxiating, poisonous, or other gases, and all analogous liquids, materials, or devices, including bacteriological methods of warfare.

Judge Boyle stated in his turn that "[u]nder article 38(1)(d) of the Statute of the International Court of Justice, this Opinion" — by himself and his two fellow judges — constitutes a "subsidiary means for the determination of rules of law." It could therefore be relied upon by some future international war crimes tribunal. This case has thus become the seminal case in the field and could be referred to by litigants in any country.

The trial was the result of an initiative by Leon Vickman, a California attorney, for whom it became clear, after some research, that bringing a lawsuit about nuclear weapons in the United States would not result in a ruling on the merits, since domestic courts consider such matters to be "political questions," which require abstention. It also seemed futile to him to turn to the International Court of Justice in the Hague, since defendants in any suit must agree to the jurisdiction of the Court and only nations can sue.

The lawsuit was filed on behalf of all the persons of Earth, against 28 "nuclear nations".

Vickman describes his six-year battle in a pamphlet, *Why Nuclear Weapons Are Illegal*, from which the following is extracted.

It was necessary to search for a court that was empowered to hear such matters. And it came to pass that such a court was in a formative stage, within a provisional world government called the Federation of Earth. Under its Constitution, a complete court system could be formed. Upon the author's urging, a Bill was passed at the Federation's First Provisional World Parliament in Brighton, UK, in 1982, establishing such a court in Los Angeles. The lawsuit was filed soon thereafter, on behalf of all the persons of Earth, against 28 "nuclear" nations. The defendants were divided into three groups: the superpowers, the nuclear host nations, and the nuclear-capable nations.

Every step of the process was conducted with meticulous care to conform to generally accepted legal procedures. The defendant nations were served numerous times with legal pleadings. (India was the only state to file a responsive pleading, stating it was against the use of nuclear weapons.) Attorney Gaither Kodis of Bellevue, Washington, was appointed to serve as an amicus to the Court, representing the viewpoint of the defendants in briefs and oral argument.

C

During the almost six-year duration of the lawsuit, perhaps the most dramatic event, other than the court hearing itself, was the appointment of three highly qualified judges to the panel that was to decide the case: Judge Francis A. Boyle, Professor of International Law at the University of Illinois Law School at Champagne; Judge Alfred P. Rubin, Professor of International Law at the School of Law and Diplomacy at Tufts University; and Judge Burns H. Weston, Professor of International Law at the University of Iowa School of Law. The fact that the three judges are leading experts in the field of nuclear weapons law resulted in the three lengthy written opinions by the judges having a far-reaching legal effect.

The principal cause of action on the court summons stated: "Plaintiffs are informed and believe and on said basis allege that the following defendants possess nuclear weapons that are poised for use against human population centers, as well as numerous other target areas which inevitably drastically affect human populations: China (People's Republic), France, Union of Soviet Socialist Republics, United Kingdom and the United States."

We are a people of law. We now have the law on the most horrible of weapons. Let us observe it.

The finding against the defendants could prove influential, concludes Vickman. "It will only take a few persons to start a peaceful international protest against nuclear weapons that can ultimately impact on the very core of nuclear policy. Remember the pioneering work of Linus Pauling against atmospheric testing, and the crusade of Helen Caldicott against nuclear arsenals .... We are a people of law. We now have the law on the most horrible of weapons. Let us observe it."

→ Why Nuclear Weapons Are Illegal, *by Leon Vickman, is booklet number 20 published by the Nuclear Age Peace Foundation, 187 Coast Village Road, Suite 123, Santa Barbara, CA 93108.*

Criteria for sane transnational structures

NICHOLAS ALBERY

MANY IDEALISTS BELIEVE IN THE DISSOLUTION OF THE NATION STATE and a gradual progress towards a World Government. But the latter would inevitably become just one more tyrannous empire, even more remote and inaccessible than the present superpowers. To quote from a book I co-edited, *How to Save the World: A Guide to the Politics of Scale* (published by Thorsons), "We believe that the movement we are supporting for a new localism in world affairs, involving as it does the breakdown of giant nations, needs to be balanced by a sane internationalism.

We must evolve criteria and safeguards for the federalist and transnational structures that are necessary to confront the complexity of the planet's problems.

Any form of political or economic power which is not controlled by those affected by it is a threat to peace or freedom or both. Questions that need to be asked center on control:

- Who appoints whom?
- Who elects whom?
- Who hires and fires?

Who decides policy? Who settles the budget?

- Who decides policy?
- Who settles the budget?
- Who checks the books?
- And who controls those who make these decisions?"

. My exemplar of a sane transnational structure is not the slightly grotesque United Nations, but rather the humble international postal union, which is based in Berne and quietly gets on with the specialist job of facilitating international mail. Thus my criteria for worthwhile global organizations would include the following:

- They should be based in various places around the world, not all in one country.
- They should have an incentive to dissolve once their specialist task is completed.
- They should be separate organizations, with separate names, and not be under one central or global authority, whether that be the United Nations, the World Parliament, or something similar.
- They should, wherever possible, consist of concerned professionals and experts getting together on an ad hoc basis, subject to national political supervision and interest group lobbying as required. Thus the international postal union could continue to be based in Switzerland, with a center for tackling transnational pollution in Kenya, and regional commissions for human rights. There would also at times no doubt need to be ad hoc regional poolings of

national armies or militias for service in emergencies, as in the grouping of countries that confronted Iraq.

• These transnational bodies should have as little power as possible.

• They should incorporate the principle of subsidiarity, leaving powers devolved to the most local levels possible.

Internationalism was part of communism's doomed love affair with the curse of bigness.

Communism's internationalism was not the least of its failings. Internationalism was all part of communism's doomed love affair with the mass scale, with the curse of bigness. Politicians and constitution designers have an obligation to learn the principles of scale, as must architects, town planners, engineers, industrialists, economists, and all those who have blighted this century with their over-bloated giantism.

→ *Please send feedback to The Institute for Social Inventions, 20 Heber Road, London NW2 6AA, UK (Phone: Int.+44 [0]20 8208 2853; Fax: Int.+44 [0]20 8452 6434; E-mail: rhino@dial.pipex.com; Web: www.globalideasbank.org).*

Curitiba's civic virtues revisited

From an e-mail by Michael O. Patterson in which he summarizes a story from the book *Hope, Human and Wild: True Stories of Living Lightly on the Earth* by Bill McKibben (published by Hungry Mind Press).

CURITIBA, BRAZIL. JUST AN AVERAGE BRAZILIAN CITY, REALLY. It has the best mass transit system in the world, has housed its street children, and uses sheep to trim the grass in the parks. For those who look at livability indexes, Curitiba is almost off the charts. In recent surveys, more than half the residents of American cities like Detroit and New York City would like to get out. Yet over 98 percent of Curitibans are happy with their city. Even the Japanese do not have those kind of stats. This city was built around people, rather than having the people forced into the city. It has a government that works with the people, with the organizations, to create a good place to live. Oh, it has its slum housing — but it is clean, because a sack of garbage can be exchanged for a sack of food from a municipal truck.

Jaime Lerner, a major part of this, started out by fighting an overpass that would have destroyed a neighborhood. He had grown up in a real neighborhood, and for him his street — the Rua Quinze — was the city. He decided to make it into a walking mall, with no cars allowed. As mayor, he sat with his public works guy and planned it out. They knew the merchants would never approve it. Like Edwin Moses, the legendary New York planner, they tore up the pavement, replaced it with brick and cobblestone, and put in decorative elements including thousands of flowers, lights, and kiosks. They also had it done by the following Monday morning. Later that day, other merchants wanted the walking mall extended to be in front of their stores.

People took the flowers at first, but the city kept replacing them till they were left alone.

A group of car owners decided to drive down the street to get it back for cars. The mayor put paper down the length of the mall and had many children sitting on the street, painting on the papers.

People took the flowers at first, but the city kept replacing them till they were left alone. The city respects its citizens and the citizens return that respect. Bus stations are made out of glass and are not vandalized.

Other things were done. Traffic was rerouted into three groups of parallel avenues — the outer ones were one way, either in or out, and the middle street was for buses, which meant no costs for tearing down buildings to make highways and kept streets to human scale. Zoning was fixed so that apartment complexes were allowed only close to bus routes. The city grows in lines, preserving varied kinds of housing, with people at different income levels, organically, as D'Arcy Thompson recommends in *On Growth and Form*. They plant trees everywhere and fine people who cut them without permission, even on their own land. Where there are problem trees — trees that are getting too big — they plant other trees and wait till the new trees are a good size before cutting down the problem trees.

The city regulates where factories can be built and what they can do. They note that the quality of life attracts good corporations, the kind that pay good wages, and they do not have to use tax concessions. Companies help pay for municipal childcare. The city often employs single mothers from the slums and sometimes helps people get materials to build homes. Architects help people design homes that they can build one room at a time, which is all most can afford.

Children who sort out plastic by categories can exchange it for bus tokens

---

The city has kids' programs — and they treat all children like their own, with foster homes that care, or dorms and jobs. The head of the department is most concerned that they get food and love. City daycare is free to toddlers and older kids and runs almost 12 hours per day. It even serves meals.

Kids plant community gardens, using seed supplied by the city. Some new arrivals in the 1980s tried to make a living from pushcarts, competing with merchants. The city, instead of destroying the carts as they would in an American city, licensed them instead and put them in locations that helped the city. The city authorities found it was cheaper to buy food from farmers and trade it for bags of garbage — especially since the trucks do not fit in the narrow streets of the favelas.

They put up an opera house in a month.

Several million people ride the buses each day. Some buses go to special shelters where passengers load through several doors, having already paid their fares, as on a subway. Buses are self-supporting and get no money from the government. Passenger levels increase because the buses are faster. Children who sort out plastic by categories can exchange it for bus tokens. Old buses become classrooms for job skills training.

There is much less crime in this city. The lack of opportunity, constant frustration, and resentments that reduce the veneer of civilization, so common in US cities, are much less in evidence here.

The city looks to recycle buildings rather than tear them down, converting old buildings to new uses. Curitiba took federal money, available for building concrete levees to keep rivers from flooding, and spent it on land for parks and on small dams to make lakes. The city went from two square feet of green per person to 150 square feet, which increased property values.

The city runs on about ten percent of the average expenditure per person of major cities in the US; they find ways to do things cheaply, simply, and quickly. They put up an opera house in a month.

The mayor finds people who find ways
to get things done and has brainstorming sessions.

They cannot afford research or consultants, so they find something that works and implement it as soon as possible. Lerner says you cannot leave problems to experts. He finds people who find ways to get things done and has brainstorming sessions. One product of such a session was the 24/7 street, which has shops and so forth that are open 24 hours per day — this uses the space more efficiently and reduces the force that ties up space with buildings used only a few hours each day.

The mayor believes that at work you have to have fun, laughter, and the creative things that make people happy. Designers come from other cities for the workshops. One group designed a mobile tent factory so that children could create toys from recycled items. His staff love seeing their ideas come into form; in most places they would be unable to get anything done.

Americans live in cocoons, watching TV programs designed to fill them with fear of their neighbors. Often they have no idea who their neighbors are. Fr. Thomas O'Brien notes that the worldwide breakdown of community leads directly to addiction. Mother Teresa noted that the major deficit in the first world is love and attention from friends and family. Curitiba starts by making kids happy — so they feel secure, have hopes for the future and opportunities. The city has bike paths, soccer fields, and pleasant, safe public space. It has public concerts, street fairs, and volleyball courts, and a real, living downtown, not a fake one. It is a place to enjoy life. Some Saturdays, city workers put out paper for kids to draw on, to remember the original act that started it all.

No, it's not all perfect, but it's much closer to perfect than any American big city.

→ *Michael O. Patterson (E-mail: MedicineOwl@angelfire.com).*

D

Damanhur and the Temple of Mankind

SINCE 1978, A GROUP THAT STYLES ITSELF THE NATION OF DAMANHUR has created, without planning permission, one of the great wonders of the modern world: interlinked underground halls, domes, corridors, a labyrinth, a moving wall, and an alchemical laboratory, all secretly carved out within a mountain near Turin, in the Piedmont foothills of the Italian Alps — an underground temple that is equivalent in volume to an 11-story building.

One of the great wonders of the modern world

Art for these Damanhurians is considered a "spiritual path. The process of giving shape and consistency to raw matter symbolically corresponds to the refining of the artist's soul. Inert matter is brought to life by the artist's thought and action."

D

The artists have decorated the underground temple, reviving techniques that have almost disappeared, using glass and stone mosaic, stained and cathedral glass, frescos and paintings, marquetry, embossed copper, marble and stone sculpture — there are now 480 square yards (400 square meters) of paintings and frescoes and 360 square yards (300 square meters) of mosaics.

The Damanhurians only revealed the existence of the temple in 1992, when a disgruntled former member tried to blackmail them, threatening to reveal their secret if they didn't pay 700 million lira ($440,000). The authorities seem to have decided that the temple is too beautiful to be closed down (on April 27, 1996, a judge canceled a seizure order on the temple), but the Damanhurians are battling for the right to continue its expansion. The group's founder, Oberto Airaudi, says it is only one-tenth complete — he would like to have one or two miles (two or three kilometers) of corridors.

The Nation of Damanhur is a long-lasting social experiment, with its own flag, currency (the Credito), and daily newspaper.

The Nation of Damanhur is a large and long-lasting social experiment, having evolved in a more democratic direction over the years, and now has — besides a flag, a currency (the Credito), a constitution, and a daily newspaper — Guides, elected every six months, who have a spiritual function, overseeing long-term plans; a Senate, which liaises with each community's president (no community is allowed to have more than 200 citizens); and a College of Justice, which rules over violations of the community's norms and constitution. The latter states: "Spirituality and global ecology are the inspiring principles by which we relate to the land and the animals, avoiding all forms of pollution and waste."

Damanhur owns 460 acres (185 hectares) of land in various patches of the region and presently has over 350 resident members, with connected groups in Italy, France, and Germany. It runs schools, farms, a cashmere and silk factory, and various artist workshops. It gets mineral water from a well in the temple, and its Company of the Good Earth sells goods such as preserved fruits at Fortnum and Masons.

Damanhurians have been criticized by the Catholic Church for their beliefs. Their temple is, Damanhurians say, at the meeting point of three energy rivers ("synchronic lines") that surround the earth. Their respect for nature includes conventional conservationist credos, but also extends to a pantheistic (and some might feel rather flaky) belief that individual plants may be able to communicate with humans — a belief enshrined in their attempts to produce musical collaborations between the plant and human kingdoms. "We connect plants' leaves and roots, via electrodes, which measure minute changes in electrical resistance, to two machines which convert the signal into MIDI — the digital language read by all modern electronic instruments. Thus the plants can learn to play the synthesizer ... and they respond to the simultaneous performances of human musicians. The Concerts of the Wood, starring chestnuts, birches, and oaks together with human [sic] musicians, are always among the most successful events of Damanhur's summers." They have also developed their own esoteric Sacred Language, whose ideograms can have several different meanings "according to the level of logical framework adopted," with the language used to develop sounds, music, dances, decorations, and paintings.

Damanhur's public relations are handled in part by Esperide (people can take new names on joining; hers means "butterfly"). The place allows in occasional visitors for events such as the temple concerts.

→ *See Damanhur's own illustrated website at <www.damanhur.it/html/visit_the_temple.html>. The group can be contacted c/o I-Damanhur 10080, Baldissero, Canavese (T.O.), Via Pramarze 3, Italy (Phone: Int.+39 [0]124 512150; Fax: Int.+39 [0]124 512205; E-mail: dhvisit@damanhur.it).*

Depreciating community-owned currencies

DAVID WESTON

The following piece is updated from one first published in *New Economics*.

THERE WAS A TIME WHEN PEOPLE WERE SO CONVINCED THE EARTH WAS FLAT that the idea it was round was inconceivable. Likewise today, the idea of a community or region issuing and using its own currency and running its own bank may seem impossible.

But it has happened.

The Wörgl schillings

In the early 1930s the small town of Wörgl in the Austrian Tyrol, suffering like every other town in Europe and America from the Great Depression, took the unlikely step of issuing its own currency.

Its burgomaster, Michael Unterguggenberger, faced an empty treasury because the unemployed citizens could not pay their taxes; roads and bridges needed repair and parks needed maintenance, for which the town could not pay; and idle men and women earned no wages.

He recognized that all three problems could be solved if he could find the connecting link.

That link was money. The three problems coexisted because no one had any of it, and his simple solution was to create money locally.

He issued numbered "labor certificates" in denominations of one, five, and ten schillings, to the value of 32,000 schillings. These certificates became valid only after being stamped at the town hall, and they depreciated monthly by one percent of their nominal value.

It was possible for the holders to "revalue" them by purchasing, before the end of each month, stamps from the town hall, in the process creating a relief fund.

The small town of Wörgl, suffering from the Great Depression, issued its own currency.

The depreciation encouraged not only rapid circulation, but also the payment of taxes, past, current, and upcoming. These taxes were used to provide social and public services.

At the end of each year, it was required that the notes be turned in for new ones. No charge was made for the transaction if the required stamps had been affixed. Subject to a two percent deduction, the labor notes were also undertook into Austrian schillings.

To facilitate this conversion at any time — and thereby provide a cover for the relief certificates — the trustees deposited at the local Raiffeisen Bank (credit union) an amount in Austrian currency equivalent to the issued local currency.

The money was loaned out to trustworthy wholesalers at six percent interest. Interest thereby flowed back into the town treasury, further facilitating transactions with the "outside world."

Wages paid in the new money

The burgomaster put this money into circulation by paying 50 percent — later raised to 75 percent — of the wages of the town's clerical and manual workers in the new money.

The workers found that all businesses in Wörgl accepted the currency in payment and at face value, and the notes returned to the parish treasury as dues and taxes. Economically, there was no inflation, and politically, the money was unanimously acceptable to all the municipal parties.

Because it was a depreciating currency, it circulated with rapidity, boosting the local economy.

Because it was a depreciating currency, it circulated with rapidity, boosting the local economy. Also, not only did people pay their current taxes in the currency, but they also discharged their tax arrears. Further, many paid their taxes in advance because it was financially advantageous.

Apart from the obvious employment benefits, physical assets were created. These included improvements in the main street and its drainage system, street lighting, new road construction, manufacturing of curbs and drainage pipes, construction of a ski-jumping platform, and fencing and construction of a new water reservoir.

Although the Wörgl money was unanimously accepted at the local level, there was great opposition from two centralist forces — the Tyrol Labour Party and the Austrian State Bank.

In both cases, there seemed to be fear that the experiment would spread, for the idea was copied by the neighboring town of Kirchbichel. The town monies were valid in both places. Other towns in the Tyrol also decided to issue depreciating money, but did not proceed because of threats from the State Bank.

Ultimately, the State Bank threatened Wörgl with legal proceedings, and on September 1, 1933, the experiment was terminated.

In an analysis, Unterguggenberger concluded that depreciating currency fulfills the functions of money much better than unvarying nationalized currency. He noted that no difficulties or complaints had arisen in making payments in the new currency or in affixing stamps, and that the local currency was accepted by all businesses very shortly after the project started.

He also suggested that not only did it work at the town level, but it could also be applied in larger entities including regions, provinces, and the state.

Although the experiment was terminated in Austria, it was noted and tried elsewhere. In Canada, for instance, the government of the province of Alberta set up a provincial depreciating currency in the mid-1930s in the form of Prosperity Certificates.

The "danger" of its success prompted the central government to ban it.

What lessons?

What lessons can be learned? First and foremost, that there is nothing sacred about the "national" money with which we grew up.

Money — as information technology, metal chips, paper slips, and electronic blips — is what people will accept in payment for goods and services and taxes.

The community money could be used to pay taxes and also be exchanged for national currency.

If they will accept community or regional money, then it is as good as pounds or dollars or deutsche marks. It was the fact that the community or regional money could be used to pay taxes and also be exchanged for familiar national currency that made it acceptable and successful.

A depressed community found a way of ending the problems of unemployment.

The most important lesson, however, is that a depressed community in an apparently hopeless situation found a way of ending the seemingly insoluble problems of unemployment, local decline, and lack of a reliable tax base symbiotically through the use of a community-owned currency.

The prime candidate for the cause of community and regional decline is the centralized banking and money system. By definition, national money is political.

The banks are also political inasmuch as they make policies to siphon off local wealth and value into their central financial vortex.

The centralized banks collect money from the regions in a nation and invest in a booming area.

This vortex is well described by Myrdal's "cumulative causation effect." The centralized banks collect money from the regions in a nation and invest in a booming area, creating a further boom, which demands more national money from the regions, which creates ....

Conversely and concurrently, the communities and regions are deprived of their wealth — via the national money — to feed the voracious appetite of the center. Even if some of that money is reimported into the community or region, it is their externally controlled capital.

In the process, the communities or regions lose control of their economy and also their political systems, becoming dispensable Regions of Sacrifice. Scotland is a prime example.

A duplication of the process is now evolving in the push for a European central bank and a single European currency.

From observation and experience, there is no doubt that the European Monetary System will be used to enhance a corridor of centralized financial power running from London to Zürich and connected to the other major financial centers of Europe, including possibly Moscow. The centralization of power has always created problems, and its abuse comes as no surprise.

The appropriate decentralization of power, known as the Principle of Subsidiarity, can and should take place. This principle states that the priority for decision-making and action-taking should be at the most decentralized level possible. Only when those decisions and actions impinge upon the well-being of the next larger communities or regions should those too have an influence.

The decentralization of power will require that authorization be given to local governments to create their own currency.

In practical terms, this will require that authorization be given to local and regional governments to create their own currency in the form of non-interest-bearing local bonds to be used as money.

Community Barter

In this context, it is also important to understand the difference between community currency and community barter systems.

A community barter system — like the LETSystem, which is *not* community currency — is usually based on a voluntary organizational sharing of information about goods and services available from individuals in an area. The accounting is usually based either on time (hours) or the nationalized currency (pounds, dollars, etc.).

Such a system has three basic weaknesses:

- It tends to be limited in scope to a handful of dedicated practitioners, usually in largely rural or semi-rural areas.
- It does not cater to transactions outside the community.
- It encourages hoarding rather than the circulation of wealth and energy, and can only expand by recruiting new producers — there are no built-in inducements to encourage the circulation of goods and services.

A community currency, on the other hand, can be used by *anyone* in the community as a means of payment for *any* commodity or service.

The only limit to the expansion of its circulation is its acceptability, so it encourages all forms of economic activity. If suitable provision is made for convertibility, it can facilitate transactions with people and organizations outside the community and encourage community "import replacement."

Also, of course, communities may agree — as they did in the Tyrol — to accept each other's currency at par.

Workable now?

The example of Wörgl suggests several prerequisites for success:

- The currency must be *accepted* by local government and other "official" organizations in payment for taxes, rents, licenses, etc., and be used by them for their own local payments.

- It must be exchangeable into national currency, though some deterrents to conversion — a discount on face value, perhaps — may be needed to prevent the whole issue from disappearing from circulation.
- It is essential to encourage the circulation of community money and to discourage hoarding by implementing automatic depreciation.

The demise of the Wörgl experiment has its lessons, too. It will be necessary to amend the present situation under which only the state can issue money as legal tender. Otherwise the issuers of community currency, and perhaps even its users, will face state sanctions.

It will also be necessary to persuade workers that they are not being cheated if part or all of their pay is in community currency.

The experiment is surely worth trying, and the growing strength of the regional movement in Britain, Europe, and parts of the US suggests that there would be political support in many places for such initiatives.

↷ *David Weston, 24 Howe Close, Wheatley, Oxford OX9 1SS, UK (Phone: Int.+44 [0]18677 2832; Fax: Int+44 [0]18677 3351).*

Design your own ten commandments

NICHOLAS ALBERY

AS PART OF THEIR RELIGIOUS EDUCATION, all schoolchildren could be encouraged to design their own ten commandments. Adults might care to do the same. Quakers, a correspondent has suggested to me, might prefer questions to commandments. Here, to get you thinking, and inspired by helping Rev John Papworth improve his own version of the ten commandments, are my ten for now:

1. Show reverence towards creation in all its manifestations.
2. Maintain and care for your network of family, friends, and neighbors.
3. Preserve your health for old age.
4. Procreate only with respect for population limits.
5. Choose work that is life-enhancing.
6. Resolve disputes without resort to unnecessary violence.

Resist enslavement to television, computers, and similar virtual realities.

---

7. Resist enslavement to television, computers, and similar virtual realities.

8. Refrain from acts that seriously impinge on the well-being of others.

9. Create human-scale societies of small neighborhoods, small firms, and small nations.

10. Preserve the beauty and diversity of the planet for future generations.

↪ *Please send feedback to The Institute for Social Inventions, 20 Heber Road, London NW2 6AA, UK (Phone: Int.+44 [0]20 8208 2853; Fax: Int.+44 [0]20 8452 6434; E-mail: rhino@dial.pipex.com; Web: www.globalideasbank.org).*

DIPEx — A database of patients' experiences of medical treatment

Summarized from an article by Andrew Herxheimer, Ann McPherson, Rachel Miller, Sasha Shepperd, John Yaphe, and Sue Ziebland entitled "Database of patients' experiences (DIPEx): A multimedia approach to sharing experiences and information," in *The Lancet*, and from the DIPEx website <www.dphpc.ox.ac.uk/primarycare/research/medical_communications/dipex/index.htm>.

TO FILL A MAJOR GAP IN HEALTHCARE INFORMATION, a specialist medical team in Oxford, UK, is proposing the formation of a database of patients' experiences (DIPEx), to be accessible via the internet or by CD-ROM. Their aim is to improve understanding of people's experience of illness and to promote a more balanced encounter between patient and health professional. Patients will be able to use the database as a resource, which will provide them with some indication of the feelings of others who have experienced similar procedures. Health professionals, on the other hand, will get an indication of patients' priorities and of details of many procedures with which they may not be as familiar.

A collection of interviews with people about their experience of illness, information about support groups, and other resource materials

---

DIPEx will combine a systematic collection and analysis of interviews with people about their experience of illness with evidence of the effects of treatments, information about support groups, and other appropriate resource materials. The aim is for each condition, from hypertension to breast cancer to atrial fibrillation, to have its own offshoot site with all such information, but all under the general DIPEx umbrella.

Interviews with patients will be collected and analyzed for each illness, and the sampling method used will aim to represent the fullest possible range of experiences. For each condition, a steering group (consisting of clinicians, support group members, academics, etc.) will be responsible for identifying and approving the information included. This will be just part of a rigorous monitoring process of DIPEx to ensure the quality and current nature of the information contained in the database. If the project gets the backing it needs, DIPEx could fulfill the patients' need for better information and radically improve the relationship between the health professionals and those they treat.

✦ *To contact DIPEx for information or with questions and suggestions, write to DIPEx, c/o Pamela Baker, GPRG, Institute of Health Sciences, Headington, Oxford, OX3 7LF, UK (E-mail: pamela.baker@dphpc.ox.ac.uk).*

The Direct Charge Co-op Supermarket

NICHOLAS SAUNDERS

IN NANAIMO, BRITISH COLUMBIA, CANADA, THERE IS A NOVEL STRUCTURE for a consumers' co-op. The system is that members pay a high subscription, which is sufficient to pay the overheads of the shop or supermarket, and non-members are excluded. Members may then buy goods at little above wholesale price, as the major costs have already been covered by their subscription. This encourages member loyalty.

The Direct Charge Co-op does best if it sells less —
providing it keeps its members satisfied.

The result is profound. Instead of competing with other supermarkets, trying to sell more with "special offers" and other come-ons, the co-op does best if it sells *less*, providing it keeps its members satisfied. The co-op thus becomes a true agent of its members, aiming to satisfy their needs rather than to sell them more than they want.

The system also involves many other sophistications, such as compulsory investment in the co-op by means of a checkout levy. This generates capital for expansion and provides an essential stabilizing effect — if a rival supplier tries to seduce away members, their subscriptions would be paid out of the levy until the required six months' notice has elapsed.

✦ *Nicholas Saunders died in a car accident in South Africa. A book about his ideas is online at <www.globalideasbank.org/Saunders.HTML>. Please send feedback to The Institute for Social Inventions, 20 Heber Road, London NW2 6AA, UK (Phone: Int.+44 [0]20 8208 2853; Fax: Int.+44 [0]20 8452 6434; E-mail: rhino@dial.pipex.com).*

DIY tutors

Alan Stern

Alan Stern's proposal for do-it-yourself (DIY) tutors is entitled "The Institute for Domestic Engineering Advancement and Learning (IDEAL)."

IDEAL's AIM WOULD BE TO ENROLL STUDENTS WHO WISH TO LEARN the skills of "domestic engineering" and hence to develop and keep their homes, contents, and attachments in an attractive, comfortable, and well-maintained condition.

The tutor would offer practical tutorials in DIY in the student's own home

---

IDEAL would create a register of independent consultant craftsmen or tutors, in much the same way as the Open University – which exists likewise in the US — maintains a local tutor and counselor network. The IDEAL tutor would offer practical tutorials in the student's own home or the place that needs to be worked on, with the objective of helping that student become both proficient and self-sufficient with respect to the problem at hand. Domestic engineering skills that could be taught at such tutorials include painting and decorating, plumbing, wiring and electrical installation, general household and building repairs to both internal and external fixtures and fittings as well as furniture, mechanical appliances, motors, and bicycles, plus guidance in gardening and horticultural projects.

Not to do the job itself but to teach the students how to do it for themselves

---

This new educational institution would be financed by student fees paid (via IDEAL) to the tutor, matching the market rate for the standard job. The tutors would, in effect, be paid not to do the job itself but to teach the students how to do it for themselves.

IDEAL will need to take steps to deal with issues such as the selection and ongoing quality control of tutors, the establishment of criteria for student assessment, and the awarding of a diploma in domestic engineering (Dip. Dom. Eng.).

Initial funding and the foundation of IDEAL could well find benefaction from one or more of the several large retail hardware store chains such as Home Depot which would all benefit from both a financial and public relations perspective as they'd help to create a nation of DIYers.

IDEAL would in turn serve an ever-growing market of home owners desperate to know everything there is to know about DIY, but afraid to experiment on their own.

To summarize the benefits of IDEAL:

- Society would become more self-sufficient on the DIY front, resulting in renovated, revitalized, and refurbished communities.

- Legitimately skilled and empathetic local craftsmen would find a growing and grateful market that would continue to employ their tutorial service as new skills are required to tackle ever more demanding domestic engineering tasks. Moreover, their image and community standing would be enhanced by their IDEAL tutor status, no doubt resulting in increased job satisfaction.

- Industry and commerce would find a new and potentially lucrative outlet for their social responsibility policies.

The chairman of the UK's Wickes Building Supplies, W.J. McGrath, has responded encouragingly to the scheme: "We would be delighted to discuss the possibility of developing our current innovation, product development, and design department into a far more proactive Wickes institute."

➔ *Alan Stern, 5 Walker Close, London N11 1AQ, UK*
(Phone: Int.+44 [0]20 8361 5323).

Dolphin midwives

Summarized from a piece by Vicki Mackenzie in the *Daily Telegraph*.

IGOR CHARKOVSKY, THE RUSSIAN MALE MIDWIFE, is known for helping pregnant women give birth underwater in the Black Sea, aided by dolphins. "Dolphins have an affinity with the baby in the womb and are automatically attracted to pregnant women. They sense when a woman is about to give birth and gather round. They give both the mother and child a sense of protection and safety," says Charkovsky.

Dolphins sense when a woman
is about to give birth and gather round.

"Sometimes when the baby is born, the dolphins nuzzle it to the surface to help it breathe."

Charkovsky began to experiment with dolphins and children in 1979 at a dolphin research station. He discovered that the nine-foot mammals were exceptionally gentle with the children, aged between eight days and eight years, allowing them to ride on their backs and handling them with extraordinary care, understanding, and purposefulness.

More specifically, he realized how powerfully beneficial the animals were for the newborn, who lay peacefully sleeping in the sea with the dolphins swimming around them. He concluded that dolphins, through their benign energy, take the stress off the baby and mother alike, during and after the birth.

→ *Igor Charkovsky, 127254 Moscow, Rustaveli 15a, Kv61, Russia (Phone: Int.+7 [0]7095 219 5937).*

E

Earthquakes predicted by lost pet ads

Based on an article by Jim Berkland in *True News*, monitored by Roger Knights.

SAN JOSE GEOLOGIST JIM BERKLAND HAS PREDICTED OVER 270 EARTH TREMORS and earthquakes since 1979 by watching for sudden increases in the number of lost pet ads in the papers. He has been right in his predictions three out of four times. One of his most famous predictions occurred in October 1989 when he counted 27 lost cat ads in the classified ads — normally there are three or four. Based on this data and other information, such as forecasts of unusually high tides, Berkland predicted in the newspaper that San Francisco would be rocked by a quake registering 6 or higher on the Richter scale. Four days later the nearby San Andreas Fault suddenly shifted, producing a quake registering 7.1 that killed nearly 70 people.

> When he counted 27 lost cat ads in the classified ads, he predicted that San Francisco would be rocked by a quake.

"Animals somehow sense changes in our magnetic field that precede these kinds of disasters," says Berkland.

Eccentrics are healthier

Adapted from the *Examiner,* monitored by Roger Knights; an article by Victoria McKee in the *London Times;* and another article in the *Economist.*

NOT ONLY DO ECCENTRICS LIVE FIVE TO TEN YEARS LONGER than the norm; they are also, on average, healthier (visiting the doctor only once every eight years compared to about three times a year for the general public), happier, and more intelligent than the rest of the population. Dr. David Weeks, author of *Eccentrics: The Scientific Investigation* (published by Stirling University Press), came to admire the sense of humor, creative imagination, and strong will which he discovered are common characteristics of the 1,100 eccentrics he interviewed — and he believes that these traits help keep them healthy. They have an overriding curiosity that drives them on and makes them oblivious to the irritations and stresses of daily life that plague the rest of us.

A sense of humor, creative imagination, and a strong will are common characteristics of eccentrics.

"They don't try to keep up with the Joneses, they don't worry about conforming, and they usually have a firm belief that they are right and the rest of the world is wrong," Weeks says.

Eccentricity, he stresses, is not a mental illness. In a sense it can act as a protection against more serious mental disorders, as the mild cowpox vaccine prevents a full-blown case of smallpox. Eccentrics are creative, highly curious, aware of their differentness from an early age, and happily obsessed by their hobbyhorses. They are often single, the oldest or only child, and poor spellers. They tend to be cheerful and idealistic, full of projects to improve or save the world. They may tinker with perpetual motion machines, discover how to assemble cars from rubbish, or, in the case of John Chapman (better known as Johnny Appleseed), traverse America planting zillions of apple trees.

"I am already using what I've learned from my study of eccentrics in treating the patients referred to me for depression," Weeks says, "and I'm certainly getting better results than I was before. I tell them to loosen up — to use their sense of humor and their imagination. Neurotic patients are over-serious."

✦ Dr. David Weeks, Jardine Clinic, Royal Edinburgh Hospital, Morningside Terrace, Edinburgh, EH10 5HF, UK (Phone: Int.+44 [0]131 447 2011, ext 4614 / 4414).

✦ Dr. Siegried Munser, Professor of Psychiatry at the University of Vienna, has carried out a similar study.

Eco Lavatory

THE ECO LAVATORY, DEVELOPED BY DAVID STEPHENS, a consultant building scientist, is an "earth closet in a polythene grow-bag." It has been piloted by Agribo, an agricultural cooperative in Kinshasa, Zaire, and Oxfam has sent the details to all its field officers, who, the organization believes, "will be stimulated and informed by this excellent idea."

The system is intended as an alternative to the village latrines promoted by the World Bank and the UN for use in the developing world, which not only cause embarrassment and tend to create a nauseating environment but also completely waste the fertilizer value of feces and risk contaminating the groundwater.

Feces are excreted into a black polythene bag and covered with earth after each use. These bags are then used to nurture vegetables and trees.

It is a very simple waste-recycling scheme. In the Eco Lavatory system, feces are excreted into a black polythene bag and covered with earth after each use. These bags are then used to nurture vegetables and trees.

For instance, the bag (half full of feces) is tied at the neck and sunk four inches (ten centimeters) below the ground; ten holes are made in the bag with a pointed stick; tree seedlings or seeds are planted and watered each week with waste water and urine (in the Eco Lavatory system, urine is collected separately, waste water from washing and cooking is added, and the mixture is used to water crops). After two years the sides of the bag are pierced to allow shallow tree roots to spread. Meanwhile, the bag has retained water around the roots, allowing maximum use of available water. Trees planted in bags are protected from salinity.

The Eco Lavatory, as Oxfam sees it, "could transform Third World prospects, reducing water pollution, fly-borne disease, and bilharzia, and enabling food and trees to be grown in infertile and arid regions. People would also have more energy to tend their fields, output from small family farms would be greatly increased, and people would no longer have to seek work in cities or large farms to earn money to buy food. The men could stay at home, increasing the available labor, giving further production gains."

For those in the UK whose septic tank is leaking and causing pollution, "it will be far cheaper to start using an Eco Lavatory and thus get free organic fertilizer."

Stephens has had an Eco Lavatory in his inside bathroom since 1984. "There is no fly or smell problem in the bathroom or garden, and the garden is abundantly fertile with no artificial fertilizers, animal manure, or pesticides. Good crops of tomatoes, cucumbers, etc., have been eaten raw."

Stephens is seeking £50,000 (about $75,000) funding to set up an institute to promote pilot trials of the Eco Lavatory and other resource-saving ideas. Meanwhile he is trying to persuade aid volunteer bodies to get their volunteers to set up such systems in the developing world.

→ *David Stephens, Tir Gaia Solar Village, Rhayader, Powys LD6 5AG, UK*
  (Phone: Int.+44 [0]1597 810 929).

80-hour labor tax for co-op residents

The following is adapted from an item entitled "Selegrand co-operative housing movement," which appeared in the Norwegian Ideas Bank.

NORDAS, AN UNUSUAL HOUSING CO-OP NEAR BERGEN IN NORWAY, requires each family to contribute 80 hours of work each year to maintaining the garden and other co-op facilities; single people have to do 40 hours work. Hours that are not done for whatever reason have to be paid for.

Each family contributes 80 hours' work per annum towards maintaining the garden.

Houses are clustered around shared open space, promoting easy daily contact (while verandas provide a sense of privacy, as they are designed to be out of sight of the neighbors). The community building, with its kindergarten, youth club, and meeting room for the monthly co-op meetings, is the natural focal point for the co-op.

The overall result is that there is a strong community spirit and feeling of mutual aid — voluntary cooperation that has led to the provision of care for children and those who are elderly and infirm or handicapped.

The members were directly involved in all stages of the co-op, from planning to building; in fact many were involved as laborers. The housing is felt to be both inexpensive and tailored to the individual needs of the residents.

→ *Edvard Vogt, Hestehaugen Selegrend Borettslag and Selegrendbevegelsen*
  (Phone: Int.+47 [0]55 18 62 20). Hestehaugen, which is run on similar lines
  to Nordas, is another project developed by Selegrend Co-operative Housing.

→ *See also Stiftelsen Idebanken, PO Box 2126, Grünnerlokka, Norway,*
  (Phone: Int.+47 [0]2203 4010; Fax: Int.+47 [0]2236 4060;
  E-mail: idebanken@online.no; Web: www.idebanken.no).

Electronic scheme for per capita carbon quotas

Summarized from a paper entitled "Domestic Tradable Quotas (DTQs)" by Richard Starkey and David Fleming.

DOMESTIC TRADABLE QUOTAS WOULD INVOLVE EVERY CITIZEN being given, free, an equal number of carbon units to cover domestic fuel needs, including private transport. Businesses and other organizations would have to buy their units from government. Those who used less than their entitlement could sell their surplus units to others who needed more. The scheme would embody an obligation to pay for using the capacity of the environment to absorb carbon emissions and a right for every citizen to share in its value. It would complement at a national level the international contraction and convergence model for sharing carbon emission rights proposed by the Global Commons Institute. Unlike previously proposed rationing schemes, this is an electronic scheme, not one based on paper coupons.

The scheme embodies an obligation to pay for using the capacity of the environment to absorb carbon emissions.

In the first half of the 21st century there will be a virtual phase-out of dependency on fossil fuels. This will be in response to the need to reduce carbon emissions sufficiently to stabilize the climate, and it may happen in the setting of supply constraints affecting crude oil and gas. An economic instrument is therefore required that will reduce demand for fossil fuels without causing profound economic damage and that will distribute reduced supply without injustice and intolerable hardship. Domestic Tradable Quotas is an efficient solution that allocates emission rights by a combination of entitlement and tender, and maintains a secondary market that is open to all.

Domestic Tradable Quotas are an economic instrument to enable national economies to reduce their carbon emissions. They are designed for application within the economy and are to be distinguished from international instruments designed for trading between nations. They allow national authorities to take control over the rate at which fossil fuel consumption is reduced, while allocating the available resource fairly and maintaining price flexibility so that the economy can distribute it efficiently.

The nation implementing the scheme sets an overall Carbon Budget that is reduced over time. The "carbon units" making up this budget are issued into the market in two ways. First, there is the unconditional entitlement for all adults. The share of emissions for households is issued to all adults on an equal per capita basis. (Children's carbon usage would be provided for in the existing system of child allowances.) The remaining share is issued through a tender to commercial and industrial companies and to the public sector, using the system already established for the tender of government debt. It is distributed by the banks to organizations using direct credit (for the units) and direct debit systems (for the payments). The government receives revenue from the tender. Trading revenues are earned by the market-makers — quoting bid and offer prices.

There is a national market in carbon units in which low users can sell their surplus for revenue, and higher users can buy more. When they make purchases of fuel or energy, consumers and firms surrender quota to the energy retailer, accessing their quota account (for instance) by using their QuotaCard or by direct debit. The retailer then surrenders carbon units when buying energy from the wholesaler. Finally, the primary energy provider surrenders units back to the Register when the company pumps, mines, or imports fuel. This closes the loop.

It is a hands-off scheme, with virtually all transactions being carried out electronically, using the technologies and systems already in place for direct debit systems and credit cards. The scheme has been designed to function efficiently not only for people who participate in it but also for those who do not participate — e.g., for overseas visitors, for the infirm, and for those who refuse to cooperate. The advantages claimed for the scheme are that it is effective, equitable, and efficient.

Some fuel purchasers will not have any carbon units to offer at point of sale — for example, foreign visitors, people who have forgotten their card, people who have used all their quota, and small firms and traders that do not bother to make regular purchases of units through their banks. All these must buy quota at the time of purchase in order to surrender it. Individuals who cash in all their quota when they receive it and who then have to buy quota to cover their fuel purchases pay a cost penalty for this; they have to buy carbon units at the market's offer price and surrender them at the (lower) bid price — and the difference between these two prices is the cost of their non-participation.

There is a national market in carbon units in which low users can sell their surplus for revenue, and higher users can buy more.

The task of achieving a massive decarbonization of society by a reduction in the market economy's dependency on fossil fuels should not be underestimated. It will require the substitution of the market's central technology and energy resource, and it will require solutions to be developed at speed. Although it is often assumed that alternatives can be achieved by efficiency gains and technological shifts, this view fails to acknowledge the scale of the task.

What will be required is an energy revolution that penetrates every vein and tissue of the economy, changing behavior, land-use patterns, and expectations, and bringing every individual along willingly in the collective task of adapting to a world almost without fossil fuels.

An instrument that engages every individual with the personal challenge to achieve the required deep reductions

---

Taxation is an indirect instrument that assumes business-as-usual, a robust economy, a widely distributed ability to pay taxes, and a steady and strong supply of oil. These assumptions may not all apply in the present case. Domestic Tradable Quotas would directly reduce carbon emissions, maintain price flexibility, and build in long-term quantity signals to allow time for major adjustments. They would achieve a fair distribution of access to fuel while bringing about a rapid reduction in the total quantity, and would engage every individual with the personal challenge to achieve the required deep reductions in carbon dependency.

→ *Richard Starkey, CCEM, HUBS, University of Huddersfield, Huddersfield HD1 3DH, UK (Phone: Int.+44 [0]1484 472946; Fax: Int.+44 [0]1484 472633; E-mail: R.STARKEY@hud.ac.uk).*

→ *Dr David Fleming, The Lean Economy Initiative, 104 South Hill Park, London NW3 2SN, UK (E-mail: ellerdale@gn.apc.org).*

Energy dollars

SHANN TURNBULL

THE UNIT OF ELECTRICAL POWER OUTPUT, the kilowatt hour (kwh), has much appeal as a universal unit of value for an autonomous community banking and monetary system.

Money would be in the form of a voucher to supply a specified number of kwhs at a specified time in the future.

Money would be created by the owners of the power generator. It would be in the form of a voucher or contract note to supply a specified number of kwhs at a specified time in the future. These notes would be created and issued by the owners of the generator to pay for its purchase and installation.

The value of notes, which could be used for redemption in any given time period, would be limited by the output of the generator. The notes that had a specified maturity date would represent the "primary" currency. Such currency notes would be held mainly by investors, investment banks, and banks. Commercial banks would hold primary currency notes as a reserve currency, just as a bank currently holds gold or a merchant banker holds grain or other commodities.

Similarly, the commercial bank would issue its own notes, which the holders could convert or cash in for the primary notes or reserve currency and which could be used to pay their power bills at the time specified. The secondary notes could be denominated in kwhs but without any specified redemption time. They could thus be used as hand-to-hand money in the community.

Some of the more important issues to be considered in comparing the suitability of kwhs or gold as a basis for a monetary system are set out in the table below:

EVALUATION CRITERIA	KWH $	GOLD $
UNIT OF VALUE	KWH	OUNCES/GRAMS
QUALITY TESTING	NOT REQUIRED	DENSITY
INTRINSIC CONSUMABLE VALUE	100%	10%
SUBJECTIVE VALUE	NIL	90%
CHANGES IN CONSUMPTION	RELATED TO TOTAL ECONOMIC ACTIVITY	LITTLE RELATED TO ECONOMIC ACTIVITY
GLOBAL AVAILABILITY	UNIVERSAL	HAPHAZARD
CHANGES IN PRODUCTION	RELATED TO CONSUMPTION	LITTLE RELATED TO CONSUMPTION
RATE OF CHANGE	RELATIVELY STABLE	LESS STABLE
COST OF PRODUCTION	RELATIVELY STABLE BY REGION AND IN TIME	FLUCTUATES WITH REGION AND IN TIME
COST OF STORAGE	NOT REQUIRED	1% OF VALUE P.A.
COST OF INSURANCE	NOT REQUIRED	1% OF VALUE P.A.
COST OF DISTRIBUTION	INCREASES WITH DISTANCE	CHANGES LITTLE WITH DISTANCE

→ Shann Turnbull, GPO Box 4359, Sydney, NSW 2001, Australia
(Phone: Int.+61 [0]612 233 5340; Fax: Int.+61 [0]2 9327 1497).
The full pamphlet, Selecting a Local Currency, is available from Centre 2000,
2 O'Connell Street, Sydney, NSW 2000, Australia, for Aus $1.50.

Excursion bus to promote neighborliness

The following is adapted from an item entitled "Inner-city dwellers run own excursion bus," which appeared in the Norwegian Ideas Bank.

FOR THE INHABITANTS OF LUNDTOFTEGATE HOUSING COOPERATIVE in central Copenhagen, a bus called Lundte has become an important meeting place. AKB Association, which owns the housing co-op, bought the bus for the cooperative in 1995.

The residents have used the bus to go everywhere from Legoland to the local supermarket. One of the residents, Lissi Dohr, tells how she went abroad for the first time when she went on holiday to Poland with the bus.

Before the days of the bus, the neighbors rarely even said hello to each other.

Before the days of the bus, the neighbors rarely even said hello to each other. Now they get to know each other intimately through the various outings and activities.

The bus was bought secondhand for 112,000 kroner (about $13,000). The chairperson of the residents' association is very happy with the investment, believing that it has helped reduce vandalism in the neighborhood, which in turn has saved the association a great deal of money.

➔ *AKB Lundtoftegate, Beboernes prosjektkontor, Lundtoftegate 57, DK-2200 Copenhagen, Denmark (Phone: Int.+45 [0]35 81 24 57).*

➔ *See also Stiftelsen Idebanken, PO Box 2126, Grünnerlokka, Norway (Phone: Int.+47 [0]2203 4010; Fax: Int.+47 [0]2236 4060; E-mail: idebanken@online.no; Web: www.idebanken.no).*

Exporting the Swiss constitution

NICHOLAS ALBERY

THE UK-BASED INSTITUTE FOR SOCIAL INVENTIONS INITIATED A SYMPOSIUM for Eastern and Central European politicians and constitution designers that took place in Lausanne in 1990, financed by the Swiss government and organized by the Swiss Institute of Comparative Law. I had always admired the Swiss constitution from afar, and I felt that the 50 or so constitutional experts from the emerging democracies who were present for the three days of deliberations could only have benefited from the painstaking immersion into every aspect of the Swiss system. The Swiss, with typical, if misplaced, modesty, made no efforts to sell their constitutional set-up to the easterners and were scrupulous in drawing attention to Switzerland's failings.

Positive aspects

I learned a great deal at this symposium about the essential ingredients that have made the Swiss constitution so suitable for export to troubled "hot spots" around the world.

The most vital aspect of all, I believe, is the rural Swiss commune at the village level, each with a couple of thousand inhabitants enjoying a fair degree of autonomy. These communes have their own constitutions and some meet once a year to debate and vote at open meetings.

In Switzerland, final sovereignty resides clearly
with the people, and so there is not the same
chasm of distrust between governors and
governed that is apparent in most other countries.

The main constitutional safeguard against over-mighty government is the right of the Swiss citizen to gather between 50,000 and 100,000 signatures, depending on circumstances, so as to trigger a referendum on a topic they have stron feelings about. These referenda are relatively popular. The average Swiss citizen can vote perhaps three to five times a year in federal referenda, once every two years on a cantonal issue, and once every three years in a communal referendum. There is virtually no limit to the odd and diverse topics that citizens can attempt to add to the constitution in this way. Thus article 32 forbids the sale of absinthe, and there was even a referendum recently that, had it been successful, would have required the abolition of the Swiss army. In Switzerland, final sovereignty resides clearly with the people, and so there is not the same chasm of distrust between governors and governed that is apparent in most other countries.

Minorities are safeguarded in that a referendum,
once passed by the voters, must also be
passed by a majority of the cantons.

Furthermore, minorities are safeguarded in that a referendum, once passed by the voters, must also be passed by a majority of the cantons. As for minorities within cantons, those that feel sufficiently oppressed can follow the example of the Jura, which through a complex series of referenda broke away to form its own canton. Although the Swiss constitution makes no allowance for secession, we were assured that if Jura had wanted to leave the federation and join France instead, it would not have been prevented from doing so; in practice, such a misguided impulse would not have survived a closer look at the centralized nature of the French Napoleonic system.

At the federal level, sweetness and light between the different language groups is preserved by reserving each of them a permanent place in the cabinet. And presidential ambitions are curtailed by having a presidency that rotates among the seven ministers. Many Swiss do not even know who their current president happens to be. (Uruguay once copied the Swiss constitution, only to have its president rebel at his lack of power, with an army coup promoting him to military dictator.)

Improving the Swiss constitution

How could the Swiss constitution be improved by a country in Central or Eastern Europe or elsewhere seeking to adopt it for its purposes? What are the failings of the Swiss system?

- It all works so slowly. A Swiss referendum can take four or five years to achieve its by then obsolete aim. No commercial business that took four years to make a simple yes/no decision could succeed. A total revision of the Swiss constitution has been underway for 25 years, and the end is still not in sight.

I suggest that to prevent the constitution from becoming over-encrusted with obsolete elements, lawmakers should ensure that any additions lapse automatically after a hundred years unless renewed. Also, the whole referendum process should be dragged into the modern era by devoting in-depth television programs to referenda debates, followed by voting within a few weeks.

Give lottery tickets to all those who turn up to vote.

- People in Switzerland apparently feel that they suffer from a surfeit of democracy, with apathy spreading among the young and the working classes. On several occasions only just over 20 percent of the electorate has bothered to vote in a referendum. It might be worth trying Peter Mucci's idea to attract working-class voters in particular: give lottery tickets to all those who turn up to vote.

The lowest turnouts are for referenda on abstract constitutional issues beloved by law professors. The highest turnouts are for issues that hit the Swiss citizen in the pocket. The suspicion lurks that the Swiss refused to join the United Nations less for reasons of principle than because it was going to cost them. They prefer to buy into particular programs a la carte, which might indeed be a sensible way for other nations to fund the UN while keeping firm control of the purse strings.

E

The Swiss prefer to buy into particular UN programs a la carte.

- Swiss cities need subdividing into a network of communes. John Papworth in the *Fourth World Review* has highlighted the lack of political subdivision within Swiss urban communes. A city commune of half a million voters is absurdly large compared with its rural counterpart. Perhaps this lack of meaningful representation has contributed to the alienation of the young, reflected in the fact that the Swiss have the highest proportion of drug addicts (and AIDS victims) of any country in Europe.
- A tax on the size of firms is needed to control the powers of the large corporations, which otherwise tend to ride roughshod over any constitutional or other safeguards.
- The main present threat to the Swiss constitution is an external one. There are signs that the Swiss economy may be heading for troubled times as multinationals and banks (pressured by the United States into becoming no longer so secret) move elsewhere in search of the European community market. It is possible that financial fears may push the Swiss into the Common Market, a move that would not only, I believe, diminish their long-term prosperity, but would also homogenize their cantonal diversity and replace a highly evolved system of local autonomy and human-scale government with dictates from Brussels.

I am sure that the Swiss "peasant" farm in the mountains visited by our coachload of East European constitution designers would not survive among the EC's industrialized farms. The 82-year-old grandfather sang and yodeled for us, saying that he felt like a millionaire. His gold was his life in the mountains and his bevy of grandchildren. His son, with occasional help from the neighbors, looked after 40 cows. As good a test as any of whether a country's agriculture is sufficiently human-scale is, I believe, to find out if the cows have individual names. In this case each had not only a name over her stall (Amoureuse, Bourgeoise, etc.), but also a posy of flowers and a heavy bell waiting for the ceremonial autumnal descent to lower lands. I bought a distinctive Gruyere cheese that would probably not have met EC pasteurization standards, and I learned that farming is more heavily subsidized in Switzerland than even the EC would allow, for it has to take into account the difficult mountainous nature of the terrain.

✦ Fourth World Review, *The Close, 26 High St, Purton, Wiltshire SN5 9AE, UK (Phone: Int.+44 [0]1793 772214; Fax: Int. 44 [0]1793 772521; E-mail: john.papworth@btinternet.com).*

✦ *The Swiss Constitution – Can it be Exported by Nicholas Gillett is available for £8.50 incl. shipping from YES, 14 Frederick Place, Clifton, Bristol BS8 1AS, UK.*

Extending the living room to the street

The following is adapted from an item entitled "Residents furnish the street in Stavanger," which appeared in the Norwegian Ideas Bank.

RESIDENTS IN THE NORWEGIAN CITY OF STAVANGER (population 108,000) have transformed a whole street into a permanent social space by furnishing it with benches, tables, a pergola, potted plants, a notice-board, wiring for those who want to sit in the street with their computers and surf the internet, and a flag-pole (a flag is hoisted on the pole to celebrate residents' birthdays).

It all started one day when Trond Sigvaldsen took his father's garden bench out in the street to give it a polish, taking with him his newspaper and a coffee flask. People started to gather around his bench for a chat. So, they thought, why not make the whole of Vikesdalsgata street into an open-air living room?

Having first knocked on doors to get the agreement of all the residents, they spent tedious months negotiating with local authorities and then more months furnishing their new dwelling space.

The launch took place in the spring of 1999, and nowadays the street has become something of an attraction for surrounding neighborhoods. The improvements are much appreciated by the elderly waiting for their buses and by schoolchildren in their lunch hours.

✦ *Olav Stav, City of Stavanger, 4005 Stavanger, Norway*
(Phone: Int.+47 [0]51 50 70 90; Fax: Int.+47 [0]51 50 70 21;
E-mail: infoavd@stavanger.kommune.no; Web:www.stavanger.kommune.no).

✦ *See also Stiftelsen Idebanken, PO Box 2126, Grünnerlokka, Norway*
(Phone: Int.+47 [0]2203 4010; Fax: Int.+47 [0]2236 4060;
E-mail: idebanken@online.no; Web: www.idebanken.no).

Eye signs on the road

DAVID WADE, A WRITER OF BOOKS ON ISLAMIC DESIGN, suggests that "ambi-per-plexity" — his term for the confusion people have in telling their left from their right, which is the bane of all drill sergeants — is a far more widespread condition than is generally recognized.

Children, tourists, and sufferers from ambi-perplexity all have their lives endangered, especially when crossing one-way streets, by traffic coming from an unexpected direction. "Look Left" or "Look Right" signs are not readily taken in, and the arrows sometimes used, although more direct, are ambiguous because they can be taken to indicate the direction of traffic.

Wade suggests that if white eyes and eyebrows were painted on the roads, with the pupils indicating which way to look, it would save lives. It would also add to the growing stock of what Wade terms the "international pictogram language" found on road signs, cleaning labels, and so on, which is fast becoming like "a Chinese Esperanto of the eye."

Arrows are ambiguous because they can be taken to indicate the direction of traffic.

Mr. M.J. Read, the director of road safety at the Royal Society for the Prevention of Accidents, commented: "This suggestion is both simple and complete. We receive many, many 'bright ideas,' most of which are commendable in that they are trying to tackle the terrible road accident problem. Most, however, are usually impracticable for a variety of reasons. I have pleasure, therefore, in commending this proposal."

→ *David Wade, Plas Tylwych, Tylwych, near Llanidloes, Powys, Wales
(Phone: Int.+44 [0]1597 88627).*

F

Family noises transmitted to babies

Summarized from an article by Meredith Small entitled "Bringing up baby" in *New Scientist.*

"THE INFANT'S EVOLUTIONARY HISTORY, and just about every psychological study of infants, reveals that they are designed to respond favorably to sensory stimulation," suggests James McKenna, an anthropologist at Pomona College in Claremont, California. He believes that the idea of monitoring a sleeping baby through an intercom is all wrong. Instead, we should switch the amplifiers to let sleeping babies listen to family noises.

"Babies' heart rates and breathing are known to change and be positively affected by listening to mother speak, laugh, or sing," says McKenna. "Family noises promote healthy infant sleep."

Forest gardens

ROBERT HART'S LIFETIME STUDY OF AGROFORESTRY CULMINATED in his establishing a small model forest garden on his farm on Wenlock Edge, Shropshire, UK. The forest garden he made there could be repeated many thousands of times, even by those who possess only small town gardens.

A forest garden can enable a family to enjoy a considerable degree of self-sufficiency, with minimal labor.

A forest garden can enable a family to enjoy a considerable degree of self-sufficiency, with minimal labor, for some seven months of the year, providing the very best foods for building up positive health. It is a miniature reproduction of the self-maintaining ecosystem of the natural forest, consisting entirely of fruit and nut trees and bushes, perennial and self-seeding vegetables, and culinary and medicinal herbs.

Robert Hart writes: "It is no good waiting for the Powers-That-Be to take decisive action in the infinitely serious crisis caused by wholesale forest destruction, curbed and restricted as they are by blind prejudice and vested interests. Those who care, the ordinary people, should take action themselves to restore the earth's depleted forest cover, even though they may live in cities."

Once established after about two years, a forest garden is
- self-perpetuating, because all plants are perennial or active seed-seekers, such as borage and cress;
- self-fertilizing, because deep-rooting trees, bushes, and herbs draw upon minerals in the subsoil and make them available to their neighbors, and because the complex should include edible legumes such as lucerne, which inject nitrogen into the soil;

A forest garden is self-watering, because deep-rooting plants tap the spring-veins in the subsoil.

- self-watering, because deep-rooting plants tap the spring-veins in the subsoil, even at times of drought, and pump up water for the benefit of the whole ecosystem;
- self-mulching and self-weed-suppressing, because the scheme includes rapidly spreading herbs, such as the mints, and perennial vegetables, such as Good King Henry, which soon cover all the ground between the trees and bushes, thus creating a permanent

mulch. In fact, one main problem is to check their pervasiveness in the interests of less-dominating plants;

• self-pollinating, because all the fruit and nut trees are chosen to be mutually compatible for pollinating purposes — unless self-fertile — and also because the scheme includes many aromatic herbs and vegetables such as tree-onions and wild garlic, which undoubtedly exert curative influences on their neighbors;

• resistant to pests and diseases, not only on account of the aromatic plants, but also because any complex consisting of a wide spectrum of different plants does not allow the build-up of epidemics, such as occurs in monocultures.

A forest garden is also self-healing. The only work required is pruning, controlling plants that seek to encroach on others, and mulching with compost once a year, after the herbaceous plants die down in the late autumn. The scheme is highly intensive, making use of all seven "stories" found in the natural forest for the production of economic plants. These stories are

• the canopy formed by the tops of the higher trees;

• the planes of low-growing trees such as dwarf fruits;

• the shrub layer, comprising bush fruits;

• the herbaceous layer of herbs and vegetables;

• the ground layer of plants that spread horizontally rather than vertically, such as creeping thyme;

• the vertical layer occupied by climbing berries and vines;

• the rhizosphere, with shade-tolerant plants.

In order to achieve a maximum economy of space, the following devices are employed:

• Some of the vegetables and herbs are grown on mounds, erected in accordance with the German Hügelkultur system.

• Full advantage is taken of fences for training climbing berries, such as the Japanese wineberry, and fan-trained plums.

• An apple hedge has been created according to the French Bouche-Thomas system, where the trees (Allington Pippins) are planted diagonally so that they grow into each other.

• A hardy Canadian Brant vine is trained over the tool shed and another is to be trained up an old damson tree.

There is a "family tree," comprising three compatible varieties of English eating apples — Sunset, Discovery, and Laxton's Fortune — grafted onto a single root stock.

Conventional horticulturalists will object that food plants cannot achieve full productivity when planted in such close proximity to each other. But as the natural forest and even the herbaceous flower border demonstrate, many plants thrive best when grown close to plants of other species. The reasons for this are contained in the science of plant symbiosis, about which very little research has been undertaken since Ehrenfried Pfeiffer invented his system of "sensitive crystallization." This is a study that must be extensively developed if agroforestry is to attain its full potential.

Many plants thrive best when grown close to plants of other species.

The forest garden's produce is health-promoting, just as in the 16th and 17th centuries, when England produced an amazing number of men of exceptional hardihood and genius and a standard article of diet was a salad, called "sallet" or "salgamundy," comprising a wide variety of cultivated and wild vegetables, fruits, and herbs.

As for the forest garden helping restore the earth's forest cover, if ten trees were planted in a hundred thousand gardens, that would amount to a million trees. Quite a forest!

→ The Forest Garden, *a booklet by Robert Hart (who died in 2000), is available from the Institute for Social Inventions.* Forest Gardening, *a full-length book with color photos, and* Forest Gardening, *a video (48 minutes VHS format), are both published by Green Books. There are now a number of forest gardens around the world.*

Former inmates mentoring prisoners

Michael Patterson

Manitonquat is an elder and storyteller of the Wampanoag Nation. He has run prison rehab programs in three states since the 1970s, with a recidivism rate of under six percent, which is far lower than the overall rate.

Manitonquat says that the great majority of prisoners he worked with over the years — well over 90 percent — have never had so much as one person they could trust in their lives. He notes that when he runs his Medicine Circles in prisons, many inmates state that this is the first time in their lives they have ever experienced respect.

Former inmates who have completed his program mentor current inmates to ensure their healthy return to society.

Manitonquat proposes a mentor program, in which former inmates who have completed his program mentor current inmates to ensure their healthy return to society.

→ *Manitonquat, 173 Merriam Hill Rd, Greenville, NH 03048. Contact him for details of his book* Ending Violent Crime.

→ *Michael Patterson, POB 332, Granville, MA 01034-0332 (E-mail: MedicineOwl@lycosmail.com).*

Forum Theater — A new way to resolve children's fights

MICHAEL SOTH

Michael Soth ran a Social Invention Workshop with a class of 22 seven- and eight-year-olds at Earlsfield School in London, UK. He showed them a creative way to resolve their fights — to reenact these fights twice, the second time with elegant variations — as he describes in this article.

ONE MORNING, WHEN THE CHILDREN CAME INTO THE CLASSROOM, one girl had a bleeding lip. She had been involved in a fight on her way to school. The children were excited and talked among themselves: "Next time I'm really going to beat him up"; "No, he's much stronger," and so on.

The teacher asked what had happened and was immediately flooded with six different versions of the event at the same time. She told all of them to be quiet and asked the injured girl. While recounting what happened, the girl was interrupted by the other children, who were getting impatient and making comments, and then by the teacher, who asked the interesting question: "Why is it always *you* who gets into fights?"

The girl got defensive. "I'm sticking up for myself," she responded. Raised eyebrows from the teacher, and another child saying "This is boring," finally made the girl give up and subside into sulking. The teacher was not entirely satisfied with this conclusion, but she knew of no other way to deal with it, except to warn, "If I were you, I would be more careful in future."

This example, with an exceptionally patient and well-meaning teacher, is quite typical. My feeling is that nothing has really been resolved and that the same thing will happen again the next day.

What is lacking is the belief that human beings can actually resolve conflicts to the satisfaction of everybody involved. Most children operate on the assumption that human beings are basically hostile to each other and are only held back by the guarding and policing forces of law, order, and authority.

I understand this belief as the children's accurate perception of most adults they come into contact with. The children mirror, in an unmediated and raw form, the largely unconscious underlying assumptions by which most of us shape our social reality (although a lot of well-intentioned adults

would vehemently disagree that they are in fact operating on these assumptions). The violence and distress in the ordinary schoolyard is an eloquent
reminder that the slogan "Don't do as I do — do as I say!" doesn't actually
work very well in education.

To my mind, this situation calls for urgent social invention. We need
structures that make conflict resolution possible without violence.

The method I used with this class, and which worked astonishingly well,
is called Forum Theater. It was developed by the Brazilian Augusto Boal, who
was inspired by the writings of Paolo Freire and worked in South America
with those suffering from oppression.

The basic method is as follows: The conflict is first discussed. When the
situation, behavior, and feelings of those involved are clear and understood
by everybody, they "perform" this "original" once from beginning to end
without interruption.

**The whole audience is encouraged to say "stop" at any point
where they feel that an alternative behavior is possible.**

Then they repeat it a second time, but this time the whole audience is encouraged to say "stop" at any point where they feel that something is wrong or that
an alternative behavior is possible. They are then invited to take somebody's
role in the original and to act it differently. Somebody acting differently
changes the whole course of the interaction, and it is possible to observe
whether a more satisfactory and less oppressive conclusion is reached. If not,
the original is played a third time and is again open to changes and alternatives. In this way, different ways of behaving are tried and the possible results
elucidated. This collective process of replaying and transforming the original
oppressive situation into one that everybody is happy with involves everybody's creativity and makes reaching a consensus possible.

With the children, we took up conflicts that happened in playtime and
used all the emotional "charge" that the children brought with them to keep
them motivated in, for once, investing energy in actually resolving the conflict.

Usually we spent quite some time listening to everybody's version of
what had happened before we could agree on what the sequence of events
had been. It was very important to give everybody space in creating this
"original" (the reproduction of what had actually happened). If we did not do
this, the children dropped out and gave up, feeling ignored or misrepresent-
ed, and were not interested in working out alternatives.

In the beginning they needed a great deal of guidance until they all
understood the ground rules of Forum Theater. Thereafter the process was
quite smooth, and my main work was to hold them back from all shouting
"Stop!" and wanting to suggest alternatives at once.

It was important that we made it very clear that we were not on anybody's side. By the end of term, the groupings that used to form, threatening the other side with retribution — which seemed to me like a Lilliputian version of super-power politics — were no longer necessary. We had provided a structure for conflict resolution that they all accepted and felt safe with, for they were confident that they would be able to establish their needs and position through it.

The children got so involved that they wanted to demonstrate Forum Theater to their school assembly, which they did. In the last session of term they discussed what they had learned: mainly, they said, "How to avoid fights, how not to be greedy and hog things, how to listen to each other, and how to respond to name calling." The feedback from parents and teachers was that they felt the children had learned something that would be useful for the whole of their lives.

➔ *Michael Soth, 16 Riverside Road, Oxford OX2 OHU, UK (Phone: Int.+44 [0]1865 723613).*

Free and Independent Republic of Frestonia

NICHOLAS ALBERY

THE FREE AND INDEPENDENT REPUBLIC OF FRESTONIA was founded on October 27, 1977. The residents in Freston Road, Notting Dale, London W11, threatened with eviction to make way for a giant factory estate, held a referendum. A 95 percent majority was in favor of independence from Great Britain and a 73 percent majority in favor of joining the European Union. An application for membership, complete with coat of arms, was sent to the United Nations, along with a warning that a peacekeeping force might be required.

Everyone became a minister; there was no prime minister.

There were 120 residents in Frestonia, living in about 30 houses on one acre of land. Everyone who wanted to take part became a minister; there was no prime minister. The Minister of State for Education was a two-year-old, Francesco Bogina-Bramley, and the Minister of State for Foreign Affairs was a dwarf, the actor David Rappaport-Bramley (who wore a T-shirt saying "Small is Beautiful"). The nation's motto on its coat of arms was "Nos sumus una familia" — "We are one family" — and everyone adopted the surname Bramley (just in case the Greater London Council were to succeed in evicting us, for they then might have to rehouse us together, as one family).

The media descended on Frestonia from around the world. The *Daily Mail* newspaper printed a leader column and a report "from our Foreign Correspondent in Frestonia." Japanese TV filmed New Zealand TV filming nothing much going on in our uneventful communal garden. Coachloads of young tourists, mainly from Denmark, arrived and were shown round the borders in ten minutes or so, receiving their Frestonian passport stamps and leaving, rather dissatisfied.

A National Film Theater of Frestonia opened in the People's Hall, with the first showing being *Passport to Pimlico* and films by the Sex Pistols. The National Theater of Frestonia opened with the international premiere of *The Immortalist* by Heathcote Williams, preceded by no less than three national anthems. (The *London Evening Standard* had urged its readers to submit suitable anthems to us.) Frestonia applied to join the International Postal Union and printed its own postage stamps, with replies to our letters coming in from around the world.

If you did not exist, it would be necessary to invent you.

It all worked like a dream. The Greater London Council, which previously had refused to deal with us, now told the media that it would negotiate with us "in New York or wherever," and the GLC's Tory leader, Sir Horace Cutler, sent us a letter saying, "If you did not exist, it would be necessary to invent you." We replied, "Since we do exist, why is it necessary to destroy us?" Sir Geoffrey Howe, MP, wrote to us that as one who had "a childhood enthusiasm for *Napoleon of Notting Hill Gate*," he could hardly fail to be moved by our plight.

We were suddenly transformed in the GLC's eyes from a bunch of squatters, hobos, and drug addicts into an international incident that was providing them with an opportunity to show how enlightened they were — while threatening them with the prospect of negative media coverage if they carried on with their plans to evict us.

A public enquiry was ordered. The Greater London Council had its lawyers, and I represented Frestonia as the Minister of State for the Environment. We proposed that Frestonia become a mixed-use site for houses and craft workshops. We won the enquiry.

Frestonia was eventually rebuilt to our design with several millions of pounds of foreign aid from Great Britain, channeled via the Notting Hill Housing Trust to our own cooperative. We used Christopher Alexander's superb book on timeless architecture, *Pattern Language,* to vote as a co-op on the various architectural patterns we wanted incorporated in our new development (see the item "Pattern Language for community architects" later in this volume).

Today, I am immensely proud of the development that was built, complete with its overhanging roofs, decorated brickwork, and enclosed communal gardens.

In 1998 there was a great party in a marquee in the communal garden to mark the 21st anniversary of independence. The spirit was still strong.

Frestonia goes to show that with imagination and humor you can run rings round the establishment.

✦ *For more details about Frestonia, as well as photographs and stamps, see <www.globalideasbank.org/Frestonia.html>.*

Free transmitter alarms for battered women

Based on an item in *Time* magazine, monitored by Roger Knights.

ADT Security Systems of Tampa is offering panic button pendants to battered city women as part of a pilot program. Pressing the panic button within 200 feet of the home relays a signal through the telephone line to ADT, which in turn notifies the police. To be eligible for the test program, the woman must agree in advance to press charges if the assailant is caught.

Friday made the third day of the weekend

Alexandre Potolitsyn

Adapted from an e-mail to the Global Ideas Bank from Russia.

Friday should be the third day of the weekend. The advantages are many:

- The Saturday/Sunday weekend is a symbol of Judeo-Christian unity. This in a way has soothed the problem of coexistence of these two cultures: if you are free to party the same day as your neighbor, you have less opportunity to envy or offend. Adding Friday to this weekend means adding Muslim believers into the same club — leading to less tension and more respect.
- Longer weekends will create more jobs, allowing more people to feel socially included.

There will be more time to pay attention to one's children.

- There will be less stress as jobs become less tiring. There will be more time to spend with the family, more time to pay attention to one's children.
- There will be more access to distant parts of the country than is possible during the current weekend, leading to greater development of remote parts of the country.

✦ *Alexandre Potolitsyn (E-mail: shurikp@cityline.spb.ru).*

Fruit trees in urban downtown areas

Adapted extracts from an e-mail by Chris Gensic to the Institute.

I HAVE ALWAYS WONDERED WHY FRUIT TREES were not planted in urban downtown areas. These trees could provide food for the economically deprived inhabitants of cities.

Fruit trees could provide food for the economically deprived inhabitants of cities.

The trees could come out of seed stock generated in national and state parks, thereby eliminating the high cost of purchasing saplings from private firms. Once the trees are planted and established, they would generate food for many years.

I would gladly volunteer for such a program here in Washington, DC. I am looking into the possibilities.

→ *Chris Gensic, 1642 Center Avenue, Charlottesville, VA 22903 (Phone: 804 982 5538; E-mail: cgensic@cstone.net).*

Editorial comment

A one-acre site in Queensland, Australia, has been turned into an "edible" public park. Designed on permaculture principles, the park provides fruit, herbs, flowers, and vegetables to anyone walking by. Local residents and schools carry out any necessary work and maintenance.

Fuel from wind and water

THE MISSION OF HYDROGEN NOW! (www.hydrogennow.org) is to bring hydrogen into the world energy market by educating and motivating the public.

One of the most inspiring developments has been the very successful hydrogen "Welgas" experiment in the town of Harnosand, Sweden, financed by the Swedish steel industry, SAAB, and other firms. In Harnosand, Olaf Tegstrom designed and lived in a house where the electricity came from a small computer-controlled Danish windmill in the garden. The electricity was used to electrolyze filtered water into its constituents (hydrogen and oxygen), with the hydrogen gas used for cooking and heating the house and as fuel for a SAAB car.

The electricity was used to electrolyze filtered water into its constituents: hydrogen and oxygen.

The car was non-polluting as the exhaust consisted almost entirely of water vapor, and the safe storage problem was solved as the potentially explosive hydrogen gas was absorbed to form a metal hydride, with the hydrogen only released as required.

Hydrogen needs to become the world's prime provider of energy, a technological revolution that will help solve the problem of atmospheric pollution, and at the same time gradually replacing nuclear power. Hydrogen is an excellent fuel with an energy content three to four times higher than oil, and it can be produced from all known energy sources, besides being a by-product of many industrial processes.

→ *Further information on hydrogen cars may be obtained by visiting the websites for the Palm Desert Project <www.humboldt.edu/~serc/>, Mercedes-Benz research <www.mercedes-benz.com>, and the American Hydrogen Association <www.clean-air.org/>.*

Fundraising using web-based Common Application Forms

NICHOLAS ALBERY

IN MY VISION OF THE FUTURE, all that a non-profit project seeking funding would need to do would be

- to have internet access or to go to the local library or any other place that provides this;
- to get help if necessary to complete a simple web-based application form;
- to use software such as Funder Finder on the web to identify appropriate funders;

E-mail the web-based application form to 50 or so foundations

---

- to e-mail the completed application to the 50 or so foundations that appear to be most relevant;
- to answer online any supplementary questions that the funder may insist on before allowing an application to be e-mailed to a particular foundation with its own specific requirements;
- and finally, and most onerously, to print out and "snail mail" applications to those Neanderthal and antisocial foundations that couldn't be bothered to make themselves approachable via the web.

Either way, the first stage of fundraising would have be completed in an afternoon.

Many foundations insist on their own forms — forms that can't even be filled in using a word processor.

Contrast this with the unhappy present situation. At present in the UK, for instance, a small non-profit organization can spend at least half a day per application, filling in special forms for those foundations that insist on their own forms — forms that can't even be filled in using a word processor. Often it is necessary to approach at least 50 different foundations with one's project application (and one foundation then insists on 13 copies of the completed application pack). Assuming that at least 35 of the UK's major grant-giving bodies, and some of the smaller ones, require their own forms to be filled in, this can mean that over a week can be spent on this work by the average charity, days that could have been spent on fulfilling the charitable objectives for which it was set up.

Our calculations show that the small UK non-profits could save a total of £117 million (about $175 million) a year in office and labor costs if the above recommendations were implemented. From the perspective of partic-ipating foundations, the long-term advantages would include the following:

Less diversion of money intended for charitable purposes to the applicant admin and fundraising organizations' costs

---

- Applicant organizations would divert less money intended for char-itable purposes to admin and fundraising.
- Foundations would receive more, but better targeted, applications that would be more likely to be within their areas of interest.
- A wider range of applicants with less fundraising expertise would be empowered to approach foundations, especially applicants that can-not afford full-time or professional fundraisers.
- There would be a cut in the cost of responding to applications.

→ *For more about this project, see <www.globalideasbank.org/SD/SD-49.HTML>.*

G

Gaviotas —
A self-sufficient community in a harsh environment

The following is summarized from an article by Alan Weisman entitled "Gaviotas, oasis of the imagination," in *YES! A Journal of Positive Futures* and from a radio documentary by Alan Weisman (the full text of this interview is on the web at <www.loe.org/html/books/gaviotas.html>).

PAOLI LUGARI, A COLOMBIAN ENVIRONMENTALIST, HAS WORKED SINCE 1971 to develop Gaviotas, a self-sufficient community in the nutrient-poor savanna grassland of Los Llanos, the huge eastern plains in Colombia.

As he puts it: "They always put social experiments in the easiest, most fertile places. We wanted the hardest place. We figured if we could do it here, we could do it anywhere. The only deserts are deserts of imagination. Gaviotas is an oasis of the imagination."

Rain forests and excess people were a foolish mix.

Lugari was also motivated by the need to find alternative habitats for Colombia's increasing population, having realized that "rain forests and excess people were a foolish mix" and that, because population and development pressures were ever-intensifying around the world, people would eventually need to learn to live in even the harshest of the planet's ecosystems.

Starting with some abandoned concrete sheds at the midpoint of the failed trans-llano highway, and using the labor of Guahibo Indians, llanero workers, and keen students from the universities, Lugari and colleagues developed prototype windmills, solar motors, water heater panels, micro-hydro turbines, biogas generators, and various pumps. In 1976, the settlement, christened Gaviotas, was designated as a model community by the United Nations and given a research grant.

They plant more trees than the Colombian government through its entire forestry program.

Later, inspired by a Catholic missionary settlement in Brazil, the Gaviotas residents started hydroponic nurseries, germinating plants in trays of sawdust and wood chips with added minerals. They also planted over a million tropical pines (*Pinus caribaea*), having obtained the seedlings from Guatemala, Nicaragua, Belize, and Honduras — indeed, they plant more trees than the Colombian government through its entire forestry program. Instead of cutting them for timber, they're selling the renewable sap for making paint and turpentine.

In the moist understory of the Gaviotas forest, birds have returned to redistribute seed — dormant seeds of native trees probably not seen in Los Llanos for millennia are sprouting. Biologists have now counted at least 40 species that are sheltered by Caribbean pines. Over the coming decades, Gaviotas will let these new native trees choke out the pines (which are sterile anyway) and return the Llanos plains to what many believe was their primeval state, an extension of the Amazon. Already the population of deer and anteaters is growing.

While coping with intrusions by military, guerrillas, and paramilitary groups, the Gaviotans have also had to develop ways to become self-sufficient once the UN grant ran out.

The factory at Gaviotas employs many of the 130 Gaviotas residents as well as people from surrounding communities. Here they produce the innovative devices that Gaviotas uses and sells, such as the windmills and a double action pump that pumps water six times deeper than normal models. Instead of raising and lowering the heavy piston inside a pipe, this one leaves the piston stationary and lifts the pipe made of plastic tubing. This simple, inexpensive pump has revolutionized rural life across Colombia for people who used to haul their water in buckets from muddy tropical rivers.

The seesaw is actually a pump in disguise.
Over the years, Gaviotas technicians have installed
these in thousands of schoolyards.

In the open-air Gaviotas preschool, the seesaw is actually a pump in disguise. As the children rise and descend, water gushes from a vertical pipe into an open cement tank. Over the years, Gaviotas technicians have installed these in thousands of schoolyards, using kid power to provide villages with clean water.

Besides schooling for the children, housing, healthcare, and food are free in Gaviotas, and everyone earns the same above-minimum-wage salary. With no poverty, families remain a manageable size and there's no crime problem in Gaviotas. And apparently no one gets married in the Gaviotas utopia. Couples live in free union.

No one gets married in the Gaviotas utopia.
Couples live in free union.

The settlement's hospital building is set on a rise, a maze of angles formed by skylights, glass awnings, solar collectors, and brushed steel columns. A Japanese architectural journal has named this 16-bed Gaviotas hospital one of the 40 most important buildings in the world.

Inside, the air-conditioning system is a blend of modern and ancient technology. The underground ducts have hillside intakes that face north to catch the breeze. Egyptians used this kind of wind ventilation to cool the pyramids.

In the hospital kitchen, methane from cow dung provides the gas for stovetop burners, but most of the cooking is done with solar pressure cookers. Photovoltaic cells on the roof run a pump; solar heated oil circulates around the stainless steel pot.

In a separate hospital wing, a large thatch *ramada* has been built for llanos-dwelling Guahibo Indians. Instead of using beds, these patients lie in hammocks hung from wooden beams.

While the doctor treats the sick, their families stay with them because the Guahibo believe that to wall someone off away from his people is the ultimate unhealthy confinement. To earn their keep, the relatives tend vegetables in an adjacent greenhouse — Lugari hopes that this greenhouse will form the foundation for one of the finest medicinal plant laboratories in the tropics.

A new village is planned for the 600 resin-collecting workers they expect to need by the year 2004, with additional factories to encourage women to come — factories producing drinking water, fruit preserves, and harps.

More recently, Gaviotas has decided to sell its cattle herd and to allow Gaviotans to raise rabbits, chicken, and fish as private enterprises. "Too much red meat is bad for us," says Lugari, "too many cow pastures are bad for the environment, and too much *hamburgerizacion* is bad for the world."

Meanwhile, in Bogota, Colombia's capital, rooftop solar collectors developed by Gaviotas are now heating water for more than 50,000 apartments.

✦ *The whole story of this remarkable community is told in* **Gaviotas**! A Village to Reinvent the World *by Alan Weisman (published by Chelsea Green).*

✦ *Centro Gaviotas, Paseo de Bolivar #20-90, Avenida Circunvalar, Bogota, DC, Colombia (Phone: Int.+57 [0]1 2286 74466 / 2969; Fax: Int.+57 [0]1 281 1803).*

Giving gardens to the needy

DAN BARKER

Dan Barker, a poet and novelist, has been giving away vegetable gardens in Portland, Oregon, since the 1980s. Funded by private foundations and trusts, Barker builds gardens in the backyards of recipients — at no cost to them. He constructs soil frames and brings in a trellis, seeds, fertilizer, tomato cages, pest controls, instructions, advice, and cooking tips. Barker does his work in the needier neighborhoods, where the proceeds — material, psychological, and spiritual – can make the greatest difference. Barker has built many hundreds of gardens. He wrote the following article, summarized from the *Sun*, monitored by Roger Knights.

When you plant, use three seeds – one for you, one for your neighbor, one for God.

THE CHARITABLE TRUSTS AND FOUNDATIONS WANT TO KNOW if the gardens work. Do they dissolve the current anguish ripping the dignity from the impoverished? I can't say with certainty that one gang kid has been deflected from his run toward a violent end or prison, or that I've passed out sandwiches to people who have no reason to vote or given shelter to homeless families. But I've saved thousands of people considerable money, time, and trouble, trips to the doctor, despair, sessions with their therapists, longing for death. I tell the gardeners that this is the store you don't have to go to. You get hungry, come on out and pick yourself a meal. When you plant, use three seeds – one for you, one for your neighbor, one for God. They always laugh when I mention God, or silently let the word slide on by. I go home knowing that I've planted the possibility of self-caring. But the donors want a figure; I tell them that each garden is capable of producing at least $500 worth of food a summer, if you don't count gas, time, etc., and that 95 percent of the gardens are productive the first year, 85 percent the second — I don't keep track after that, though often I run across a garden still producing after five or six years. Some people even load their gardens onto trucks when they move.

What is more difficult to convey is the health and joy alive in a 70-year-old woman showing me her beans and tomatoes, or the pride of accomplishment beaming from the face of the 12-year-old son of an ex-prostitute who put him in charge of the garden. Or the envy of neighbors – I put down a garden and the next year two or three neighbors will call for theirs. We're strictly word of mouth. I wouldn't know how well it was working otherwise. There's never been a shortage of recipients, only a shortage of money, time, and energy.

The original idea was a reaction to the diaspora of the perpetual garden, a way to reverse what is so celebrated now: the deprivation of the many for the gain of the few. Too ambitious a thought. The free market/welfare system victimizes those unprepared for its complexities; it's too large, too pervasive to be countered by something so small as a garden, extended metaphor or not. Still, the notion contains the whole cycle of life, incorporating use of local materials (dairy and racetrack manures, construction subsoil, compost, surplus seed), reducing use of fossil fuels, reconnecting people with life — thus serving all.

Everything necessary is already in place: parks departments have trac-
tors, trucks, working space, and greenhouses, much of the time underused;
thousands of people desire to be of service to their neighbors; workers could
be recruited from extension agents and agricultural programs. All we have to
do is put it together and get it paid for. One announcement on TV and there
would be no end to the requests for gardens. People in need want all the help
they can get. They will be the ones, and are the ones, who quiet the neighborhood. They will endure and will invite peace from others.

It's taken me seven years to get the project into the black, and it could
not have happened without the goodwill and generous hearts of my wife and
friends. We lift ourselves. Accolades go to the foundations and trusts that
have sponsored and believed in the work. They call it charity, but it is simply service, a providence that can even be employed by the recipients, as
shown by several older women who wanted — and got — double or triple
gardens so they could provide vegetables for the entire neighborhood.

Don't you think trying to lift the weight
of suffering by one micron is real?

They ask me why I do this, and I say it needs to be done. Don't you need
a vegetable garden, one you can get to, one you can use without too much
physical effort to maintain? There, now you've got one, good luck, happy to
do it. Or, once, when I was tired and being interviewed, the young reporter
asked, "Why?" and I said, "I'm out to change the world." And when she
asked, "What do you do in real life?" my tact left me, and I replied, "Don't
you think giving away gardens is real life? Don't you think trying to lift the
weight of suffering by one micron is real?" To affirm the good in you, in life;
the Tao speaks of neighbors who do not tread on each other but live their
lives in quiet wonder, grow old, and die. And the way to affirm the good life
is to deliver it. If such an act challenges the men on the corner, good; shovels are easy to come by.

What is bothersome is not that giving away gardens is so wonderful, but
that it is so rare.

→ *Dan Barker, Home Gardening Project Foundation, 8060 Upper Applegate
Road, Jacksonville, OR 97530
(E-mail: hgpf@teleport.com; Web: www.teleport.com).*

GPS bracelet for lost children

SCOTT SNYDER
Summarized from an e-mail to the Global Ideas Bank.

THIS IS A PROPOSAL TO WHICH I HAVE GIVEN AN ENORMOUS AMOUNT OF THOUGHT. I would like to design a wrist bracelet for children that could give Global Positioning System coordinates on their current location.

The bracelet would reply with the location and child's heart-rate.

It would also reply to a query (if someone were to call that particular bracelet) with the location and child's heart-rate. Currently this technology is being used in the United States for pagers that are able to reply with one of three preset responses.

The bracelet would be adjustable so there would be no need to purchase additional sizes as the child grows; and it would be removable by a responsible parent or law enforcement officer (in the US this would be the FBI).

As an option, any time the bracelet is removed, it could send a signal (silent) to the local law enforcement agency. The responsible parent would need to telephone that agency within a few minutes to reassure them that it was a routine removal.

The bracelet's casing would be made of titanium alloy and should not make any sound when the device is queried.

I am all too aware of the increasing numbers of children being abducted or kidnapped, and I'm convinced that this would deter any such attempts.

❖ *Scott Snyder, Moline, Illinois (E-mail: storm2000@home.com).*

Golf carts as the only vehicles allowed in city areas

CORINNA GALLOP
Summarized from an e-mail to the Global Ideas Bank.

THE FOLLOWING PROPOSAL MAY NOT BE POLITICALLY ACCEPTABLE, but it would solve urban transport problems.

It is pretty difficult to get road rage when you're sitting in a golf cart.

Cars would be banned from cities (with park-and-ride only for private vehicles). A fee would then be charged for use of golf carts. These would be run electrically so there would be no exhaust fumes. They only travel up to 20 miles per hour, which would be sufficient for use within a city. Anyone wanting to get to a destination more rapidly would have to use the bus, which would travel faster due to the paucity of other traffic. Parking would no longer be a problem as golf carts are so much smaller. The number of accidents would also be significantly reduced, the golf cart being both lighter and slower.

The quality of life would be vastly improved for everyone.

I reckon that road rage incidents would also decrease. It is pretty difficult to get road rage when you're sitting in a golf cart.

↪ *Corinna Gallop, Flat 4, 56 Belsize Park, London NW3 4EH, UK (Phone: Int.+44 [0]20 7722 7038; E-mail: corinnagallop@hotmail.com).*

Grameen Banks for the poorest of the poor

GUY DAUNCEY

Summarized from Guy Dauncey's book *After the Crash: The Emergence of the Rainbow Economy* (published by Green Print/Merlin Press).

THE GRAMEEN BANK IN BANGLADESH WAS SET UP IN 1977 by Muhammad Yunus. Instead of insisting on personal collateral, the Grameen Bank asks landless villagers to form into groups of 50 people of the same sex — Bangladesh being a Muslim country — and then to form into smaller groups of five. The ten groups of five each meet regularly with a bank worker for training, and with each other to discuss their business ideas. Each loan has to be approved by a smaller group of five, by the larger group, and finally by the bank's officer in the field; Grameen does not believe in having huge city banks. Two people in a small group can then apply for a loan. The average loan size is 135 Takas, equivalent to about $10,700, given the annual incomes of landless peasants.

Women borrowers use their loans for such things as buying a milk cow, paddy husking, and cattle fattening, while men tend to invest in paddy and rice trading, cattle fattening, and setting up grocery shops. After six weeks, if the first two have been regular in their payments, the next two members get their loan, and after another six weeks, the final member. The loans are not analyzed by the bank — they leave it up to the villagers to do the analysis. As they depend on each other's success in repaying them, the system works. The default rate is only 2.7 percent — there is a 97.3 percent on-time repayment record, and in recent years the bank has made a profit on its activities.

The bank is active in 15,000 villages, employing 8,000 workers, and lending to half a million people, and it is growing all the time. Grameen banking operations are being developed in India and in South America, where people in 60 cities and towns in 12 countries are benefiting from loans organized by Accion International. The South Shore Bank in Chicago has experimented in rural Arkansas with Grameen principles linked to other community economic development strategies. The annalists of the 23rd century might well be able to write that for the poorer people on the Earth, the invention of social collateral and peer-group lending was the single most significant economic breakthrough of the 20th century.

The single most significant economic breakthrough of the 20th century

---

The success of the Grameen philosophy of fostering an effective entrepreneurial culture among the very poor has been a notable success in Bangladesh. As a result, Grameen has been encouraged (and found itself with the resources) to expand beyond providing credit. Struck by the plight of self-employed handloom workers in Bangladesh whose products were being marginalized by bigger-scale suppliers, Grameen stepped in with a scheme whereby it acted as a broker for these individual producers, lending them a presence and clout on the international market they would otherwise lack.

The same spirit informs the Grameen Agricultural Foundation, which owns no land itself but enters into agreements with individuals to become a partner in production. In return for an agreed portion of the harvest, the GAF supplies training, funding, and marketing. This set-up appears to have helped dislodge a traditional production cycle which tended, by its inefficiency and lack of market awareness, to reinforce their poverty. GAF encourages its partners to experiment with unfamiliar crops and to acquire new (sustainable) techniques. Both GAF and the small farmers profit through these arrangements, creating a natural momentum for the growth of the scheme.

Yunus's zeal to show that a responsible capitalism is the best way forward for the developing world has also been extended into healthcare. "Bangladesh has a very elaborate health service infrastructure which is built to provide free medical services to all citizens. As a result, the service is extremely poor and it is available only to a handful of privileged people," he maintains. As an alternative, Grameen has set up a private health insurance scheme, on a cost-recovery basis, which Yunus insists is both affordable for people poor even by Bangladesh standards and more efficient than the free state service.

→ *Guy Dauncey, Sustainable Communities Consultancy, 395 Conway Rd, Victoria BC V8X 3X1, Canada (Phone/Fax: 250 881 1304 at work, or 250 881 1555 at home; E-mail: guydauncey@earthfuture.com; Web: www.earthfuture.com).*

→ *See also* **Grameen Dialogue**, *newsletter of the Grameen Trust, Mirpur Two, Dhaka 1216, Bangladesh (Phone: Int.+88 [0]2 801138; Fax: Int.+88 [0]2 803559; Web: www.grameen-info.org).*

→ *Microfinance Network, 733 15th Ave, NW, Suite 700, Washington DC 20005 (Phone: 202 3472953; Fax: 202 3472959; Web: www.bellanet.org/partners/mfn).*

G

The Great Ape Project

Summarized from *The Great Ape Project: Equality Beyond Humanity*, edited by Paola Cavalieri and Peter Singer (published by Fourth Estate).

THE GREAT APE PROJECT BRINGS TOGETHER AN INTERNATIONAL GROUP of distinguished ape researchers, philosophers, and writers who support a declaration of the rights of great apes. At the core of their argument is an encounter between ethology and ethics — between our study of animal behavior on the one hand and, on the other, our rhetoric about the basis of equality between humans.

The declaration urges that in drawing the boundary of our moral community, we should focus not on a common sense of humanity, but rather on the fact that we are intelligent beings with a rich and varied social and emotional life.

Like humans, great apes can solve problems,
deceive others, plan ahead, and make moral judgments.

These are qualities we share with the great apes. Like humans, great apes can solve problems, deceive others, plan ahead, and make moral judgments. All of which suggests, according to the book's contributors, that we should make membership of the larger group sufficient entitlement for inclusion within our sphere of moral equality.

Within this "community of equals," certain basic moral principles or rights would apply, which would govern our relations with each other. Among these rights, which would be enforceable by law, are the following:

The Right To Life

The lives of members of the community of equals are to be protected. Members of the community of equals may not be killed except in very strictly defined circumstances, for example, self-defense.

The Protection of Individual Liberty

Members of the community of equals are not to be arbitrarily deprived of their liberty; if they should be imprisoned without due legal process, they have the right to immediate release. The detention of those who have not been convicted of any crime, or of those who are not criminally liable, should be allowed only where it can be shown to be for their own good, or necessary to protect the public from a member of the community who would clearly be a danger to others if at liberty. In such cases, members of the community of equals must have the right to appeal, either directly, or, if they lack the relevant capacity, through an advocate, to a judicial tribunal.

The Prohibition of Torture

The deliberate infliction of severe pain on a member of the community of equals, either wantonly or for an alleged benefit to others, is regarded as torture, and is wrong.

The Great Ape Project aims to restore ethics to its proper place in determining the shape of the society in which we live. At its heart is a highly innovative social project born of an enlightening historical parallel. The Project's instigators explain:

Aristotle refers to human slaves as "animated property." The phrase exactly describes the current status of non-human animals. Human slavery therefore presents an enlightening parallel to this situation. At the root of the master's power over the slave is the fact that the slave is not acknowledged by the community.

Political action on behalf of animals today focuses on abolishing abhorrent practices and forms of treatment. But a look at the history of slavery shows that this type of approach had only a marginal impact. Gladiatorial games were abolished, but this did not influence the general condition of slaves. Neither was this condition fundamentally changed by the undoubtedly desirable regulations that ruled out the most blatant forms of mistreatment — for example, branding on the face or castration.

Just as manumission was the only way out for slaves,
so it appears to be needed for animals.

In antiquity there was one way to leave the no man's land of the slave: manumission. The term, which means literally "to emit or release from one's hand," vividly conveys the sense of giving up control over something. Just as manumission was the only way out for slaves, so it appears to be the kind of response needed for animals. Not only does it address directly the question of status, it is also a long-standing and well-known instrument for the bestowal of freedom on those who cannot win it for themselves.

In a sense, extending equality to the great apes through a process of actual and symbolic manumission is a cautious step. There are relatively few of them in the world, and the move would require a much more modest rearrangement of our lives than, say, the extension of equality to all animals. Some animal liberationists, among them some of the contributors to *The*

Great Ape Project, would like to see a much larger extension of the moral community, so that it includes a wider range of non-human animals. But here the book's editors consider that the tactic of selective manumission exhibits one of its advantages when tied to the broader ethical aim of extending our community of equals.

The initiative can weaken the spurious species boundaries that serve to justify our current limited understanding of moral obligation

---

If we are to dismantle the barrier that serves to keep non-humans outside the protective moral realm of our community, then, they argue, we could do worse than to begin by applying pressure to one of the weaker areas underpinning the certainties of human chauvinism. Since we now have sufficient information about the capacities of chimpanzees, gorillas, and orangutans to make it clear that the moral boundary we draw between them and us is indefensible, it makes sense that we begin by extending full moral equality to these, our closest cousins among non-human animals. But, they continue, though it cannot be used for all animals at once, this reformist measure can still create a precedent. From this first step, the initiative can be extended across the evolutionary tree, weakening the spurious species boundaries that serve to justify our current limited understanding of moral obligation.

Implications for society

In *The Great Ape Project,* Richard Dawkins writes of our difficulty in accepting that humans are genetically part of the Great Ape family, and of the implications for society of accepting such a perspective.

Politics would never be the same again, nor would theology, sociology, psychology, or philosophy.

I can assert, without fear of contradiction, that if somebody succeeded in breeding a chimpanzee/human hybrid the news would be earth-shattering. Bishops would bleat, lawyers would gloat in anticipation, conservative politicians would thunder, socialists wouldn't know where to put their barricades. The scientist that achieved the feat would be drummed out of politically correct common-rooms; denounced in pulpit and gutter press; condemned, perhaps, by an Ayatollah's fatwah. Politics would never be the same again, nor would theology, sociology, psychology, or most branches of philosophy. The world that would be so shaken, by such an incidental event as a hybridization, is a speciesist world indeed, dominated by the discontinuous mind.

→ *The Great Ape Project, PO Box 1023, Collingwood, Melbourne, Victoria, Australia 3066 (Fax: Int.+61 [0]39 2 481 4784; Web: www.envirolink.org/orgs/gap/gaphome.html).*

→ *Etica & Animali, Corsa Magenta 62, 20123 Milan, Italy (Phone: Int.+39 [0]2 481 5514; Fax: Int.+39 [0]2 481 4784; E-mail paolac@planet.it)* Etica & Animali *journal is edited by Paola Cavalieri, who co-edited the original edition of* The Great Ape Project.

Groningen — The car-free city for bikes

Summarized from articles by David Nicholson-Lord in the *London Independent* and in *Resurgence* magazine.

IN GRONINGEN, THE NETHERLANDS' SIXTH LARGEST CITY, the main form of transport is the bicycle. In the 1970s, ruinous traffic congestion led city planners to dig up city-center roads. In the 1990s they set about creating a car-free city center. Now Groningen, with a population of 170,000, has the highest level of bicycle usage in the West, as 57 percent of its inhabitants travel by bicycle.

---

57 percent of Groningen's inhabitants travel by bicycle.

The economic repercussions of the program warrant some examination. Since 1977, when the six-lane road intersection in the city's center was replaced by greenery, pedestrianization, cycleways, and bus lanes, the city has staged a remarkable recovery. Rents are among the highest in the Netherlands, the outflow of population has been reversed, and businesses, once in revolt against car restraint, are clamoring for more of it. As Gerrit van Werven, a senior city planner, puts it, "This is not an environmental program, it is an economic program. We are boosting jobs and business. It has been proved that planning for the bicycle is cheaper than planning for the car." Proving the point, requests to ban car traffic now regularly arrive from shopkeepers in streets where cyclization is not yet in force.

Businesses, once in revolt against car restraint,
are clamoring for more of it.

A vital threshold has been crossed. Through sheer weight of numbers, the bicycle lays down the rules, slowing traffic, determining the attitudes of drivers. All across the city, roads are being narrowed or closed to traffic,

G

cycleways are being constructed, and new houses built to which the only direct access is by cycle. Out-of-town shopping centers are banned. The aim is to force cars to take longer detours while providing a "fine mesh" network for bicycles, giving them easy access to the city center.

Like the Netherlands nationally, Groningen is backing bicycles because of fears about car growth. Its ten-year bicycle program is costing $30 million, but every commuter car it keeps off the road saves at least $255 a year in hidden costs of noise, pollution, parking, health, etc.

Cycling in Groningen is viewed as part of an integral urban renewal, planning, and transport strategy. Bicycle-friendly devices seen as exceptional in the UK — separate cycleways, advanced stop lines at traffic lights, and official sanction for cyclists to do right-hand turns at red lights — are routine.

New city-center buildings must provide cycle garages. There are tens of thousands of parking spaces for bikes, either in guarded parks — the central railway station has room for over 3,000 — or in street racks. Under the City Hall a nuclear shelter has been turned into a bike park.

"We don't want a good system for bicycles; we want a perfect system," says Mr. van Werven. "We want a system for bicycles that is like the German autobahns for cars. We don't ride bicycles because we are poor. We ride them because it is fun, it is faster, it is convenient."

→ *Gerrit van Werven, Bestuursdienst, Gemeent Groningen, Grote Markt 1, Groningen, NL-9712-HN, The Netherlands (Phone: Int.+31 [0]50 679111; Fax: Int.+31 [0]50 673070).*

Gurus — How to rate them

THERE HAVE BEEN SO MANY SCANDALS SURROUNDING CULT RELIGIOUS SECTS that the Institute for Social Inventions has compiled a list of questions that a would-be disciple could ask before joining up with a guru or new cult. The total number of "yes" answers to questions such as the following provides a rough-and-ready comparative rating of gurus.

1. Is what the guru offers free?

2. Is the guru relatively poor (i.e., he or she does not have personal control — or control in practice — over more wealth than he or she needs to live in normal comfort and dignity)?

3. Can you gain access to the teachings without having to join the organization (i.e., are there books, tapes, open meetings, etc., that transmit the knowledge needed)?

4. Is it easy to leave the guru, are ex-disciples treated satisfactorily, and are "opponents" of the guru treated fairly?

Is there respect for quality in the work of the guru's organization (no ugly architecture, for instance)?

---

5. Does the guru refrain from sexual involvement with the disciples?

6. Is free contact allowed with families and friends?

7. Is there respect for quality in the work of the guru's organization (no ugly architecture, for instance)?

8. Are the guru's words in harmony with past spiritual insights, such as contained in Huxley's anthology *Perennial Philosophy*?

9. Is the organization non-authoritarian — are there signs of democracy, for instance, i.e, are questions and debates and thinking for oneself welcome?

10. Is the guru's legitimacy anchored in a tradition that points back to previous gurus, rather than the guru claiming to be the sole arbiter of his or her legitimacy?

11. Does the guru avoid claiming to be a perfect master, offering the only route to enlightenment? Is the guru open about his or her own "feet of clay," if they exist?

12. Does the guru recognize that his or her authority is "phase-specific," e.g., lasting only long enough to bring you up to his or her level of understanding?

13. Does the guru's organization, in its methods and in all aspects of its daily regime, successfully avoid brainwashing psychologically coercive or any other techniques?

14. Do the guru's or the organization's replies to these questions agree with evidence from other sources? For instance, ask the Cult Information Service for its perspective (Box 867, Teaneck, New Jersey 07666; Phone: 201 833 1212; Web: www.cultinformationservice.org).

15. Does the guru have fewer than 1,000 signed-up disciples? (Gurus with large followings seem to be more prone to succumb to the temptations of power.)

"Guru Quotient" ratings table

Having looked at the available literature, with additional information coming from present and past disciples (and having answered the questions as if all the gurus rated were still alive), we have produced the following very approx-

imate table of gurus dead and alive. The number shows the percentage of "yes" answers to the questions in our checklist, which is, admittedly, very basic.
- Bhagwan (Osho) 17
- Maharishi 23
- Leonard Orr of the Rebirthing movement 53
- Swami Bhaktivedanta of the Hare Krishna movement 60
- Krishnamurti 73
- Stephen Gaskin (from the Tennessee farm commune) 77

These ratings do not necessarily reflect what a disciple can learn from a particular guru; they are more an indication of how "safe" the guru is. Potential disciples would be well advised to steer clear of becoming organizationally involved with "low GQ" gurus. Almost all traditional gurus for the last 3,000 years would have had little difficulty scoring in the 70s and above.

→ *Please send improved checklist questions (or examples of trying out the test on a guru that you know) to "Guru Quotients," c/o The Institute for Social Inventions, 20 Heber Road, London NW2 6AA, UK (Phone: Int.+44 [0]20 8208 2853; Fax: Int.+44 [0]20 8452 6434; E-mail: rhino@dial.pipex.com; Web: www.globalideasbank.org).*

Health Quotients

DR. JOHN HART
The following is an extract from the book *Wealth and Well-Being* (published by Oxon Publishing).

HQ is a measure of a person's health and well-being on the lines of the IQ measure of intelligence.

ONE THING PEOPLE LACK IS A MEMORABLE, QUANTITATIVE ASSESSMENT of their health. The HQ concept meets this need. First mooted in a *Social Inventions Journal* (No. 4), HQ stands for Health Quotient. It is a measure of a person's health and well-being on the lines of the IQ measure of intelligence. By definition, average health is 100. The advantage of the idea is that individuals gain a precise view of their health and can establish clear objectives for improvement. The HQ would need to measure objective indicators of health such as blood pressure, but also behavioral elements such as drinking and smoking, and well-being elements such as stress and even the difficult-to-define "contentment." Sir Douglas Black, chair of the British government commissioned inquiry "Inequalities in Health: The Black Report" published in 1980, said in a Christie Gordon Lecture, "Of their nature, health statistics relate to morbidity and mortality, not to positive health, which in a euphoric passage we define as a 'positive expression of vigor, well-being, and engagement in one's environment or community.'"

The HQ concept could be an integral part of a preventive screening program. Screening specific groups for cervical and breast cancer is already justified, by smear and X-ray mammography respectively, as is measuring blood pressure to detect hypertension and assessing blood cholesterol for predisposition to coronary heart disease. Furthermore, a battery of tests becoming available from biotechnology companies enables identification of those who are most likely to die from common conditions such as diabetes, emphysema, heart disease, several types of cancer, and even, it is said, alcoholism, long before they actually do so. New pregnancy tests have been developed enabling the identification of genetic disorders such as cystic fibrosis and Huntingdon's Chorea. A new generation of "physician office" diagnostic tests is arriving. Among these is a kit allowing plasma cholesterol to be determined in two minutes using a pinprick blood sample. Screening is an idea whose time has come — particularly combined with an HQ component that leads to the adoption of healthier lifestyles.

The HQ part of the screening process might well comprise three stages: a preliminary questionnaire, the test itself, and a follow-up interview. The pretest questionnaire would seek to establish dietary pattern, behavior, social circumstances, typical levels of psychological stress, information on vaccinations previously received, present and previous illnesses and disabilities, and use of health service facilities in the recent past. Also obtained would be information relating to disease and death among the subject's parents, grandparents, and blood relatives to establish the genetic background.

The HQ test itself would be a comprehensive medical.

The HQ test itself would be a comprehensive medical. Conventional height, weight, and other measurements would be made; hearing and sight tests done; blood and urine samples analyzed; and so on. The patient would also be subject to treadmill exercise stress tests with computer-assisted monitoring to assess cardiovascular and lung function. Other screening assessments would be made in what would clearly be an extensive test schedule.

The follow-up interview would inform the individual of the HQ findings and identify the potential for improvements, focusing on key risk factors relevant to that person. Subjects with an HQ under 100 would be given particular attention in this regard. The intention would be to develop a Personal Program for Risk Reduction, covering diet, exercise, etc. The opportunity could also be taken to give information, where appropriate, on family planning, sexual diseases including AIDS, dental hygiene, availability of government and personal social services, sickness support groups (of which there are almost 9,000, including one for people with diseases so rare they thought no one else had them), local sporting activities, counseling services, welfare benefits (e.g., heating grants), accident prevention, and so on. The HQ follow-up could also be used to improve immunization relating to polio, measles, rubella, and whooping cough.

Who to screen? A representative sample of the entire population, and members of high-risk groups. The representative sample would enable a "national HQ" to be determined. This would provide the basis for determining progress against a target of a ten percent improvement in the nation's health by a given year. It would also facilitate broad-based international comparisons in the health sphere in the way that gross domestic product (GDP) figures permit in the economic sphere. It will have a further advantage: it will enable us to determine "productivity" in the health business in terms of the HQ score added by a certain measure, health team, or hospital.

↠ Dr. John Hart, 16 Burleigh Court, Cavendish Place, Brighton BN1 2HR, UK (Phone: Int.+44 [0]1273 720879).

Health tips — The ten best

THE INSTITUTE FOR SOCIAL INVENTIONS HAS PUBLISHED 1,001 Health Tips From Recent Medical Research — a book intended to help people regain control of their health. It is so much easier to safeguard your health than to regain it once it has gone. Here are some of the best or less well-known tips from the book.

- Lycopene, derived in the diet from tomatoes, can have health benefits. One large study has shown that those with high levels of lycopene had half the risk of a heart attack, and another study has shown that eating tomato products more than twice a week, as opposed to never, reduced the risk of prostate cancer by up to 34 percent. Processed tomatoes appear to offer the most benefit (tomato sauce, puree, and ketchup), with tomato juice showing little or no benefit. Lycopene is also found in watermelon, pink grapefruit, and apricots.

- Researchers believe that a low-fat diet may reduce the risk of Alzheimer's. Sweden, with its high fish and low-fat diet, has the lowest incidence of Alzheimer's.

- Robert Swain and colleagues at the University of Wisconsin have found that the brains of active rats sprouted more capillaries than those of sedentary rats. Swain believes that a similar explosion in capillaries would take place in human brains within a month of physical exercise and as a result of mental "cognitive work-outs," and may protect against age-related decline.

- Kiwi is the most "nutritionally dense" of the commonly eaten fruit, scoring high for Vitamins C and E, magnesium, potassium, fiber, serotonin, arginine (used to treat impotence), and nutrients recommended to combat cancer and heart disease.

- In a study of 11,000 volunteers — meat-eaters, semi-vegetarians, and vegetarians — over a 13-year period by the University of Otago, New Zealand, and others, it was found that for those who ate more nuts on a regular basis, death rates from all causes were cut by almost a quarter. Nuts are good sources of vitamin E, antioxidants, nutrients, and linoleic aid.

- Low selenium intake has been linked to cancer, cardiovascular disease, and infertility. HIV patients with low selenium levels are 20 times more likely to die of AIDS than those with normal levels. Selenium, described as "a birth control pill for viruses" by Will Taylor of the University of Georgia, is found in kidneys, liver, poultry, fish, cereals, and bread made with high-protein

- By donating three units of blood a year, a man could possibly reduce the risk of heart disease by reducing the amount of iron in the body (just as menstrual bleeding protects women's hearts). A new study has demonstrated a direct link between heart disease and high iron levels in nearly 2,000 Finnish men.

- Brussels sprouts contain sinigrin, a compound that helps protect against breast, lung, and bowel cancer. The sinigrin is particularly rich in the more bitter sprouts.

- Professor Allan Ebringer of the Ankylosing Spondylitis (AS) Research Clinic at the Middlesex Hospital in London has published research arguing that a high-fluid, high-fructose diet would help in many cases of rheumatoid arthritis. Infection of the upper urinary tract by the microbe *Proteus mirabilis* can in some cases trigger relapses in rheumatoid arthritis. To reduce such infections, Professor Ebringer recommends patients drink four pints (two liters) of fluids (tea, coffee, lemonade, soft drinks of any kind) per day. A further way of reducing urinary tract infection is to have a high intake of fructose-containing substances such as orange juice, lemon juice, and vegetables of all kinds. Fructose competes for binding sites with urinary bacteria, thus enhancing the bacteria's removal.

- Professor Ebringer also advises those suffering from ankylosing spondylitis to follow a diet low in complex carbohydrates, especially at times of flare-up. His advice is to reduce intake of bread, potatoes, chips, rice, spaghetti, cereals, cakes, and cookies, and to compensate for the calorie loss by increasing the amount of meat, fish, beans and peas, nuts, vegetables, salads, milk products, and fruit you eat. Simple carbohydrates such as dietary glucose and sucrose can be consumed normally, and no restriction needs to be placed on beverages or spices such as pepper, salt, or herbs. Professor Ebringer considers ankylosing spondylitis to be a form of "reactive arthritis" that follows infection by the bowel microbe Klebsiella.

→ For further details on Professor Ebringer's work, see <www.globalideasbank.org/reinv/RIS-79.HTML>.

Hippocratic Oath for Scientists

NICHOLAS ALBERY

AN OATH FOR MACHINE DESIGNERS AND MAKERS should have been in place centuries ago; likewise a ban on the development of new weapons. Our religious leaders have betrayed us. The Pope most worthy of respect is Pope Innocent II, who, in the Lateran Council of 1139, forbade under anathema the use of the crossbow, at least against Catholics and other Christians. The crossbow was the new ultimate weapon of the 12th century, piercing the armor of the nobility, yet wielded by non-nobles. The Pope's edict seems to have had some effect, too — King Louis VII of France, otherwise known as Louis the Pious, is recorded as having had a troop of crossbowmen before the council but not afterwards, and they were only reintroduced in France after England's Richard I had popularized their use against infidels in the Crusades.

Pope Innocent II, in the Lateran Council of 1139, forbade under anathema the use of the crossbow.

Even today, now that most weapons are dangerous boomerangs, it is perhaps not too late to make a stand against the military and technological evils that threaten to engulf us. Professor C.G. Weeramantry in Australia has made clear that a number of interacting initiatives are needed: technology assessment boards, future scanning agencies in government departments, committees for alternative futures, centers for the study of scientific policy, committees of the bar, legislative and judicial restructuring, international covenants and treaties, court-imposed moratoria, referenda, and the restructuring of education and law school curricula.

As part of this wider approach, an Institute for Social Inventions' working party has drawn up a new and shorter version of the Hippocratic Oath, aimed not at doctors but at engineers, scientists (pure and applied), and the executives who employ them.

Hippocratic Oath for Scientists, Engineers and Executives

I vow to practice my profession with conscience and dignity;

I will strive to apply my skills only with the utmost respect for the well-being of humanity, the earth, and all its species;

I will not permit considerations of nationality, politics, prejudice, or material advancement to intervene between my work and this duty to present and future generations.

I make this Oath solemnly, freely, and upon my honor.

As Professor Weeramantry remarks: "The idea of an ethic for science goes all the way back to Francis Bacon. In Bacon's work *New Atlantis*, scientists took an oath for concealing inventions and experiences which they thought fit to keep secret."

An Institute working party member, Peter Lewis, adds that history provides a notable precedent of ethical behavior by a scientist. This is the example of Leonardo da Vinci, who (despite offering many of his military inventions to the Duke of Milan and other patrons) suppressed his work on submarines "on account of the evil nature of men, who would practice assassination at the bottom of the sea." By Leonardo's action the world was spared submarine warfare for 300 years. Peter Lewis acknowledges that scientists have tended in the main to see their work as an amoral and dispassionate search for truth, but considers that in recent decades a growing number have begun to ask themselves if the scientific method cannot be amended so as to incorporate an ethical component. "Anyone who is bound by an oath such as the one we propose," writes Lewis, "has a powerful curb placed on their behavior. If I break the rules, even if I have concealed my transgression from other people, *I will know what I am*, and I cannot escape from that knowledge."

The long-term aim is that the oath should become part of the graduation ceremony for students.

There are over a hundred eminent signatories of this oath, including 18 Nobel Laureates. The launch signatories were Professor Maurice Wilkins, CBE FRS; Abdus Salam, FRS; and Sir John Kendrew, who is president of the International Council of Scientific Unions. Also lending their support are the vice-chancellors or equivalents of many prestigious universities around the world. The long-term aim is that the oath should become part of the graduation ceremony for students — there is not much hope of "converting" the 50 percent of scientists already working for defense industries, who have families and mortgages to worry about, but it may be possible to influence students in their choice of work at the outset of their careers.

The response has been encouraging. For instance, most of the key staff at Auckland University have signed and they have ordered hundreds of copies for their students. The Pugwash Conference in London had a working party on this theme, and Unesco is showing signs of interest.

Professor Meredith Thring, chairman of the Institute's working party and author of *Man, Machines and Tomorrow* (published by Routledge & Kegan Paul), writes: "No one wants pointless restriction, but too many scientific developments are posing moral problems by being big enough to involve survival or destruction. Not to face up to defining morality now will put mankind on a level with the concentration camp officials of the Second World War: 'It was not my job to think. I was only obeying orders.'" The wording of the oath is of course very general and is applicable to thoughtful professionals of all sorts. The expectation is that it will provide an ethical framework for the more detailed codes of practice within each discipline.

Eventually, such an oath may help reduce the social standing of technologists working in armaments and similar dubious areas — and, once aroused, there are few forces on earth more powerful than social pressure.

Probably the most important issue of them all, as far as gaining acceptance for the oath goes, is the question of what happens to scientists or engineers with ethics if they obey the oath, take a stand, and lose their jobs. If the oath became part of a profession's graduation ceremony, the professional association should bring pressure to bear on the employer. Robert Jungk and his colleagues in Austria have looked at this problem. Their initial suggestion was that any scientists leaving their research jobs for ethical reasons could receive conscience money through an insurance scheme, but this turned out to be costly. What they developed instead was a fund, which people could pay into, that would finance alternative scientific institutes to provide jobs for "refugee" scientists. There are now four or five such institutes in Europe.

✦ The Book of Oaths *and a card copy of this Hippocratic Oath for Scientists are available for £3.95 from The Institute for Social Inventions, 20 Heber Road,*

London NW2 6AA, UK (Phone: Int.+44 [0]20 8208 2853; Fax: Int.+44 [0]20 8452 6434; E-mail: rhino@dial.pipex.com; Web: www.globalideasbank.org).

Hitchhiker safety postcards

Adapted by Nicholas Albery from a suggestion by Celia Fremlin.

TO HELP REDUCE THE RISK OF BEING MOLESTED OR RAPED, hitchhikers might might find it helpful to hitch, whenever possible, from beside a mailbox. They would have a supply of postcards, addressed to a friend, and would write down the spot from which they are hitching and the date and time. When they are about to accept a lift, they will complete the card by writing down the vehicle's number and then post it — and the friend will know to raise the alarm if he or she does not receive subsequent news of the hitchhiker's safe arrival. The driver's knowledge that the card was posted would act as a deterrent to assault.

Mailboxes could be installed at the main hitching points, perhaps financed by a charity such as the Suzy Lamplugh Trust (set up after the disappearance of Diana Lamplugh's daughter).

> When they are about to accept a lift, they will complete the card by writing down the vehicle's number and then post it.

In the absence of a mailbox, hitchhikers could give the cards to passers-by or fellow hitchers to post or could leave them on the wayside in a small transparent envelope marked "Urgent. Please Post the Card Inside."

→ *Celia Fremlin, 11 Parkhill Road, London NW3, UK.*

Homes for the elderly who share the same interests

GREGORY WRIGHT

WHY NOT ESTABLISH NURSING HOMES AND SENIOR RESIDENCES that accept residents based on their sharing a range of interests, hobbies, past careers, and backgrounds? For example, there could be a Gardeners' Home, an Artists' Home, a Readers' Home, an Animal Lovers' Home. The residents of these themed homes might have much more of a sense of life being worth living and experience more personal growth and health when they are living in an environment of shared interests and accumulated knowledge. The staff could be selected according to *their* similar interests too.

→ *Gregory Wright, #3–14161 Riverside Drive, Sherman Oaks, California 91423 (Phone: 818 784 0325).*

H

The Human Kindness Foundation

BO LOZOFF

Extracts from a recent talk by Bo Lozoff about the work and philosophy of the Human Kindness Foundation.

IT'S THE PEOPLE WHO DEFEND THE PRISON SYSTEM or who want to build even more prisons and sentence more people who are the idealists, not me. They're "negative idealists" because they have a punitive ideal that reality continues to disprove. It simply doesn't work. Hurting people who hurt us just perpetuates a lot of hurting.

The vast majority of prisoners hate their lives, and they begin to shine when someone comes along and shows them that they can be of value.

I would say that over 90 percent of prisoners would love to straighten their lives out if given a decent chance. Very few people are dead-set on doing wrong. The vast majority of prisoners hate their lives, they feel like worthless losers, and they begin to shine when someone comes along and shows them that they can be of value.

That's why I'm so passionate about prisoners doing some kind of "good work" instead of just getting an education and job skills. As somebody named Susie Gomez once said, "It is an honor to be asked to help." It's an amazing experience to introduce a prisoner to that honor, and to watch the profound changes which take place.

I'm not saying that everyone should be set free. There may always be twisted people who need to be removed from society to protect the public. And sometimes somebody may even forfeit his right to ever again be trusted with his freedom — perhaps people like David "Son of Sam" or Charles Manson. Why should the public be guinea pigs?

But there are very few people like that, and we already have *more* than enough prisons to hold them. And even so, we can create optimum conditions for their redemption so that even if they're behind bars for the rest of their lives, they have an opportunity to become respected writers, inventors, thinkers, artists, or humanitarians, contributing to the world through their unique restrictions and humility for their past.

That's why I'm so passionate about prisoners doing some kind of good work instead of just getting an education and job skills.

But those are the few. The *many* are prisoners who would be better served through imaginative combinations of house arrest, community service, electronic monitoring, family counseling, restitution, drug and alcohol rehabilitation, and so forth. Prisons should be the last recourse. And prisons offer *no* solution to problems that are primarily social and medical, such as drug abuse.

→ *The Human Kindness Foundation relies on free-will donations rather than on grant applications. Their address is The Human Kindness Foundation, Route 1, Box 201-n, Durham, NC 27705 (Phone: 919 942 2138; Web: www.humankindness.org).*

I

Industries made to drink their effluent discharges

IAN GASCOIGNE

ALLOW EVERY COMMERCIAL, INDUSTRIAL, AND AGRICULTURAL ORGANIZATION the freedom to discharge effluent into all rivers and watercourses, with one condition only: that they take their drinking water out of the same river or watercourse, from downstream of the discharge, and use it without treatment in their operation as drinking water for all employees irrespective of the physical location of the site in relation to the river.

Inequality reduced by giving $80,000 to every citizen at the age of 21

Based on *The Stakeholder Society* by Bruce Ackerman and Anne Alstott (published by Yale University Press). Summarized from a review by Jack Beatty in the *Atlantic Monthly*, monitored by Roger Knights.

THE INSTITUTE FOR SOCIAL INVENTIONS IN LONDON has in the past stated the case for all young people, on reaching adulthood, to be given a large sum of money by the state at a point in their lives where they are most likely to make creative use of it. Bruce Ackerman and Anne Alstott in *The Stakeholder Society* advocate the same measure from an American perspective, with their focus being primarily on relieving inequalities within the nation.

They would like there to be a two percent wealth tax (equivalent to the cost of the US defense budget). According to their calculations, 93 percent of this wealth tax would be paid for by the richest 20 percent of society. This enormous sum of money would finance a donation of $80,000 to every US citizen on reaching his or her 21st birthday (or 18th birthday in the case of those going to college).

This scheme would make it possible for young people to buy a house or start a business or pay for a college education.

"Too many 40-year-olds look back to their twenties with bitter regret at the chances they never had," write Ackerman and Alstott. The money would disproportionately favor black people and others whose wages tend rarely to add up to wealth. The authors want young people to be able to buy a house or start a business or pay for a college education (this last, on average, costs $80,000).

The $80,000 would have to be paid back, with interest, at death, making this "stakeholding" scheme sustainable in the long run.

Their proposal would, they maintain, reduce the social harshness resulting from the new inequalities of wealth within society, provide greater equality of opportunity, and promote a sense of community, social obligation, and national loyalty.

Innovative idea e-mailed to you every day

Summarized from information on the Idea-a-Day website <www.idea-a-day.com>.

THE IDEA-A-DAY.COM WEBSITE SENDS PEOPLE AN IDEA EVERY DAY, with the hope that it can fire people's imaginations and foster creative and innovative thinking.

Once you have subscribed to idea-a-day.com, you receive an e-mail containing that day's idea directly to your computer. The service is free, and the founders of the site stress that it is not in any way a money-making scheme, just a fun one.

Subscribers and visitors to the site are encouraged to respond to the author of a particular idea as well as being invited to submit their own original ideas. Each idea, as the website puts it, is "there to be read, enjoyed, used, or abused."

As this statement might imply, none of the ideas themselves are copyrighted in any way (only the way they are phrased on the site is protected). The intention is to foster the propagation and dispersal of new ideas wherever the e-mails land.

There is also an archive of every idea the website has featured. Recent ideas have included a suggestion for parking space sensors to be introduced in multistory car parks, which would allow each driver (via a ticket system) to pinpoint the closest free space before they actually enter the car park; another suggested giving voters the chance to vote against a party with their one vote, rather than forcing disillusioned people to vote for one side or the other.

Institute for retired scientists

FARHANG SEFIDVASH

Summarized from an e-mail to the Global Ideas Bank from Farhang Sefidvash of the Research Centre for Global Governance. Farhang Sefidvash is a professor of Nuclear Engineering with a PhD from Imperial College (University of London), the inventor of a new nuclear reactor concept, and the author of more than 95 scientific publications.

Most scientists and intellectuals retire while they are still capable and willing to contribute to the development of knowledge.

I PROPOSE THE ESTABLISHMENT OF A WORLD INSTITUTE OF KNOWLEDGE for retired scientists. At present, humanity loses the potential development of knowledge as most scientists and intellectuals retire while they are still capable and willing to contribute to the development of knowledge — and the teaching of it.

There are many people worldwide, in all fields of knowledge, who retire every year and become inactive, but not of their own volition. The considerable knowledge and experience they have accumulated over many years — a non-replaceable treasure — are lost. These people still have a lot to contribute to the well-being of humanity.

While humanity loses their contributions, they themselves feel unhappy on entering a lifestyle where they find themselves, at best, less useful. Humanity lets billions of dollars spent on preparing these people go to waste.

At a World Institute of Knowledge, retired scientists and intellectuals in all fields of knowledge from around the world could come to do whatever they would like to do. They will be provided with opportunities to discuss with co-workers their wild ideas, to do research on personal projects — perhaps on the subjects that did not fit their institutional objectives — to write books and articles, to teach, and essentially to do whatever they wanted to do during their regular work but did not have the chance to.

Students and seekers of knowledge will also come to the Institute to learn and to become research assistants.

Scientists would be provided with office space, secretarial services, and basic infrastructures for their research work; with simple but adequate housing for themselves and their partners; with food, medical assistance, tickets, and pocket money. Most have their retirement pensions and do not need any assistance, although this would depend on the amount of their pension. Scientists could stay for as long as they wanted, from a few months per year to a permanent stay.

The Institute would require a beautiful place in a country with a mild climate away from population centers. It would need housing, office space, seminar rooms, an amphitheater, restaurants, a medical center, a library, computer facilities, etc.

Developing countries can be expected to compete to host the Institute as it will bring with it prestige and wealth.

Developing countries with a vision for the future can be expected to compete to host the Institute as it will bring with it prestige and wealth. The host country will benefit from a great bank of knowledge and from help with educating its people at a minimum cost. Many scientific tourists will travel to the host country to seek knowledge. The Institute will be the melting pot of all the scientists and intellectuals of the world. The interaction between these highly capable people will lead to new and important knowledge. This World Institute of Knowledge will become a center of learning.

Many international scientific organizations and individuals could be expected to donate to this project. It will receive endowments. Many of those in power will be motivated by the idea of building up a place for their own future. Many retired scientists will contribute to it during their lifetime or will leave it a donation in their will. In this way they will make themselves immortal, leaving their name on a World Institute of Knowledge project of their choice.

➜ *This idea is now beginning to become concrete reality, as the World Institute for Retired Scientists (WIRS) takes shape. Dr Sefidvash hopes that WIRS will become an organic institution that will grow and develop like a living being while maintaining its altruistic principles and using the art of consultation. Its headquarters will be in Rio Grande do Sul, but scientists will be able to consult all over the world via the internet. More information and an application form to become a member of WIRS are available from <www.rcgg.ufrgs.br/wirs.htm>.*

➜ *The Research Centre for Global Governance is a think tank looking for lasting solutions to humanity's problems, c/o Dr F. Sefidvash, Federal University of Rio Grande do Sul, Nuclear Engineering Department, UFRGS, Av.Osvaldo Aranha 99, 4 andar, 90046-900 Porto Alegre, RS, Brazil (Fax: Int.+55 [0]51 316 3983; E-mail: rcgg@orion.ufrgs.br; Web: www.rcgg.ufrgs.br).*

➜ *The National Research Council of Canada provides office space and resources to retired scientists who wish to pursue their interests. The scientists are then given the title of "guest worker." Contact the NRCC c/o Norman Vinson, Institute for Information Technology, National Research Council of Canada, M-50 Montreal Road, Ottawa, Ontario, K1A 0R6, Canada (Phone: 613 952 7151; Fax: 613 993 2565; E-mail: normvinson@nrc.ca; Web: www.nrc.ca).*

✦ *Herman Bank, an 84-year-old NASA veteran, founded the Volunteer Professionals for Medical Advancement a decade ago. It consists of a group of retired engineers and scientists from the Jet Propulsion Laboratory in Pasadena, California, who apply their knowledge and expertise to medicine. Having already designed an automated oxygen-enrichment system for premature babies, the group is currently in the process of developing a database of children's illnesses for researchers and pediatricians worldwide. Mr Bank is now starting a campaign to set up similar organizations around the US. (Summarized from an item by Susan Zjawinski, entitled "Dataspace Cowboy," in* **Must Read** *magazine, monitored by Roger Knights.)*

Insurance sold with gasoline

PAUL BLANKENSHIP

By buying a gallon of gasoline, a driver is buying a unit of insurance for the time that the gasoline is in the car.

FORTY PERCENT OF CALIFORNIA'S DRIVERS ARE UNINSURED. The core of my proposal is to bundle costs for gasoline and insurance. By buying a gallon of gasoline, a driver is buying a unit of insurance for the period of time that the gasoline is in the car. Gasoline stations would display both the brand of gasoline and the brand of insurance company. Prices for both would be displayed. (The retailer would select which insurance company to ally his station with.)

Consumers benefit by having a fixed cost of insurance that is directly related to their driving. If you normally take alternative forms of transportation but use a car for occasional trips, you have a much lower insurance cost.

Consumers also benefit by having greater competition for their insurance money. Insurance costs per gallon would be clearly posted, allowing much easier comparison shopping. There would also be a reduction in the inherent racial bias of insurance costs. Often lower income areas have a higher insurance cost, which shifts the highest burden onto those who can least afford it. This plan would make for truer risk sharing.

The consumer is guaranteed protection in the event of an accident. If a car has gasoline, it is insured. Of course, this implies that the insurance system works under a no-fault rule. Regardless of fault, you are fully covered.

The incentive for drivers to get into more fuel-efficient cars would increase dramatically.

The increase in gasoline costs would be beneficial. Because higher gas mileage would equal higher insurance mileage, the incentive for drivers to get into more fuel-efficient cars would increase dramatically. An increase in alternative forms of transportation and in mass transit could be expected.

A simple way to manage the system might be to issue a computer-coded driver's license, which would be needed to refuel. In addition to establishing who the most recent insurance carrier is, the driver could be ordered to surrender his card if serious driving violations occur. This would make it more difficult for dangerous drivers to get on the road, reducing risk and possibly insurance cost.

This idea is flexible. The basic concept can be stretched to add new taxes (for example, taxes for mass transit or healthcare). And driver's licenses could be coded to reflect certain risk factors (such as age or driving record).

All the main parties involved can gain by this idea: gasoline retailers would be induced to participate because they would have a second profitable enterprise: insurance. Depending on the cost of insurance-per-mile, retailers could perhaps make an additional profit of 50 to 100 percent.

Insurance companies would be attracted to the idea because currently uninsured drivers would be paying insurance. (Such companies would also continue to supply additional comprehensive cover.)

There would be secondary savings to the government from not having to pay for property and healthcare costs incurred by uninsured motorists.

→ *Paul Blankinship, 1661 Gateway Drive, Vallejo, California 94589 (Phone: 707 645 7445).*

Ithaca HOURS – Better than dollars

PAUL GLOVER
Adapted from an e-mail to the Global Ideas Bank.

HERE IN ITHACA, NEW YORK, WE'VE BEGUN TO GAIN CONTROL of the social and environmental effects of commerce by issuing over $85,000 of our own local paper money to thousands of participants since 1991. Tens of thousands of purchases and many new friendships have been made with this cash, and millions of dollars of local trading have been added to the Grassroots National Product.

We printed our own money because we watched federal dollars come to town, shake a few hands, then leave to buy rainforest lumber and fight wars.

We printed our own money because we watched federal dollars come to town, shake a few hands, then leave to buy rainforest lumber and fight wars. Ithaca's HOURS, by contrast, stay in our region to help us hire each other. While dollars make us increasingly dependent on multinational corporations and bankers, HOURS reinforce community trading and expand commerce that is more accountable to our concerns for ecology and social justice.

Here's how it works: the Ithaca HOUR is Ithaca's $10 bill, because $10 per hour is the average of wages/salaries in Tompkins County. These HOUR notes, in five denominations, buy plumbing, carpentry, electrical work, roofing, nursing, chiropractic, childcare, car and bike repair, food, eyeglasses, firewood, gifts, and thousands of other goods and services. Our credit union accepts them for mortgage and loan fees. People pay rent with HOURS. The best restaurants in town take them, as do movie theaters, bowling alleys, two large locally owned grocery stores, many garage sales, 55 market vendors, the Chamber of Commerce, and 300 other businesses. Hundreds more who are not on the Ithaca Money list have earned and spent HOURS.

Ithaca's new HOURly minimum wage lifts the lowest paid up without knocking down higher wages. For example, several of Ithaca's organic farmers are paying the highest farm labor wages in the world: $10 of spending power per HOUR. These farmers benefit by the HOUR's loyalty to local agriculture. On the other hand, dentists, massage therapists, and lawyers charging more than the $10 per hour are permitted to collect several HOURS hourly. But we hear increasingly of professional services provided for our equitable wage.

Everyone who agrees to accept HOURS is paid one or two HOURS ($10 or $20) for being listed in our "HOUR Town" directory. Every eight months they may apply to be paid an additional HOUR as reward for continuing participation. This is how we gradually and carefully increase the per capita supply of our money: once it's issued, anyone may earn and spend HOURS, whether signed up or not, and hundreds have done so.

Ithaca Money's 1,500 listings, rivaling the Yellow Pages, are a portrait of our community's capability, bringing into the marketplace time and skills not employed by the conventional market.

Residents are proud of income gained by doing work they enjoy. We encounter each other as fellow Ithacans, rather than as winners and losers scrambling for dollars. The success stories of 300 participants published so far testify to the acts of generosity and community solidarity that our system prompts. We're making a community while making a living. As we do so, we relieve the social desperation that has led to compulsive shopping and wasted resources.

At the same time, Ithaca's locally owned stores, which keep more wealth local, make sales and get spending power they otherwise would not have. And over $10,000 of our local currency have been donated to 60 community organizations so far, by the Barter Potluck, our wide-open governing body.

We regard Ithaca HOURS as real money, backed by real people, real time, and real skills and tools.

As we discover new ways to provide for each other, we replace dependence on imports. Yet our greater self-reliance, rather than isolating Ithaca, gives us more potential to reach outward with ecological export industry. We can capitalize new businesses with loans of our own cash. HOUR loans are made without interest charges. We regard Ithaca HOURS as real money, backed by real people, real time, and real skills and tools. Dollars, by contrast, are funny money, backed no longer by gold or silver but by less than nothing — $5 trillion of national debt.

Ithaca's money honors local features we respect, like native flowers, powerful waterfalls, crafts, farms, and our children. Our commemorative HOUR is the first paper money in the US to honor an African-American. Multicolored HOURS, some printed on locally made watermarked cattail (marsh reed) paper, all with serial numbers, are harder to counterfeit than dollars.

Local currency is a lot of fun, and it's legal — HOURS are taxable income when traded for professional goods or services.

Local currency is also lots of work and responsibility. To give other communities a boost, we've been providing a Hometown Money Starter Kit. The kit explains, step-by-step, how to start up and maintain an HOURS system, and includes forms, laws, articles, procedures, insights, samples of Ithaca's HOURS, and issues of Ithaca Money. We've sent the kit to over 1,000 communities in 49 states and beyond, and our example has attracted international attention.

➔ *Paul Glover, PO Box 6578, Ithaca, NY 14851 (Phone: 607 272 4330; E-mail: hours@lightlink.com).*

➔ *Kits are $25 (2.5 HOURS option in NY) or $35 from abroad. A 17-minute video is also available for $17, or $15 if bought with the kit ($40 for kit and video). Orders to Ithaca HOURS, Inc., Box 6731, Ithaca, NY 14851 USA (Phone: 607 272 3738 between 9 a.m. and 9 p.m.; E-mail: ithacahours@lightlink.com; Web: www.lightlink.com/ithacahours). The Ithaca HOURS website features color samples of HOURS notes.*

➔ *See also time dollars (on the web at <www.cfg.com/timedollar>).*

J

Jaisalmer — One traveler's initiative to save it

Summarized from an article by Sue Carpenter entitled "Last chance to save Jaisalmer" in *New Scientist*.

DURING A THREE-MONTH TRIP TO INDIA TO GATHER TRAVEL STORIES, I spent a week in Jaisalmer, a glorious fortress city perched on a remote hill on the edge of the Great Indian Desert in Rajasthan, nine hours by train from the nearest metropolis of Jodhpur. The place has stood for more than 800 years, a testament to the riches and skills of its present citizens' ancestors, its intricately carved sandstone buildings glowing golden in the sun.

The city's water had previously been collected manually from a reservoir lake. Now the much larger amount being pumped into the city is more than the open drains can handle. The resulting seepage into the foundations has rendered many structures unstable. Battered by unprecedented monsoons in 1993, more than 80 historic buildings trembled like houses of cards. Yet locals were ignoring their crumbling heritage, said a despondent architect, preferring an instant return from erecting concrete hotels or rebuilding on the cheap. Only by bringing Jaisalmer's dilemma into the international spotlight could the town be saved.

Back home, I wrote an article for *New Scientist* ("Collapse of the golden city") on how one of the world's most beautiful cities was falling apart. I was invited to speak about it on a national radio program, and a London-based architect, who had visited Jaisalmer ten years earlier, contacted me to express his consternation. We really ought to do something, we said.

So I drew up a mailing list — from the Prince of Wales to the Chief Minister of Rajasthan — and launched the Jaisalmer in Jeopardy campaign, with the initial intention of raising international awareness. The money for the campaign's running costs came from a peculiarly fitting source. My visit to Jaisalmer happened to coincide with the filming of Rudyard Kipling's *The Jungle Book* in the magnificent fort of Jodhpur. I had been hired as an extra for the ballroom scene in which Mowgli gets pushed into the banqueting table by a pair of irate Bengal lancers. When the film opened in London, I persuaded the Disney Company to hold a special screening, at which I gathered donations for the Jaisalmer cause.

My letters stirred up a good deal of concern and interest. Both the Chief Minister and the Chief Secretary of Rajasthan wrote to say that they welcomed the campaign and that a conservation plan was ready to be implemented when resources were forthcoming. Given that a positive approach in India towards conserving Jaisalmer is a prerequisite for its survival, this was an encouraging response. The Indian National Trust for Art and Cultural Heritage also wrote to pledge its support, enclosing a long statement headed "Jaisalmer in Jeopardy." The Nehru Centre of the Indian high commission in London asked me to give a lecture, which further spread the word.

The Prince of Wales' aide specializing in architecture and planning suggested people and organizations to contact and brought Jaisalmer to the attention of the World Monuments Fund (WMF) in New York. It in turn has written to me to inquire about sending a WMF representative to Jaisalmer to consider it as a potential project for the near future.

It may be a long haul, but I feel that Jaisalmer in Jeopardy, like Venice in Peril, has acquired an identity and momentum of its own. And Jaisalmer has one big advantage. We are not fighting an endless war, but a contained battle, and the finances — millions rather than tens of hundreds of millions — are attainable. Perhaps one individual can make a difference.

➔ *If you can help in any way, please contact Jaisalmer in Jeopardy (registered charity no. 1055433), 3 Brickbarn Close, London SW10 0TP, UK (Phone/Fax: Int.+44 [0]20 7 352 4336;*
E-mail: jaisalmerinfo@yahoo.co.uk; Web: www.jaisalmer-in-jeopardy.org).

Judge lets victims take from burglars' homes

Based on an item by Woody Baird in the *Seattle Times,* monitored by Roger Knights.

SINCE HIS ELECTION TO THE CRIMINAL COURT IN 1990, Joe B. Brown has built a reputation as a tough, street-wise judge willing to try new ways to sentence criminals. He has ordered several burglars to open their homes to former victims. With deputies in tow, the victims can take what they want, up to a limit set by Brown that approximates the value of what they lost.

"He learns what a good citizen feels like, worrying whether he's going to come home and find all his stuff there," said the judge.

Victims can take what they want, up to a limit set by the judge.

One victim made several visits before he was satisfied. "The first day he didn't find anything, but the second time he came back, he bagged a color television and a stereo-component set."

Criticism has come from Scott Wallace of the National Association of Criminal Defense Lawyers, who argues that it may be difficult to tell if items seized by a victim really belong to the burglar.

However, Robert Jones, assistant administrator of the Shelby County public defender's office, is in favor of the judge's approach: "He's being very creative. A lot of things that have been done in the past aren't working, so somebody needs to be creative."

Jurors can interrupt and ask questions

Summarized from an Associated Press item in the *Seattle Times,* monitored by Roger Knights.

SINCE 1994, CIRCUIT JUDGE ROBERT JONES IN PORTLAND, OREGON, has allowed the jurors in the civil trials in his courtroom to interrupt with questions, even when witnesses are on the stand.

He has had switches installed under the lawyers' desks. If either lawyer objects when a juror asks a question, they flip the switch, which lights a button on Jones' bench, and he can dismiss the question.

"This makes the jurors more involved in the case. It is the people's courtroom," Jones said.

Any trial lawyer will say it scares them to
death when a juror puts his hand up.

"Any trial lawyer will say it scares them to death when a juror puts his hand up," said attorney David Miller, who often works in Jones' courtroom.

→ *Robert P. Jones, Circuit Court Judge, 706 Multnomah County Courthouse, 1021 SW Fourth Avenue, Portland, Oregon 97204 (Phone: 503 248 3038).*

→ *David Miller (E-mail: c/o KCB@hhw.com).*

K

Scale model of the solar system

The following is from a proposal entitled "St Joseph's School Garden, An Outdoor Classroom." The garden has been designed by Steve Parry and colleagues for St Joseph's School (Oakhill Road, Wandsworth, London), where the new building uses sustainable timber, non-toxic paint and polishes, etc.

DESPITE MAN'S LANDING ON THE MOON, the universe is still an intriguing mystery to us, and children are fascinated by the concept of space. The idea is to develop a "solar walk" in which scaled models of the planets are placed within scaled distances from the sun. The models will be built at a scale of one to one billion, which means that each step one takes symbolizes a distance of 62 billion miles (100 billion kilometers) in space. The Sun will be four feet (1.2 meters) in diameter. The school grounds are not large enough to accommodate both the Sun and Pluto, which is the planet farthest from the Sun. If the Sun model is near the River Wandel, Pluto needs to be placed some 4.5 miles (7.4 kilometers) away in Greenwich, and a solar walk along the Thames would pass the other planets, from Venus, Mercury, and Earth to Saturn, Uranus, and Neptune.

This project is an ideal way to teach about astronomy and to help people visualize abstract concepts.

→ *Steve Parry, Wandsworth Education Business Partnership, Office A 104/105, The Fruit and Veg Market, New Covent Garden, Nine Elms Lane, London SW8 5EE, UK (Phone: Int.+44 [0]20 7 498 0577; Fax: Int.+44 [0]20 7 498 2433).*

Knee bends to soothe a crying baby

MARTIN RAYMAN
The following is summarized from an e-mail to the Global Ideas Bank.

HERE IS MY TECHNIQUE FOR CALMING A CRYING BABY: Most attempts to rock a baby seem to be close to shaking the baby, involving rapid changes in direction that often do more to unsettle the baby. I hold a baby in my arms, supporting the head against my chest, and, in a standing position, bend at the knees so my body bounces up and down relatively gently. The baby gets its rocking (in a vertical direction rather than horizontal) but with fairly gentle movements.

> **I time my downward stops to coincide with the moment that the baby is breathing in.**

But this is just the start of the technique. I time my downward stops (i.e., when I am at my lowest point) to coincide with the moment that the baby is breathing in — in crude terms, I am knocking the air out of the baby; in gentler terms, I am reducing the amount of air the baby has to scream at me with.

I know this may sound a bit strange, but it is, in my experience — four children of my own and plenty of friends' babies — just what the baby wants. The effect it seems to have on the baby's crying is that it dampens the intensity (imagine a spring with a weight attached that is bouncing) and slowly soothes the baby (I decrease my "knee bending" corresponding to the baby's submission). This can happen fairly rapidly, such as after four or five bobs up and down.

> **It does wonders for my calf muscles, but at 3 a.m. I am not too concerned about that.**

It gives me a rewarding feeling that I am actually achieving some success. I can vary the motion by bending on alternate legs (producing a dance-like motion). It does wonders for my calf muscles by the way, but at 3 a.m. I am not too concerned about that. I just want some peace and quiet.

Let me point out that this approach is not 100 percent effective — and rightly so, because sometimes with babies there is something very much wrong that needs addressing: diaper change, illness, etc. This technique should not be used to smother the baby's genuine distress.

What about more extreme cases? I mention the following with a bit more trepidation as you need to be very careful. I shall carry on and describe it, however, as it could avert the very real possibility of a distressed adult doing the baby some serious physical damage out of blind frustration and rage. (I know, I've been close.) So for a very distressed baby for whom all else seems to fail, use the same technique, but apply it a bit more vigorously. You are moving up higher and dropping down deeper. I have even jumped a couple of inches off the ground, but again, the motion must be smooth, especially when you come down. Remember to have the baby properly supported, especially the head.

I discovered these two techniques 11 years ago when my daughter Giselle became very distressed as a baby — we were going through a time of homelessness. As a physicist (yes, if the descriptions above sound a bit cold and technical, it's my training that's at fault), I wondered whether the crying of a baby could be subdued in the same way that the motion of a spring is

subdued by absorbing the motion, just as the shock absorbers subdue the
rocking of a car.

I have shown the technique to total strangers in restaurants.

I was surprised at my success and felt sure that somewhere before in the
history of humanity this technique must have been used, so I only mentioned
it to friends. As the years have gone by, I have noticed so many frustrated,
anxious parents in the predicament I found myself in that I thought maybe I
should mention this here. I have shown the technique to total strangers in
restaurants, who, apart from the initial irritation of having someone strange
suggest something to them about their child, have been extremely grateful.

→ *Martin Rayman, 29 All Saints Terrace, Cheltenham, Glos GL52 6UA, UK
(Phone/Fax: Int.+44 [0]1242 575521; E-mail: C.Brain@bath.ac.uk).*

L

A Labor Tax

FRED ALLEN

A LABOR TAX THAT YOU COULD EITHER FULFILL or pay someone else to do is a
good idea. It solves the problem of getting nothing from the unemployed.
The form that labor should take must be left to the taxpayer.

→ *Fred Allen, 13 Shelly Row, Cambridge, CB3 OBP, UK.*

Response from Nicholas Albery

I ran a pilot project along these lines years ago for the hundred residents of
a housing co-op in Shepherds Bush. Residents could either pay a £2 tax each
week or sign up on the circulated worksheet for an average of 20 minutes
work on a community project. Unpopular jobs such as fixing the sewers
might pay off the tax at a quicker rate, say ten minutes. This allowed residents to work off weeks of tax with one job. The job coordinator would
accept the least "expensive" bid. Conversely, popular jobs such as watering
the flowers were worth a much slower rate — a full 30 minutes might be

required to pay off the week's requirement. Residents could also propose jobs that needed to be done.

Residents could either pay a £2 tax each week or sign up on the circulated worksheet.

The scheme worked well for a time, but needed an element of compulsion (such as eventual loss of one's place on the co-op rehousing list) to prevent residents from gradually dropping out as the initial spirit faded.

Obviously such a scheme could be expanded to cover a whole neighborhood, with the labor tax being a small allocated part of your tax payment to the council, which you could recoup through labor. It would be a way for unemployed people to top up their dole money, while at the same time improving the local environment. It would need to be supervised by a neighborhood committee, working through a jobs coordinator. But the formation of such neighborhood committees, with a real task to get their teeth into, would be a major positive step forward anyway.

→ *The Institute for Social Inventions, 20 Heber Road, London NW2 6AA, UK (Phone: Int.+44 [0]20 8208 2853; Fax Int.+44 [0]20 8452 6434; E-mail: rhino@dial.pipex.com).*

Ladakh — A global model

Summarized from Ladakh Project newsletters.

"EVERY YEAR, MORE THAN 10,000 TOURISTS VISIT LADAKH," writes Helena Norberg-Hodge, who has worked among the Ladakhis in Kashmir, on the borders of Tibet, for the last 14 years. "The picture most Ladakhis have of life in the West is a very distorted one. As they have seen it only in its seemingly attractive form of digital watches and camera-laden tourists (who spend — in the Ladakhi context — the equivalent of $150,000 a day!), their own lives, by contrast, seem slow, primitive, and inefficient. They are made to feel stupid for being farmers and for getting their hands dirty. Our educational program is helping to correct some of these misconceptions. We are showing them the parallels between the new 'post-industrial' age of which Westerners speak and what they — the Ladakhis — already have. We have to encourage young Ladakhis to maintain respect for their own culture."

The picture most Ladakhis have of life in the West is a very distorted one, as they have seen it only in its seemingly attractive form of digital watches and camera-laden tourists.

The Ladakh Project's newsletter tells how progress has been maintained. The son-in-law of Ladakh's Queen has become full-time director of the Ladakh Ecological Development Group, and his wife is coordinator of its handicrafts program. There is increasing demand for the Ladakh Project's solar greenhouses, Trombe walls, ram pumps, and improved water mills. The exhibition at the Centre for Ecological Development in Leh provides a graphic representation of what life could be like in Leh if development is not carefully controlled. There is also a game that allows children to see the effects of increasing economic dependence on the outside world. .

A new indigenous group, the Students' Educational and Cultural Movement of Ladakh, has been founded primarily as a means of promoting the traditional culture. Its young founders, all in their 20s, come from the very segment of Ladakhi society that is most at risk from the region's modernization. The SECMOL recently mounted its own theater production, "A Journey to New York," conceived as a corrective to the prevailing mythology of the West. It follows a young Ladakhi's American Dream as it goes sour. After initial infatuation with the speed and snazz of New York, the dream gives way to its nightmare flipside of crime, drugs, greed, and loneliness — and the hero hangs up his "I love NY" T-shirt to return to his roots.

→ *Helena Norberg-Hodge, The Ladakh Project, 21 Victoria Square, Clifton, Bristol BS8 4LS, UK (Phone: Int.+44 [0]117 9731575). Ladakh Project newsletters are available for a donation from the Ladakh Project. Also available are the video* Development, a Better Way? *(£ 12); other publications including* Ladakh in a global context: Energy, Ecological steps towards a sustainable future, *and* Ecology and principles for sustainable development, *all at £5 each; and, for a donation, a short pamphlet,* Guidelines for Visitors to Ladakh. *Helena Norberg-Hodge is sometimes available to give lectures or slide shows about Ladakh in the UK. She makes a most interesting presentation of her subject.*

Ladakh — Reviving traditional medicine

Summarized from information distributed by the Rolex Awards for Enterprise.

LAURENT PORDIÉ, A FRENCH ANTHROPOLOGIST and ethno-pharmacologist, is attempting to reintroduce traditional Amchi medicine to the region of Ladakh in northern India. Such a reinstatement of Amchi skills should not only revive and perpetuate the tradition but also, in doing so, improve the healthcare in one of the world's least hospitable environments.

In the past, the local doctors known as Amchis provided their skills free of charge to their village in return for their farming chores being done. With the other villagers doing their communal duties of raising livestock, plowing, and harvesting, the Amchis were allowed to concentrate on consultations, treatment, and gathering medicinal minerals and plants.

The Amchi medical system is suffering because it is based
on a strong sense of community, which is now declining.

But in the last 20 years, things have dramatically changed. Increasing
social mobility has eroded the rural communities; people are much less likely to remain in the village they were born in. In addition to this, market forces
have to some extent replaced the barter systems of before. The Amchi medical tradition has also been undermined by government initiatives to introduce conventional Western medicine to these impoverished areas. Their
intent may have been worthy, but the result has been a marginalization of the
holistic skills upon which such communities used to depend. As a result, the
traditional Amchi skills have begun to disappear. As Laurent Pordié says,
"Modernization has brought a sense of individualism and a breakdown in the
traditional system of help between families in the villages. The Amchi medical system is suffering because it is based on a strong sense of community,
which is now declining."

That some action is needed now is unquestionable. Ladakh can be one
of the coldest places on earth, with temperatures as low as minus 40 degrees
in winter, and its communities are often as isolated as they are impoverished. The government initiatives have failed to provide an adequate substitute for the traditional system, with drugs too expensive, knowledge scarce,
and hospitals and clinics few and far between. With the Amchis no longer
passing their skills from father to son, Ladakhis have neither the traditional
nor the Western medical systems to rely on. The standard of health in the
region has suffered as a consequence, and it now has the highest infant mortality rate in India.

Pordié's aims, therefore, are threefold: to educate individuals from Amchi
families, and new students, in the traditional system; to set up banks of
medicinal drugs accessible to all on a fee-paying basis; and to develop Amchi
projects in alliance with government organizations.

The education program was officially launched in November 1999, and
13 people were taken on after an entrance exam (including four women and
six students with no prior knowledge of the traditional techniques).
Assuming all goes well, they should qualify with diplomas in April 2002.

With the system of medicine banks in each village, the villagers
will be able to choose to either pay for their medicinal
"withdrawals" or to barter goods and labor in the traditional way.

The medicine banks were needed because it is no longer possible for
Amchis to take the sole responsibility for gathering medicinal plants and

minerals — they now have to take care of their own farming tasks. With the system of medicine banks in each village, the villagers will be able to choose to either pay for their medicinal "withdrawals" or to barter goods and labor in the traditional way. Pordié set up a pilot project in a part of Ladakh, Senghi-La, in August 1998, and six medicine banks are now up and running there. His eventual aim is to set up enough banks to supply the whole of Ladakh.

Pordié hopes to further improve the lot of the Amchi doctors by getting the new diplomas accredited and recognized by the central government, and by producing a journal to bring the 400-odd practicing Amchis together into some sort of professional network. He also plans to run ten- or 15-day seminars to hone the skills of the existing Amchi doctors, in collaboration with the Tibetan Medical and Astrological Institute. It should also be stated that, although Amchi practitioners do use basic instruments, they normally leave major surgery to Western physicians. They view illness as an imbalance of bodily or mental states caused by climate, diet, behavior, or the influence of demons. As a result, it is possible for the two systems to work in tandem.

Perhaps most importantly of all, the local people have responded with enthusiasm to Pordié's efforts, and his work is supported by most of the existing Amchi doctors. Many observers expect the project to have a significant impact on both the healthcare of the Ladakhis and on the preservation of their culture. Furthermore, as the Amchi doctors' presence is essential for the cohesiveness and mental well-being of their communities, the revival of Amchi medicine could repair and strengthen the very fabric of life in these isolated mountain villages.

➔ Dr. Laurent Pordié can be contacted at NOMAD Health & Education, 24 chemin du Roussimort, 31270 Frouzins, France (E-mail: nomadplant@hotmail.com).

➔ Laurent Pordié is a laureate in the Rolex Awards for Enterprise. For more information about the awards, write to Rolex Awards Secretariat, PO Box 1311, 1211 Geneva 26, Switzerland, or see the website <www.rolexawards.com>.

Legalizing trade in marijuana seeds only

NICHOLAS ALBERY

I DISAGREE WITH THOSE WHO SAY THAT CANNABIS should be legalized and taxed, doubtless then to become an industry to rival the present tobacco empires. Cannabis can have harmful effects, especially, as in Europe, when mixed with tobacco and breathed in more deeply than tobacco normally is. At least one study has shown that it can promote schizophrenic episodes.

It should be illegal to promote the use of marijuana through advertising or to trade in anything but the seeds.

Marijuana leaves, drunk as tea or smoked on their own without tobacco, as tends to happen more in the US, might be less harmful. My proposal is that it should be legal to grow marijuana for personal consumption or to obtain cannabis syrup on prescription, but that it should be illegal to promote its use through advertising or to trade in anything but the seeds.

Californian decriminalization

Summarized from an article entitled "Mendocino Becomes First County in the US to Decriminalize Personal Cultivation and Possession of Marijuana, - unidentified source, monitored by Milena Petrova.

In Mendocino County in California, voters have passed a measure that makes their county the first in America to decriminalize the cultivation and personal use of marijuana. On the day of the abortive American presidential election, November 7, 2000, Measure G was passed by a landslide. Under the measure, the local authorities are ordered to make marijuana enforcement their lowest priority and are forbidden to prosecute any cases involving 25 or fewer plants (or the dried equivalent). Growing more than 25 plants and selling the drug remains a criminal offense.

It has been suggested that the successful passage of the measure shows the local discontent with the amount of money spent on the war on marijuana, when it could be used for more useful purposes. As Richard Glen Boire, a lawyer who has specialized in defending marijuana cases, says, "The landslide victory for Measure G shows that the people are tired of misappropriating money away from schools in order to finance a military-style war on plants." Indeed, it has been estimated that up to $8 billion is spent each year on the war against marijuana in the US, a figure that this measure will at least begin to reduce. Mendocino officials are specifically ordered by the new law to immediately halt spending county funds on investigating, arresting, and prosecuting those who grow and use marijuana for themselves. And while not all would agree with Attorney Boire's statement that there should be no difference under law "between the grape plant and the cannabis plant," the ending of wasteful law-enforcement spending and the respecting of adult individual choices are surely to be welcomed.

→ Please send feedback to The Institute of Social Inventions, 20 Heber Road, London NW2 6AA, UK (Phone: Int.+44 [0]20 8208 2853; Fax: Int.+44 [0]20 8452 6434; E-mail: rhino@dial..pipex.com).

Limit a corporation's duty
to make money for stockholders

ROBERT C. HINKLEY

Robert C. Hinkley is a partner in the New York law firm Skadden, Arps, Slate, Meagher & Flom LLP. The following is adapted from an e-mail to the Global Ideas Bank.

WHY ARE CORPORATIONS SUCH BAD CITIZENS? Corporations exist because laws have been passed that allow them to be created. These laws also place a duty on directors to use their best efforts to make money for their corporation's stockholders. Failure to satisfy this duty can result in directors being sued. Since directors are at the top of the management chain, this duty becomes the responsibility of everyone who works in the corporate system. Inevitably, it causes individuals working in the corporate system to take actions in the pursuit of profits that are not in the public's interest. How often have you heard "The corporation has to make money" as an excuse for environmental damage, discrimination, or a company leaving town?

The duty to make money ...
but not at the expense of the environment.

Corporations will accept the obligations of citizenship only when explicit boundaries are put on this duty. By way of example, corporate citizenship would be improved significantly by simply adding the following 47 words to the duty to make money:

> ... but not at the expense of the environment, the public safety, the communities in which the corporation conducts its operations, or the dignity of its employees. In meeting this duty, the corporation's directors shall foster respect for the spirit of the law as well as its letter.

This amendment would make it clear to directors that their duty to stockholders has limits. These limits include obligations to the public interest that are just as important as their obligations to stockholders.

→ *Robert Hinkley, PO Box 401, Castine, Maine 04421 (Phone/Fax: 207 326 7924; E-mail: rchinkley@compuserve.com).*

Linking retiring business people to buyers

PETER LANG

Summarized from a letter to the Global Ideas Bank.

MY PROPOSAL IS A "MARRIAGE BUREAU" to bring together small business people approaching retirement with those interested in taking on a business but lacking the capital to buy.

Small business people, including shopkeepers, skilled and semiskilled craftspeople, and those providing services are often faced, when retiring, with the choice of selling their business to a large concern, passing it to an interested son or daughter, or closing it down entirely.

If the owner's offspring does not want the business, and if there is no buyer, the retiree is left only with the memories of a lifetime of building up what could remain a flourishing business. At the same time, starting a new business is a risky proposition. Also, there is a need to promote small, locally owned businesses and to provide employment.

A "marriage bureau" to bring together small business people approaching retirement with those interested in taking on a business but lacking the capital to buy.

The bureau would probably be of primary interest to those who do not have a buyer in prospect or relatives to take their business over and who do not want it to become part of a large chain. The arrangement between the retiree and the new owner would be a matter of negotiation:

- The new owner could agree to pay over a percentage of profits for an agreed upon period, thus contributing to the retiree's pension.
- The retiree could agree to continue working for a day or two a week to give advice (and to lessen the shock of retirement).
- A fee could be paid for the lease, the machinery, and the goodwill, or as a wage to the outgoing owner.

The bureau would be a logical extension to the work of the ApprenticeMaster Alliance. If any readers are interested in taking the project forward, I would be interested in hearing from them.

→ *Peter Lang, Vicarage Cottage, Canon Frome, near Ledbury, Herefordshire HR8 2TG, UK (Phone: Int.+44 [0]1531 670 298).*

→ *See the entry on the ApprenticeMaster Alliance.*

Listening with affection and excitement

BRENDA UELAND

Brenda Ueland tried running up a mountain in her 80s, walked nine miles a day, and wrote five or six million words of journalistic columns in her lifetime — including the classic *If You Want to Write*, which has sold some 140,000 copies as a paperback (published by Graywolf Press). The following quotation and summarized extract are from her wonderful book *Strength to Your Sword Arm: Selected Writings*. A fuller version of these extracts appeared in *Utne Reader* magazine.

You cannot have enough pride or egotism or
energy or bravery, but it must be
centrifugal (generous) and not centripetal (greedy).

I BELIEVE IN WONDERFUL EGOTISM, in being "kingy," that the malaise of the world is so-called modesty, usually a form of conceit. I believe that we should all have a reckless, indomitable, arrogant, joyful blaze of self-esteem, self-trust, self-belief. You cannot have enough pride or egotism or energy or bravery, but it must be centrifugal (generous) and not centripetal (greedy).

So it is with people who have not been listened to in the right
way — with affection and a kind of jolly excitement. Their creative fountain has been blocked.

I have a kind of mystical notion. I think it is only by expressing all that is inside that purer and purer streams come. It is so in writing. You are taught in school to put down on paper only the bright things. Wrong. Pour out the dull things on paper too — you can tear them up afterward — for only then do the bright ones come. If you hold back the dull things, you are certain to hold back what is clear and beautiful and true and lively. So it is with people who have not been listened to in the right way — with affection and a kind of jolly excitement. Their creative fountain has been blocked. Only superficial talk comes out — what is prissy or gushing or merely nervous. No one has called out of them, by wonderful listening, what is true and alive.

I discovered all this about three years ago, and truly it made a revolutionary change in my life. Before that, when I went to a party I would think anxiously: "Now try hard. Be lively. Say bright things. Talk. Don't let down." And when tired, I would have to drink a lot of coffee to keep this up.

To be in their shoes when they talk, without arguing or changing the subject

Now before going to a party, I just tell myself to listen with affection to anyone who talks to me, to be in their shoes when they talk, to try to know them without my mind pressing against theirs, or arguing, or changing the subject. No. My attitude is: "Tell me more. This person is showing me his soul. It is a little dry and meager and full of grinding talk just now, but presently he will begin to think, not just automatically talk. He will show his true self. Then he will be wonderfully alive."

This person is showing me his soul. It is a little dry and meager and full of grinding talk just now, but presently he will show his true self.

Recently, I saw a man I had not seen for 20 years. He was an unusually forceful man and had made a great deal of money. But he had lost his ability to listen. He talked rapidly and told wonderful stories and it was just fascinating to hear them. But when I spoke — restlessness: "Just hand me that, will you? ... Where is my pipe?" It was just a habit. He read countless books and was eager to take in ideas, but he just could not listen to people.

When he has been really listened to enough, he will grow tranquil. He will begin to want to hear me.

Well, this is what I did. I was more patient — I did not resist his non-listening talk as I had my father's. I listened and listened to him, not once pressing against him, even in thought, with my own self-assertion. I said to myself: "He has been under a driving pressure for years. His family has grown to resist his talk. But now, by listening, I will pull it all out of him. He must talk freely and on and on. When he has been really listened to enough, he will grow tranquil. He will begin to want to hear me."

And he did, after a few days. He began asking me questions. And presently I was saying gently: "You see, it has become hard for you to listen."

He stopped dead and stared at me. And it was because I had listened with such complete, absorbed, uncritical sympathy, without one flaw of boredom or impatience, that he now believed and trusted me, although he did not know this.

"Now talk," he said. "Tell me about that. Tell me all about that."

Well, we walked back and forth across the lawn and I told him my ideas about it.

"You love your children, but probably don't let them in. Unless you listen, people are wizened in your presence; they become about a third of themselves. Unless you listen, you can't know anybody. Oh, you will know facts and what is in the newspapers and all of history, perhaps, but you will not know one single person. You know, I have come to think listening is love, that's what it really is."

Well, I don't think I would have written this article if my notions had not had such an extraordinary effect on this man. For he says they have changed his whole life. He wrote me that his children at once came closer. He was astonished to see what they are: how original, independent, courageous. His wife seemed really to care about him again, and they were actually talking about all kinds of things and making each other laugh.

The most serious result of not listening is that worst thing in the world, boredom, for it is really the death of love

---

For just as the tragedy of parents and children is not listening, so it is of husbands and wives. If they disagree, they begin to shout louder and louder — if not actually, at least inwardly — hanging fiercely and deafly onto their own ideas, instead of listening and becoming quieter and quieter and more comprehending. But the most serious result of not listening is that worst thing in the world, boredom, for it is really the death of love. It seals people off from each other more than any other thing. I think that is why married people quarrel. It is to cut through the non-conduction and boredom. Because when feelings are hurt, they really begin to listen. At last their talk is a real exchange. But of course, they are just injuring their marriage forever.

Besides critical listening, there is another kind that is no good: passive, censorious listening. Sometimes husbands can be this kind of listener, a kind of ungenerous eavesdropper who mentally (or aloud) keeps saying as you talk: "Bunk ... Bunk ... Hokum."

Creative listeners are laughing and just delighted with any manifestation of yourself, bad or good.

Now, how to listen? It is harder than you think. I don't believe in critical listening, for that only puts a person in a straitjacket of hesitancy. He begins to choose his words solemnly or primly. His little inner fountain cannot spring. Critical listeners dry you up. But creative listeners are those who want you to be recklessly yourself, even at your very worst, even vituperative, bad-tempered. They are laughing and just delighted with any manifestation of yourself, bad or good. For true listeners know that if you are bad-tempered, it does not mean that you are always so. They don't love you just when you are nice; they love all of you.

In order to learn to listen, here are some suggestions: Try to learn tranquility, to live in the present a part of the time every day. Sometimes say to yourself: "Now. What is happening now? This friend is talking. I am quiet. There is endless time. I hear it, every word." Then suddenly you begin to hear not only what people are saying, but what they are trying to say, and you sense the whole truth about them. And you sense existence, not piecemeal, not this object and that, but as a translucent whole.

Then watch your self-assertiveness. And give it up. Try not to drink too many cocktails, give up that nervous pressure that feels like energy and wit but may be neither. And remember it is not enough just to will to listen to people. One must really listen. Only then does the magic begin.

Sometimes people cannot listen because they think that unless they are talking, they are socially of no account. There are those women with an old-fashioned ballroom training that insists there must be unceasing vivacity and gyrations of talk. But this is really a strain on people.

No. We should all know this: that listening, not talking, is the gifted and great role, and the imaginative role. And the true listener is much more beloved, magnetic than the talker, and he is more effective, and learns more and does more good. And so try listening. Listen to your wife, your husband, your father, your mother, your children, your friends; to those who love you and those who don't, to those who bore you, to your enemies. It will work a small miracle. And perhaps a great one.

How to talk with kids — Advice to the shapers of the next generation

---

Don't ask your poor children those automatic questions —
"Did you wash your hands, dear?".

Don't ask your poor children those automatic questions — "Did you wash your hands, dear?" — those dull, automatic, querulous, duty questions (almost the only conversation that most parents have to offer). Note the look of dreadful exhaustion and ennui and boredom that comes into their otherwise quite happy faces. And don't say, "How was school today, dear?" which really means: "Please entertain me (mama) who is mentally totally lazy at the moment with not one witty or interesting thing to offer, and please give me an interesting and stimulating account of high marks."

Years and years ago when my child was four years old, I suddenly learned not to do this. I learned — a bolt from Heaven — never to ask an automatic question, so boring, so mentally lazy, so exhausting. No, I would myself tell her something interesting and arresting: "I saw Pat Greaves next door running and bawling because he was being chased by a strange yellow cat." My child's eyes would sparkle with interest, and there we were, in the liveliest conversation, and behold! she was soon telling me the most interesting extraordinary things, her own ideas. At our meals together I felt that it was I, not she, who must be the wit, the raconteur, the delightful one, the fascinated listener to her remarks, the laugher at her jokes. Now, the light in a child's eyes is a splendid gauge and tells you in a split second if you are failing and becoming a bore and a schoolmarm. She has liked me ever since.

Another aspect of the same thing is this: I say to those youngish parents (the vast majority these days) who are exhausted by their children and, with pale, neurasthenic frowns on their foreheads, are always pleading, "Plee-ase go to bed, dear ... Plee-ase now, Jack, Sally, Jane, go in the other room, dear, and look at television."

"No," I say, "you are doing it wrong. You are failing as parents. You should be so vigorous, healthy, in the pink of condition (cut out all the smoking and drinking and coffee breaks), so inexhaustible, rumbustious, jolly, full of devilry and frolic, of stories, of dramatizations, of actions, of backward somersaults, of athletics and tomfoolery, of hilarity, that your children at last after hours of violent exercise, worn down by laughter and intellectual excitement, with pale, neurasthenic frowns on their foreheads, cry: 'Plee ... eease, Mama, go to bed!'"

➚ *Brenda Ueland's book* Strength to Your Sword Arm: Selected Writings *is available for $16.70 incl. shipping from Holy Cow! Press, Box 3170, Mt. Royal Station, Duluth, MN 55803; Phone: 218 724 1653.*

Long-term shares

JAMIE CARNIE

A MAJOR STRUCTURAL PROBLEM WITH CAPITALISM AS IT EXISTS TODAY is that businesses, driven ultimately by the short-term interests of their shareholders, do not invest adequately in their long-term future. It is not easy for directors to justify substantial expenditure on research and capital investment designed to produce a profit in perhaps five to ten years if their shareholders are more concerned about getting a good dividend this year or about being able to sell their shares next year for a profit.

Even long-term investors such as the major building societies, insurance companies, and pension funds rarely look more than one or two years ahead, and if anything, the weight of their substantial presence reinforces the short-termist pressures of the investment marketplace. As a result, we are losing out to countries such as Japan, where a government ministry (MITI) has been responsible for encouraging and coordinating long-term research and development in industry.

This situation could be rectified relatively easily by means of a new instrument in the stock market, the heart of the capitalist system, which would provide a counterbalance in favor of a long-term industrial vision. This instrument would take the form of "long-term shares," whose issue and purchase would be a legal requirement.

A counterbalance in favor of a long-term industrial vision would take the form of "long-term shares," whose issue and purchase would be a legal requirement.

A law would be introduced requiring companies to issue a certain minimum percentage of long-term shares whenever they issue new ordinary shares. Perhaps ten percent of the total value of the issue would be required to take the long-term form. (A formula would be devised to require companies with existing shares to replace a proportion of these with long-term shares over time, perhaps with some support from government.)

The long-term shares would be traded in a special parallel long-term stock market. The new type of shares would be like any other shares except that when someone bought them they could not then be resold until a further five years had elapsed; they would then have to be sold by the owner during the subsequent year, or held for a further five years. And so on. Long-term shares would be identical to any other type of share. Owners of them would count as owners of the company in the normal way and would have normal voting rights at shareholder meetings and during takeover bids.

All individuals and companies owning more than a certain total floor value of shares would have to hold at least ten percent of them in long-term shares'

Obviously these shares, with their restriction on when they could be sold, would not be popular, so the same law would phase in a requirement that all individuals and companies owning more than a certain total floor value of shares would have to hold at least ten percent of them in long-term shares of their choice. (This floor value would perhaps be somewhere around 20,000 in order to exclude the small individual investor, who might otherwise be frightened off from investing at all, but to include the very wealthy and the major institutional investors.)

The new shares would compel boards of directors to plan and invest for the future in an unprecedented way.

What would the effect of this be? Obviously those people who held the long-term shares of a company (and who could not get rid of them until five years had passed) would be interested in ensuring the long-term health of the company, a message that would come through forcefully at shareholder meetings. The existence of the new shares would enable, and indeed compel, boards of directors to plan and invest for the future in an unprecedented way.

Some other points of detail: it may be necessary to allow the sale of long-term shares before their five-year term in exceptional but well-defined circumstances – e.g., bankruptcy of the owner. As well, investors purchasing shares on foreign markets would have to remain subject to the law. If they were not required to purchase ten percent of the value as long-term shares on their nation's market, there would be a stampede of money out of the country. The situation for foreign investors purchasing into the nation's market is less clear and would have to be thought out carefully. This requires more technical knowledge of the detailed workings of the global investment market than I possess, but there seems to be no reason in principle why foreign investors should not be allowed to carry on as now, without being subject to any requirement to buy long-term shares.

There would almost certainly be an adjustment period upon the introduction of such changes, when overall share prices would probably change considerably, but the market would soon restabilize and should then carry on as normal. The adjustment period would have to be planned carefully and may require some financial support from the government, but the long-term benefits to the economy would potentially be considerable.

→ *James Carnie, 96 Carlingcott, Bath BA2 8AW, UK (Phone: Int.+44 [0]1761 436945).*

Magic Circle to enhance children's self-esteem

MURRAY WHITE

These extracts are taken from an article by Murray White in the *Times Educational Supplement*. When it was written, he was headmaster of Kings Hedges Junior School, Cambridge, UK. He now runs self-esteem workshops, introducing these techniques in schools all over the UK. He is also the British representative on the International Council for Self-Esteem.

RESEARCH HAS SHOWN A STRONG LINK BETWEEN A CHILD'S SELF-ESTEEM and his or her academic success; children who feel good about themselves learn more easily and retain information longer. In fact, they do better in every way; if they have a sense of well-being, they are much more likely to be able to handle the ups and downs of daily life, including prejudice, abuse, addiction, delinquency, and violence.

With this in mind I instituted Circletime for every class in this junior school in 1988. Previous to this, for several years I had been taking classes and groups and spending time discussing behavior, exploring feelings, and playing games, with pleasing results. Staff had commented on the changes the activities had brought about in the children, both individually and collectively. One said, "My class doesn't like playing yours [the other class teacher is] at rounders. Yours always wins. Your class seem to be able to work together so much better."

I ask all the teachers to begin Circletime each day with the class sitting on the floor in a circle. If possible the teacher will be sitting first, waiting for the circle to form and able to greet each child individually on arrival. Before the register, the day begins with a round. The teacher says an incomplete sentence and gives an example to finish it off. Then the child next to the teacher repeats the phrase and puts his or her own ending on it, and so on. It has several purposes. It is a reestablishment of the group, an important joining together into a class. Children can "pass" if they wish, but few do.

The teacher says an incomplete sentence and gives an example to finish it off. The child next to the teacher repeats the phrase and puts his or her own ending on it.

Even in a large class, the level of listening to others is clearly high. Some enjoy the chance to be really imaginative and direct in their answers. Many quickly recognize it as a safe environment where they can say what they are thinking. "Today I'm feeling ... nervous," said a seven-year-old, two weeks into term. "I wish I was with ... my father, if I knew where he was," admitted a shy 11-year-old girl. Sensitive teachers will hear these and respond appropriately later.

Our rounds are about all sorts of things. "What makes me laugh is ..." Even a round where children choose the fruit they would like to be can reveal much. For the children, the teacher's self-disclosure in these rounds is also valuable. Rounds help the retiring child to feel included. At the beginning of the term, lots of activities are centered on getting to know each other and on the creation of a close, warm class identity.

After registration and the opportunity to share with everyone anything that has happened during the time children have been apart comes the selec-

M

tion of the Special Child for the day. This is universally popular with the children and, I would guess, for many of them an unusual experience.

Selection was first made by balloon popping. Each child wrote his or her name on a slip of paper and put it inside a balloon, which was then blown up and hung from the ceiling. Each day one balloon was popped and whoever's name appeared was Special Child for the day. After every child had had a turn, another method — riddles — was used, so that each had two special days in the term. Their importance in the children's lives was evident. On the second time round, one nine-year-old boy said, "It's Wednesday today and it was Wednesday last time I was chosen." Others chimed in to remember the days of the week when it had been their turn.

The Special Child will be asked to leave the room while a discussion takes place about all the nice things that can be said about him or her.

There is considerable opportunity for variation of the procedure, but the principles of specialness are clear. First the child is presented (often by the previous day's holder) with a badge. In our case it was made of cardboard on string; on one side it said "I am Special" and on the other side "I'm great." Then the child will be asked to leave the room while a discussion takes place about all the nice things that can be said about him or her (it is a real delight to me to see smiling children outside doors, waiting to be called back), or alternatively the Special Child will immediately begin to ask children who volunteered by raising hands to make their comments.

There are always plenty of contributions, and the vast majority are genuine. The children receive them with quiet pleasure. Some make real discoveries. Classmates told one 11-year-old boy that they admired his ability to deal calmly with other students' aggression. The next day the group was discussing "feeling" words, and he suggested "surprised." When asked to elaborate, he said he had been surprised to find out how much he was liked. He appears to have gained a lot of confidence and joins in discussions much more freely.

Faced with a barrage of compliments, children may find it difficult to remember or even believe them. It is important to get the children to preface their remarks with phrases like "I think you ..." or "I believe that you ..." In this way the recipient accepts it as an opinion and cannot contradict it. Teachers record the comments while they are being said, and the sheet is presented to the child.

Also, the children are asked to tell the class which comments mean most to them. "You are nice to be with" is always a favorite. This part of the ceremony ends with the child being asked to tell us one thing about him - or herself that causes him or her to be proud. It often causes difficulty, and here we see the measure of low self-esteem. I shall always remember the capable 11-

year-old girl who eventually said in a low voice, "I am good at math" and then in a whisper added, "sometimes."

Part of the fun of Circletime is that the Special Child is asked if he or she wants to be called by another name for the day. Nicknames used among friends become universally accepted; other children take bigger risks and choose their popular heroes and heroines. Special children are also given, or can claim, other privileges. One very popular one is to elect to sit on a chair in front of the assembly; this means the whole school will acknowledge that they are special. The Special Child also chooses the game for the day. A repertoire of games has been built up and incorporated into Circletime. These again have many purposes. One is to act as "energy raisers." They are useful at other times as well.

There are three rules in Circletime: only one person speaks at a time; everyone can have fun; no one is to spoil anyone else's fun. It is a time when the children find out a bit more about themselves and what they are capable of and how they relate to each other. There are lots of serious, lively discussions where feelings are discovered, explored, and accepted. The children come to realize that if they understand themselves it will help them better understand others. The value of cooperation and friendship is examined and emphasized during practical exercises.

At least twice a week in Circletime, each class splits into groups of three. This is the children's opportunity to talk and be listened to, where they will get close attention from peers to form and exchange ideas and opinions, which are then brought back to the big group for an airing.

Of course, arguments, quarrels, and other unpleasant situations still abound in school as children follow their old patterns of behavior in getting their needs met, but there is a growing awareness that there are alternatives. I believe children flourish when in an environment structured by definite controlled limits; but within these they must be encouraged to become responsible for their own decisions and be helped to achieve autonomy. Self-esteem develops when children have a basis for evaluating present performance and making comparisons with earlier behavior and attitudes.

Various sanctions and punishments are used, but it is important that these do not harm the child's self-concept. It is essential to differentiate between the doer and the deed: "I like you but cannot accept your behavior."

Recently, two 11-year-old boys, not generally known for their community spirit or for their need to tell me anything, told me quite casually in their classroom how they had approached two younger boys in the playground who they knew were frightened of them and said, "OK, we'll be your friends." Another boy with a reputation for aggression had gone out of his way to make friends with a first-year child.

Towards the end of term the emphasis switched to goal-setting and achieving targets. Children were asked to think of small specific targets —

things that they thought were desirable for them to do or to learn to do, either at home or school — or to keep a daily record. With encouragement from everyone and the use of simple will exercises, the children were helped to realize how they can achieve their potential.

Visitors to Circletime have been numerous and, sitting on the floor in the circle, are readily accepted by the children. Also the children were happy participants when Circletime was made into a video sponsored by the Artemis Trust.

Other activities included taking photographs of every child and displaying them in the entrance hall for all to admire, and making booklets called "All About Me." They are all aimed at enhancing self-esteem.

Jenny Mosley, one of the first to apply the Circletime approach in British classrooms and author of *Turn Your School Round,* maintains that the technique is useful to students both socially and academically. It can also be justified in terms of classroom time since it addresses specific requirements in the National Curriculum for English, enhancing listening skills and the ability to speak thoughtfully and coherently.

The importance of self-esteem is stated very eloquently by Dorothy Corkille Briggs in her book *Your Child's Self-Esteem* (published by Doubleday):

> A person's judgment of self influences the kinds of friends he chooses, how he gets along with others, the kind of person he marries, and how productive he will be. It affects his creativity, integrity, stability, and even whether he will be a leader or a follower. His feeling of self-worth forms the core of his personality and determines the use he makes of his aptitudes and abilities. His attitude toward himself has a direct bearing on how he lives all parts of his life. In fact, self-esteem is the mainspring that slates each of us for success or failure as a human being.

A person's judgment of self influences the kinds of friends he chooses, how he gets along with others, the kind of person he marries, and how productive he will be.

➜ *"Magic Circles — The Benefits of Circle Time," an account of the enthusiastic reaction of children and teachers who have taken part in this project, and details of workshops and publications describing the procedure are available from Murray White, 5 Ferry Path, Cambridge, CB4 1HB, UK (Phone/Fax: Int.+44 [0]1223 65351).*

➜ *"If a problem is not biological in origin, then it will almost certainly be traceable to poor self-esteem," writes Murray White in the inaugural bulletin of the Self-Esteem Network. Working on the premise that low self-esteem is a crucial factor in almost every personal and social problem, the network plans to help campaign for projects to enhance a sense of self-worth not only in education, but across the whole of society. Subscriptions to the quarterly newsletter cost £6. Send checks to Philippa Stone, Editor, Self-Esteem Network, 5 Harman Avenue, Woodford Green, Essex IG8 9DS, UK.*

↦ Turn Your School Round *by Jenny Mosley (published by Learning Development Aids, Duke Street, Wisbech, Cambridgeshire PE13 2AE, UK).*

Main libraries entitled to a digital copy of every book

Adapted from information and ideas in an article by Tim Jackson in the *London Evening Standard* entitled "Public libraries RIP."

AT PRESENT, UK PUBLISHERS HAVE TO GIVE SIX FREE COPIES OF ANY BOOK they publish for distribution to the main UK libraries if they are asked for them. Professor Nicholas Negroponte of the media lab at the Massachusetts Institute of Technology argues in *Wired* magazine that publishers should have to send such libraries a digital, rather than a physical, copy of their book. This would make it easier to provide computer access to books in future.

Tim Jackson suggests that libraries could offer digital online access to books for browsing free of charge to readers dialing in from their homes, but adds that readers should have to pay the copyright holder if making a print-out or if downloading the entire text.

Make the mother sit next to a disruptive student

SUE CARPENTER

In the late 1990s the UK media carried a story that demonstrated a lateral thinking approach. A boy had been so disruptive in class that the school punished him by making his mother come and sit next to him in class. He was so embarrassed that he has been on best behavior since. Sue Carpenter summarized the following from an item by Sarah Boseley in the *London Guardian*, which adds some detail to this story.

ANTHONY KIDD, 15, A STUDENT AT HATTERSLEY HIGH SCHOOL, Tameside, in Greater Manchester, had been the archetypal problem kid. He was rude to the teachers, caused trouble in class, and was eventually suspended. Teachers were at their wits' end, until his mother suggested she sit in on lessons.

The shame was just too much. Anthony has straightened himself out so fast, he's in danger of becoming perfect. "I thought my mates were going to take the mickey, but they were so afraid their own mums would come in, they just said they felt sorry for me," Anthony was quoted as saying.

↦ *Sue Carpenter, 20E Redcliffe Gardens, London SW10 9EX, UK.*

Marcel Proust Support Group

P. SEGAL
Summarized from the Marcel Proust Support Group website
<www.proust.com/proustgr.html>, monitored by Dr Julie Milton.

I LIVE IN A GRAND, CRUMBLING EDWARDIAN in the geographical center of San Francisco, in a two-story, 14-room flat with six friends and an endless succession of delightful houseguests. The inmates are, without exception, arty in one way or another; we have lived together and creatively fermented side by side for years. We are family, dysfunctional but nonetheless mutually supportive.

I just don't think I can get through *Remembrance of Things Past* without a support group.

As the birthday of one roommate rolled around, I asked him what he would like for a present. He thought about it for a few days, and then he said, "What I would really like for my birthday is for you to read Proust with me. I've tried to get through *Remembrance of Things Past* three times now, and I just don't think I can do it without a support group."

I myself had tried to read Proust twice that many times. "OK," I answered feebly, "anything for you."

"Don't look so miserable," he said. "We only have to read ten pages a day. It would only take about 11 months, and maybe we could get some other people to do it with us. It'll be fun."

I asked myself where we could find a bunch of people who would subject themselves to 11 months of purple prose, and then the obvious response suggested itself: The San Francisco Cacophony Society. Cacophony is a group that devotes itself entirely to the creation of outrageous entertainments of all sorts; some have an element of danger, others of whimsy, many have a literary bent, and all of them require participation. So I sent the following notice to the Cacophony newsletter:

> We have tried on innumerable occasions to read through to the very last pages of Marcel Proust's magnum opus, Remembrance of Things Past, some among us reaching well into the third volume of this prodigious work of literature, but succumbed to that inevitable, narcoleptic, helpless block which prevents the much-valued completion of this classic of introspective cultural history, and so we have profoundly wished to share this epic endeavor with others of like debility, gathering together in a solemn pledge, not untouched with a tinge of good-humored irony, to plow together through these three volumes at the sensible pace of ten pages a day, agreeing in advance to use the Vintage Books 1982

edition, so we might proceed at an identical pace and, therefore, at our bimonthly meetings, be able to share the delights of the literary bliss within at an equal rate of discovery ... blah blah blah.

We drank Pernod and ate madeleines.

Eight hardy literature buffs showed for the first meeting, scheduled for my roommate's birthday. We drank Pernod and ate madeleines, got acquainted with the previously unknown persons, and spoke of our anxieties about this shared venture. Curious spectators came by to examine the specimens who were voluntarily committing to a 3,500-plus-page read and to help dispose of the refreshments. One of them became the designated outside observer, charged with noting the behavioral changes of the support group members over the long haul.

When a particular dinner party had been going on for 140 pages, we had each other — co-conspirators forced to attend a dull party.

The read began on the very next day. Four of the committed ones were members of our household, and, before long, as we staggered out for morning (this term must not be taken literally) coffee, we were bearing our *Remembrances* so we might regale each other with favorite quotes. Then that wasn't enough, and we began inscribing the most deathless lines on an obscure wall over the cat food. When the going got rough, like the fortnight when a particular dinner party had been going on for 140 pages, we had each other — co-conspirators forced, as we had often been in real life, to attend a dull party.

Then we found ourselves speculating: "What is Legrandin's trip, anyway?" or "Was Odette really in bed with de Forcheville when Swann came over?" We were very hooked.

In our zeal we announced our second meeting in the Cacophony newsletter. This time 40 people showed up, but we figured that was because we had included, in our long-winded announcement, the news that we would be showing a movie as part of the evening's entertainment — *Swann in Love*, which is one of the books of *Remembrance* — and a short subject, Monty Python's hilarious skit "The Marcel Proust Summarization Contest." The crowd included numerous persons who were trying to read Proust, were thinking about trying, had been forced to read Proust, or had read it in French. People read aloud (in English and French), munched a lot of madeleines, and drank a copious quantity of Pernod.

M

Our outside observer, and anyone else who knows me, soon realized that of all of us, I had been the most altered. The existence of this Proust Support Group publication is testimony enough, but already in the earlier stages, the warning signs were clearly visible. I had dumped the generic answering-machine message and replaced it with a weekly Proust quote, a tradition I have maintained without deviation for about three years, and without having to repeat myself once. In the beginning of this manifestation I got a lot of hang-up calls, probably clients who were sure I'd finally gone round the bend. Other people began calling on a regular basis, just to hear the quote.

My callers, too, found themselves altered. Serendipitous quotes rang too many bells in their ears; their resolve not to read Proust melted away. Even the people who had been laughing at my obsession were secretly buying Volume I and indulging.

The months sped by. We were leading double lives, ours and Marcel's ("Are you still having dinner with the Swanns?" "Have you left for Balbec yet?"). Our capacity to speak in simple sentences diminished. Some readers, unable to bear it any longer, dropped out, while others joined in.

Nine months after we had begun, an impending sense of loss began setting in. Only 800 pages left...

We held our meetings in fin-de-siecle venues and amassed a library of Proustiana. Nine months after we had begun, an impending sense of loss began setting in. Only 800 pages left ... 500 pages ... 200 ... oh, no. We had long since stopped greeting each other with inquiries as to states of well-being. The first question we asked upon encountering another of our kind was invariably "What page are you on?"

It was a blustery, rainy January when the end was near for the three survivors of the original group, all of whom lived in our household. A certain rivalry ensued as to which of the three of us would finish first. John, who started the whole thing, announced that he was sure he would finish first. We soon discovered why; he had found our copies and torn out the last page.

John was, of course, correct about being the first of us to finish. He was also right about the fact that reading Proust had been fun, as shared horrors always seem in retrospect. But that wasn't the only reason.

For me, one of the great thrills of the read was the effect it had on my attitude towards books in general. They had always been some kind of sacred cow, not to be marked or mutilated in any way, but treated with utmost respect. As I read, however, it became painfully clear that discrete microdots of fine leaded pencil would not suffice to flag the gems I came across on every page. As I made my way through the first few hundred pages, I got over my bourgeois reservations about the printed page, and the margins became flooded with squiggles and exclamation marks, the text itself riddled with underlining, highlighting, brackets, and colored paper markers.

My middle-class veneration of books toppled even further as the months wore on and I, worn out, would fall asleep, frequently with the book in my hands, unable to put it down, only to be startled back into consciousness as it fell, with a resounding thunk, on the bedside floor. Within a short time the binding was so distressed that Volume I broke into multiple sections. When some of my co-readers were off on vacation, I was able to lend them chunks of text to take along, sparing them the weight of an entire volume. In these two notable deviations from my former behavior — marking and breaking great books — I felt the lightness of heart that comes with the shedding of restrictive conventions.

I now possess some kind of code to the human heart.

There was fun to be had, and another great breakthrough, in absorbing the cynical and all-too-true observations Proust made on the subject of human nature, particularly in the realm of love. It lent a sense of foreboding to every interpersonal encounter, the anticipatory irrepressible laughter I felt as a child when I knew that the jig was up and I was about to be busted. With the belief that I now possess some kind of code to the human heart, I can face all possibilities without fear, and with laughter.

→ P. Segal (e-mail: psegal@well.com).

Meeting view-sampling machines

KEITH ENGLAND

EACH PERSON IN A BUSINESS OR COMMITTEE MEETING COULD BE EQUIPPED with a control knob with positions 3,2,1,0,-1,-2,-3. The numbers signify the person's feeling on an issue, from being wholly in favor (3) to abstention (0) to being totally opposed (-3). (Eds: These devices could be similar to the electronic ones used in TV game shows where the studio audience votes for its favorites.)

The simple central computer display would then read out the vote, indicating the strength of the support for the motion. This represents value added to a decision at very little cost. Additionally, the method is quicker than counting hands or a secret ballot. At present the thinking of each person is devalued by the simple adversarial yes-no vote and by the lack of ability to express an opinion accurately or to indicate depth of feeling.

> At present the thinking of each person is devalued by the
> simple adversarial yes-no vote and the lack of ability to
> express an opinion accurately or to indicate depth of feeling.

There are other uses that would probably become commonplace. If members continuously adjusted their knobs, the chairman could see instantaneously the existing degree of support and could cease the discussion when the voters were already convinced, without further time-wasting debate. Where a chairman felt that a contribution was irrelevant, he or she could obtain a snap decision and would then be in a far more assured position to end that particular speech.

Comment by Professor Stafford Beer

Professor Stafford Beer writes that he proposed a similar Algedonic Meter for use in Chile in 1971. His son Simon constructed a trial system. The best reference is Beer's book *Brain of the Firm* (published by John Wiley), which contains a fascinating account of his cybernetics work for the Allende government in Chile.

The algedonic meter is at last an attempt to provide a metric for Aristotle's eudemony, or "state of general well-being." It is a simple analog device, with interleaved segments in different colors. Thus to turn the central knob changes the proportion of the "happy/unhappy" display — and also the electrical input to the circle of which this meter is a member.

Someone holding an algedonic meter sets the display by moving the pointer anywhere on a continuous scale between total disquiet and total satisfaction. The user does not have to explain anything — only to respond algedonically, which people may be observed to do all the time.

There could be an official locale, housing a television set and a properly constituted sample of people, having one meter between, say, three. The meters drive a simple electrical system which sums the voltage for this locale.

Now: when a broadcast is taking place, the people's eudemony is indicated on a meter in the TV studio — which everyone (those in the studio and the public) can see. The studio meter is driven by the sum of the people's meters. This closes the algedonic loop ....

> People would be able to participate in arguments broadcast
> from the People's Assembly by the continuous registration of
> a combined degree of satisfaction with events.

People would be able to participate in arguments broadcast from the People's Assembly — not by responding to questions hurled at them over the air, for this route leads to logical reductionism and to political demagoguery, but by the continuous registration of a combined degree of satisfaction with events. It has to be noted that not only would the meter be visible to those present in the Assembly, but also to the public whose meter it is ....

The problem at present is that the government communicates directly with the undifferentiated mass of the people as if it were speaking to the individual, and creates the illusion in the home that it is. The context of this false dialog is that the individual is also supplied by the news media with a proliferation of information and misinformation about things — as soon as they happen.

We see the following effects:

- Massive amplification of variety, insofar as single-sentence utterances may be developed into hour-long simulations of imagined consequences.
- Massive changes in dynamic periodicity: the government is reporting to the nation daily, instead of accounting for itself at election times.

But the return loop does not change. The variety that the people generate is attenuated as before. This situation attempts to disobey the Law of Requisite Variety and disbalances the homeostatic equilibrium in both richness and in period.

Then it is predictable that the people, thus affected, will build up pressures in the system that can no longer be released — because the filtering capacity cannot contain the flow.

This is bound to lead to unrest: demonstrations, agitation, perhaps violence, possibly revolt.

This is bound to lead to unrest: demonstrations, agitation, perhaps violence, possibly revolt.

My algedonic meter experiments were, alas, not finally undertaken by the time that the Allende government fell. At any rate, I hope that new experiments on these lines will be facilitated somewhere. A plausible experiment, for example, would be to equip a conference hall with closed algedonic loops: would the speaker become yet more steadily boring and obscure as the summation meter steadily dropped — for all to see?

Editorial comment

One requirement for a device for use in meetings is that it should be under the table, operated ideally by foot — at least in its Bore-o-meter mode. For the average person, it seems to take too much courage above the table — it would be like interrupting the speaker to tell him or her that you are bored, although Beer says that an individual in Manchester called James Baldwin used an above-table cube with six colored faces, simply exhibiting, according to his mood, one of the faces to the speaker.

The brain has evolved to decipher faces faster than any other information. The most effective view-sampling device, therefore, might be a computer-programmed face on a monitor that scowls or smiles broadly or slightly or not at all in accordance with the votes of those with access to this device (to be backed up by a corresponding numerical total displayed on the side of the screen for whenever a precise record is required).

Comment by Valerie Yule

I have long wanted a console for speakers with, say, 144 red-lit buttons. As members of the audience freak out, they can press a button at their seat and one of the console lights goes on. When 144 people are bored, the whole console flashes. Or, less technologically, there could be little pennants at seats, which can be flagged down when you stop listening.

Churches could be lit by candles at each seat. As the congregation flags, they snuff out their candle, until the whole place is in darkness and the preacher gets the message.

Or churches could be lit by candles at each seat. As the congregation flags, they snuff out their candle, until the whole place is in darkness and the preacher gets the message.

→ *Keith England, Langdale, Jordans, Beaconsfield, Bucks HP9 2ST, UK (Phone: Int.+44 [0]12407 5816).*

→ *Professor Stafford Beer, 34 Palmerston Square, Toronto, Ontario, M6G 2S7, Canada (Phone: 416 535 0396).*

→ *Valerie Yule, 57 Waimarie Drive, Mount Waverley, Victoria, Australia (Phone: Int.+61 [0]13 807 4315; E-mail: vyule@pa.ausom.net.au). She runs the Australian Ideas Bank (http://avoca.vicnet.net.au/~ozideas/).*

Meet the mayor on the park bench

The following is adapted from items entitled "Meet the mayor on a bench in the square" and "See your councillor at the library," which appeared in the Norwegian Ideas Bank.

Every Wednesday at noon, the mayor of Ringerike
sits down on a red bench in the town square.

EVERY WEDNESDAY AT NOON, THE MAYOR OF RINGERIKE — a municipality of 28,000 people northwest of Oslo in Norway — sits down on a red bench in the square at the center of its regional capital, Hönefoss. Mayor Kolbjörn Kværum has done so every week since August 1993, whatever the season and the weather. And he is never left alone — sometimes people have to line up for a chat with the mayor.

The mayor believes passionately in the importance of open dialog with his community. Some want to talk about council matters, others about their own concerns.

The idea of sitting on the bench is the mayor's own. At the outset, in 1993, he would invite people to an open hour at his office, but soon it occurred to him that the square was a better place to meet people.

Ulla Nevestad, a colleague in the neighboring municipality of Lier, has followed his example, except that she moves around, doing her bench sitting in different places each week. Kværum has also considered this option of changing benches occasionally, but has decided that the square in Hönefoss is his ideal place to be, since most people in Ringerike cross it fairly often.

In 1999, as part of an attempt to decentralize, councillors in Oslo's Uranienborg-Majorstuen district began a similar bench project. Three days a week, the inhabitants can meet politicians from their part of town and have a chat on the bench. During the winter, meetings are held inside the local library, while in summer they take place in Valkyrie Square, a natural place for local people to go.

Reactions to all these bench schemes have been very positive: people have generally enjoyed meeting their representatives in this open and relaxed setting. The bench is a place where people can meet politicians to vent their feelings and frustrations and to present their visions and ideas.

→ *Kolbjörn Kværum, Ringerike kommune, Osloveien 1, Servicebox 4, 3504 Hönefoss, Norway (Phone: 47 Int.+[0] 32 11 74 00; Fax: 47 Int.+[0] 32 12 50 30; E-mail: Inger.Moe@ringerike.kommune.no; Web: www.ringerike.kommune.no).*

→ *Bydel Uranienborg Majorstuen, Fr Nansensvei 2, Pb 5380 Majorstuen, 0304 Oslo, Norway (Phone: 47 Int.+[0] 23 36 88 00; Fax: 47 Int.+[0] 22 56 91 91; E-mail: major@bd2.bigblue.no; Web: www.bd2.bigblue.no).*

→ *See also Stiftelsen Idebanken, PO Box 2126 Grünnerlokka, Norway (Phone: Int.+47 [0] 2203 4010; Fax: Int.+47 [0]2236 4060; E-mail: idebanken@online.no; Web: www.idebanken.no).*

M

Memory Boxes — personal museums

YVONNE MALIK

MANY OF US HAVE KEEPSAKES — things of no monetary value, but sentimental or nostalgic mementoes that stimulate our memories, such as old photos, letters, coins, tickets, keys, trinkets, crockery, ornaments, holiday souvenirs, scarves, ties, medals, certificates. Individually, they may seem small or insignificant, but put together in a display, these same objects could become a decorative and pleasing personal museum.

The Memory Boxes could be converted sewing boxes,
tool boxes (the kind that opens up into two or three tiers),
circular tea trays, or shallow suitcases.

The arrangements could be displayed inexpensively in, for instance, sewing boxes, cookie tins, tool boxes (the kind that opens up into two or three tiers), circular tea trays, or shallow suitcases. These can be repainted and make excellent holders for three-dimensional objects.

When we are old, is it necessary for us to sit like potted plants in silent immobile rows, communicating nothing of what we have been, like empty people waiting for the end?

Retirement and rest homes await many of us, offering little means of expressing life's experiences or of taking a pride in having survived at all.

With Memory Boxes we would have "something to show for it." An answer to several needs. The opportunity to communicate in non-verbal ways that "I was here; I did this; I learned that; I did and do exist and live." They answer, too, the need for reassurance in visual terms, emphasizing, stimulating, and drawing attention (through memories) to the length of life experienced (rather than the shorter length still anticipated).

Language is no barrier (unlike in oral history). Pride can be taken in a tangible expression of one's past.

The collecting and putting together of possible objects could take place in our homes, with a group of friends, or could be carried out in a day center, as part of art therapy, where the camaraderie of others similarly involved could stimulate and encourage those with less initial confidence.

The participants will be surprised and pleased with the results, which could be exhibited in local libraries, etc., as a way of generating more awareness and interest from others — particularly from those of the same generation.

↬ *Yvonne Malik has made her own Memory Box as an example. Her address is Sweet Briar, Wray, near Lancaster LA2 8QN, UK (Phone: Int.+44 [0]15242 21767).*

→ *In a similar vein, Barnados — the UK's largest children's charity — have pro-duced their own "Memory Store," which comes with advice on how to fill it. Designed for parents facing a crisis of some kind, it can be used as a store of family history for the children in case the parents won't be there to pass it on directly. It comes as a large yellow box with six drawers and a matching, loose leaf memory book which can be stored inside along with family photos and mementos. It costs £34.99 incl. shipping from Barnados, PO Box 20, Tanners Lane, Barkingside, Ilford, Essex, IG6 1QQ, UK (Fax: Int.+44 [0]1268 520230).*

→ *The US alternative, the Memory Box, is a painted and lined cedar box avail-able from <www.htowne.com/boxes.asp>. A framed display case which holds both two and three dimensional objects is available at <www.mymemorybox.com>.*

Message book for visitors to sleeping patient

Extract from letter to the *Seattle Times'* "Dear Abby" column from "Ruth of Ottawa," monitored by Roger Knights.

RECENTLY I LOST MY BELOVED STEPMOTHER TO CANCER. She faced her illness with courage, humor, and determination, and she helped her family deal with it in the same way.

During her final weeks in the hospital, she slept a good deal of the time and consequently missed many of her visitors. She was disappointed when she didn't get to see them, so we placed a guest book on the table by her bed. If she was sleeping when a friend came by, the visitor signed it and left a mes-sage for her. When she awoke, she enjoyed reading the thoughts and mem-ories, humorous stories, hopes, and wishes.

This book became the text of her eulogy.

After she died, this book became the text of her eulogy. As it was read, her family and friends were able to laugh and cry together as they remem-bered this special woman.

I hope your readers will find our experience of value and use this idea in their own lives.

M

Movable theater seats for wheelchair users

Summarized from an article by Charles Krauthammer, of the Washington Post Writers Group, entitled "Handicapped people aren't to be treated like freight," monitored by Roger Knights.

THE CONCERT HALL AT WASHINGTON'S KENNEDY CENTER has been brilliantly renovated with wheelchair users in mind, according to Charles Krauthammer, a columnist in the Washington Post, who has been in a wheelchair since the age of 22.

The Kennedy Center has removed a full row of
orchestra seats and replaced them with
identical-looking but movable chairs.

Whereas a movie theater will remove a seat or two to make room for wheelchairs — only for most wheelchairs not to fit, or for the chair user to block the view of the people behind — the Kennedy Center has removed a full row of orchestra seats and replaced them with identical-looking but movable chairs.

Krauthammer writes: "Brilliant: serviceable for as many disabled and non-disabled as necessary."

The floor is depressed, so the view of those behind is not blocked, and everywhere in the concert hall there are ramps, fitting naturally into the inclined plane of the concert hall floor.

N

The Natural Step — A national plan for sustainability

DR. KARL-HENRIK ROBÈRT, ONE OF SWEDEN'S LEADING CANCER RESEARCHERS, has developed The Natural Step as a method of reaching consensus about sustainable futures within the scientific community in Sweden. With persistence, he reached an agreed-upon 22nd draft of a report on environmental problems and on the most critical avenues for action. He persuaded the king, schools, and industrial sponsors to back the report and arranged for an educational package to be sent to every household in the country, outlining the steps needed to make Swedish civilization environmentally sustainable for the long-term future. This project was backed by artists and celebrities on TV, and it has led to seminars for MPs, study circles, and an environmental youth parliament. It promises in the long run to completely reorganize the nation's way of life, bringing it "into alignment with the laws of nature."

The project outlines the steps needed to make Swedish civilization environmentally sustainable for the long-term future.

Marilyn Mehlman of the Swedish Institute for Social Inventions writes: "In my view, Dr. Karl-Henrik Robèrt's most significant social invention is his method for achieving consensus on tricky, complicated, often highly scientific matters in a way that does not reduce agreement to the lowest common denominator, but that actually produces rather radical position statements. His work has, for example, developed a position statement on energy (production and use) which has been endorsed by virtually all leading scientists in Sweden, regardless of opinions on topics like nuclear power, and which has been presented to the House of Parliament. He describes his method as leading discussion back to the 'trunk' of the problem tree rather than chattering about peripheral twigs and leaves."

Consensus-building
Dr. Robèrt gives an example of this consensus-building:

If a politician were to ask a random selection of scientists whether or not the reproductive organs of seals are destroyed by the chemical PCB, it is very unlikely that he would get the kinds of answers that would be helpful in arriving at a decision. He might hear, for instance, "That has not been definitely established yet," or "Yes, that has now been clearly established," or "Our laboratory has identified a toxin that plays a far more destructive role," and so on.

That's the sort of thing that happens with questions about the leaves of the environmental tree. But, if one begins with the trunk or branches, the answers become clearer and more consistent. For instance:

Is PCB a naturally occurring substance? No, it is artificially manufactured by man. All scientists agree on that.

Is it chemically stable, or does it quickly degrade into harmless substances? It is stable and persistent. On that they all agree as well.

Does it accumulate in organs? Yes, it does.

Is it possible to predict the tolerance limits of such a stable, unnatural substance? No, since the complexity of ecosystems is essentially limitless. Nevertheless, it is known that all such substances have limits, often very low, which cannot be exceeded.

Can we continue to introduce such substances into the ecosystem? Not if we want to survive.

The final answer is what the politician actually wanted to know from the beginning, since he is probably not particularly interested in the reproductive organs of seals. Yet most public environmental debate is preoccupied with such relatively minor details. This happens whenever we fail to proceed from a basic frame of reference, or overview, which makes it possible to focus on the fundamental issues without getting lost in a confusion of isolated details.

Networking

Dr. Robèrt explains the organizational structure:

The Natural Step is not a new organization. This is a network of people. We have a lot of good people involved from the Swedish Federation for the Preservation of Nature, the World Wildlife Fund, and so forth, but we are not getting any money from membership as those organizations do. Just the opposite — we are begging for money from industry and finding other sources, and our message is, "Please join these organizations." And that has a very big effect on their membership.

I went to the king, and asked him if he would endorse the project. He agreed.

I built networks wherever I went. When I went to Swedish TV and said that I and all the artists and scientists and this big government office wanted to educate the whole Swedish people and that we would like to have a party on TV celebrating it, they said, "Certainly. How could we refuse if you succeed with all these other things?" From there I went to the king and asked him if he would endorse the project. He agreed. You can understand that I slept worse and worse the longer I did this, because I was building a tremendous program without any money at all. I was really nervous by the time I approached the industrial sponsors. But on the other hand, by the time they saw it, it was like a parcel with a ribbon on it. It was so concrete, with dates and everything, that they understood that if they didn't buy it now, this crazy chap would take it to someone else!

In ten years, the market will be about nothing else but sustainability.

So industries must move from defending themselves to being heroes, ahead of everyone else, fighting for tomorrow's market and tomorrow's technology. In ten years, the market will be about nothing else but sustainability.

As soon as we see an enemy, we ask him for advice. We say, "Would you please help us to sort out this problem?" When you get the answer, very rarely is it a threat to what you want to do. And by following his advice, two things happen: first, he has part of the responsibility for it now, because it's his advice you are following; and secondly, the project generally improves — because most people have rather good ideas!

Next Steps

Future plans include the following:

- Emphasis on the Natural Step Institute and on intensified cooperative problem-solving by dynamic business leaders, public officials, and natural scientists.
- Papers on energy policy, agriculture, and the national economy to be distributed to members of parliament and others.
- An environmental youth parliament, featuring a closed-circuit TV symposium uniting 100,000 youths from schools across Sweden.
- Six "environmental quiz" programs on TV.
- Six humorous public service messages for movie theaters and TV, with a celebrity demonstrating how he or she has learned to act with greater environmental responsibility in everyday life.
- Eight TV variety programs, organized by Anni-Frid Lyngstad of ABBA.

➔ *The Natural Step in Sweden: Der Naturliga Steget, Slottsbacken 6, S-111 30 Stockholm, Sweden (Phone: Int.+46 [0]8 545 125 00; Fax: Int.+46 [0]8 545 125 99).*

➔ *There are long and very interesting interviews on the web about the Natural Step in Sweden, describing how the project got underway. They are part of a study by Hilary Bradbury at <http://learning.mit.edu/res/kr/rtf_learning.html>.*

➔ *The Natural Step US, Thoreau Center for Sustainability, The Presidio, PO Box 29372, San Francisco, CA 94129-0372 (Phone: 415 561 3344; Fax: 415 561 334 5400; E-mail: tns@naturalstep.org; Web: www.naturalstep.org).*

➔ *See:* **The Natural Step for Business** *by Brian Natrass and Mary Altomare (New Society Publishers, 1999), and the forthcoming* **The Natural Step Story,** *by Karl-Henrik Robèrt (New Society Publisher, 2002), and* **Dancing With the Tiger: Learning Sustainability Step by Natural Step,** *by Brian Natrass and Mary Altomare.*

N

Neal's Yard principles

NICHOLAS SAUNDERS

Nicholas Saunders initiated many of the businesses in Neal's Yard in London's Covent Garden — the first, a wholefood shop, was started in the 1970s. Others followed in quick succession: the bakery, the dairy, the coffee shop, the apothecary, the soup and salad bar, the therapy rooms, the desktop publishing studio, and the Agency for Personal Development, which have all survived to date.

MY IDEAS ABOUT WORK were influenced by Gurdjieff — fulfillment does not come from making everything easy, but from doing a variety of things that stretch your abilities, including physical work. So jobs were rotated, from cleaning to dealing with the money, and I used to encourage responsibility by giving workers turns at managing the business with authority to sign checks — often without even knowing their surnames, which shocked the bank manager.

> My ideas about work were influenced by Gurdjieff — fulfillment does not come from making everything easy, but from doing a variety of things that stretch your abilities, including physical work.

The atmosphere was one of high energy, with no nonsense, and attracted an enthusiastic lot of workers. The wholefood business was making a lot of money, too, so I divided up the profits among the workers and reduced the prices still further.

After helping set up the wholefood shop and the bakery, I had ideas of starting more shops. I was not convinced that worker co-ops or any other setup was ideal, but wanted to lay down some principles. Clare from the bakery helped me draft these Neal's Yard Trading Principles (although not all have subsequently been adhered to by all the now-independent businesses):

1. All food must be prepared or at least packed on the premises.
2. The ingredients must be wholefood, i.e., pure, without additives such as flavorings, colorings, or preservatives. Highly refined ingredients must be avoided.
3. Prices must be reasonable.

> Descriptions (both verbal and written) must be straightforward, down-to-earth, and objective. Persuasive, enticing, or glamorizing descriptions must not be used.

4. Descriptions (both verbal and written) must be straightforward, down-to-earth, and objective. Persuasive, enticing, or glamorizing descriptions must not be used.

5. The size and style of notices must be simple — not attention-seeking, enticing, image-building, or making use of any advertising or merchandising techniques.

6. "Point of sale aids" must not be used.

7. Information about recipes, ingredients, quality, and suppliers must be freely available.

8. The neighbors must be given consideration and cooperation.

9. All staff must be free to see accounts and attend meetings where they may freely express their views.

10. Jobs should be rotated as far as possible, and in particular, no one should be left with the unpopular jobs.

11. Outside contractors should be avoided if the regular staff can do the work.

12. In the event of the business growing, it should not expand or set up branches, but instead should assist and encourage some of its staff to split off and start another independent business.

What was behind these principles was my belief in direct feedback between the customer and the person producing the goods. Instead of separate experts doing each part of the process of manufacturing, packing, transporting, and selling, the same person could do all those jobs with more satisfaction — for simple but important reasons such as feeling the customers' appreciation.

Although productivity was bound to be lower as measured by output in each individual job, this could be made up for by savings in packaging and transport and by far lower overheads, as administration often accounts for half the cost of production. Additionally, there were often advantages in being able to sell fresher products — and this was particularly relevant for wholefoods, where no preservatives are used.

At the time, I was particularly against businesses expanding beyond about a dozen workers or setting up branches, because a small scale allows direct communication between people, without need for internal memos or a personnel department. In a small business, people also feel more contact with the boss — it tends to be fairer whatever the business structure.

✦ *Nicholas Saunders died in a car accident in South Africa. A 60-page booklet,* **The Neal's Yard Story,** *is available from the Institute for Social Inventions, 20 Heber Road, London NW2 6AA, UK (Phone: Int.+44 [0]20 8208 2853; Fax: Int.+44 [0]20 8452 6434; E-mail: rhino@dial.pipex.com).*

N

Negotiating the difference for charity

FREDERICK MULDER

Frederick Mulder, a dealer in old master and modern prints, describes an unusual approach to negotiating.

I asked a fair price. My client offered $20,000 less. After a certain amount of to-ing and fro-ing we were at an impasse. Suddenly I had a brainwave: why not ask if he would be willing to give the $20,000 difference away if I accepted his offer?

I HAD BOUGHT AN IMPORTANT ORIGINAL PRINT BY EDVARD MUNCH. I offered it to a good client at what I thought was a fair price; my client countered with an offer that was $20,000 less. After a certain amount of to-ing and fro-ing we were at an impasse. I had asked what I believed to be the market price for the print and did not want to accept less; my client was not prepared to pay more. Suddenly I had a brainwave: why not ask if he would be willing to give the $20,000 difference away if I accepted his offer? Plucking up courage, I asked; it was not something I had ever done or heard of being done before, although I dimly remembered the story of an art dealer who, faced with an irreconcilable difference between what he wanted and what a famous pianist wished to pay for a painting, asked the pianist what his concert fee was. The amount was that of the irreconcilable difference, and the dealer proposed that the pianist give him a private concert; both parties went away happy. My client quickly accepted and in fact generously offered to give away $25,000 instead of $20,000. I even told him my cost, and we both agreed that the remaining profit was a fair one. I had been mostly involved in funding Third World and environmental projects, and we agreed to split the $25,000 between Oxfam and Greenpeace, both organizations I knew well.

What struck me afterwards was how my suggestion changed our whole attitude to the transaction and to each other's role in it. Whereas before we were in a traditional commercial confrontation, with each of us trying to secure the best price for ourselves, the idea that we might together give away all or part of my profit turned us into allies with a common purpose. I realized also that I had not been so concerned about what my client actually paid as about ensuring that I was not unreasonably beaten down; likewise, my client was not so concerned about what he actually paid as about ensuring that he had gotten the lowest price. Introducing the "gift" element changed the tone of the discussion and made us both less sensitive about the question of who would win.

The idea that we might together give away all or part of my profit turned us into allies with a common purpose.

This was another step in helping me to look at commercial transactions in a new way. I began by seeing a transaction as a way of turning a profit and thus earning a living. When I began to use part of my profit to support Third World development and environmental work, each transaction also became a way of realizing funds for another purpose. Now I have gone a stage further and actively work with some of my clients in jointly supporting charitable projects. I understand this has had a ripple effect; some of my clients have become further involved in a particular cause that we jointly supported. I jokingly call this "cutting out the middleman."

Splitting the difference in business disputes

Summarized from a story by Don Clark entitled "Motorola agrees to an unusual settlement in patent suit with inventor Lemelson," which appeared in the *Wall Street Journal*.

A mutual interest in educational charity provided the key to breaking the deadlock in a dispute between inventor Jerome Lemelson and Motorola Inc. in the United States. Mr Lemelson, a prolific and famously litigious inventor, was embroiled in a long-term battle with Motorola over a disputed patent.

"During the course of our discussions with Mr Lemelson," a statement from Motorola ran, "we discovered a significant shared commitment to educational programs designed to stimulate inventions and innovation." The long-running dispute was settled when Motorola agreed to pay an undisclosed sum to Mr Lemelson's philanthropic foundation and to co-sponsor educational programs at the Massachusetts Institute of Technology, Arizona State University, and other selected institutions.

Donald Banner, a veteran patent attorney, termed the agreement "very unusual." He said such agreements could have positive social benefits. "We need all the innovation we can get."

Neighborhood Day

THE FIRST MONDAY IN MAY EACH YEAR IS INTERNATIONAL NEIGHBORHOOD DAY, a day to get to know your neighbors. Put out a leaflet inviting everyone on your street over for a cup of coffee, or organize a get-together, or dance in your local hall.

The Institute for Social Inventions and <www.DoBe.org> are publicizing this day and urge you to post details of your events on <www.DoBe.org> (in its "Neighborhood" section) as an inspiration for others.

N

In the Bible, Jesus talks about loving your neighbor, but it's become so bad nowadays, as the Rev. John Papworth (who first proposed International Neighborhood Day) has pointed out, that most people, Christian or other, don't even know who their neighbors are. There is nothing more vital today than to rebuild our sense of community — evidence shows it leads, for example, to increased health and less crime.

John Papworth writes:

> There is an increasing awareness that many problems of modern life are stemming from the general dissolution of community ties and structures. Young people especially are afflicted with a sense of divorce from a rooted and defined sense of reality that gives their own lives the necessary coordinates of a meaningful framework of existence in terms of relationships, rituals, traditions, and common objectives.

> One result of the stresses this imposes on people is an increasing resort to drugs, tranquillizers, fundamentalist forms of religion or politics; a growing spirit of amoral unconcern for social support factors such as family ties, care of the aged, financial and other obligations; and a general decline of caring and sharing. The results, in terms of family breakdown, lawlessness, violence, and sickness of mind, body, and spirit have become part of the commonplaces of 20th-century life. The same factors will surely characterize life even more in the 21st century — unless we take remedial action.

So International Neighborhood Day is a positive step to commemorate and celebrate the life and spirit of the local neighborhood.

On the first Monday in May, hold celebrations to signify the importance of neighborhood ties and traditions. Besides inviting neighbors in for a drink, these can include :

- having street parties
- beating the bounds
- dancing
- presenting of neighborhood civic awards
- holding an evening banquet
- planting trees

In our societies today we lack Vitamin T, the tribal vitamin. Even a nod from a neighbor counts as one unit of Vitamin T, and you need at least a hundred units a day.

↦ *For more on the philosophy behind this day, see John Papworth's journal* **Fourth World Review** *("For small nations, small communities, and a human scale"). Subscriptions cost £20 from John Papworth, The Close, 26 High St, Purton,*

Wiltshire SN5 4AE, UK (Phone: Int.+44 [0]1793 772214; Fax: 01793 772521; E-mail: john.papworth@btinternet.com).

→ *For more on Vitamin T, see the item later in this encyclopedia.*

→ *Media can contact <www.DoBe.org> at The Institute for Social Inventions, 20 Heber Road, London NW2 6AA, UK (Phone: Int.+44 [0]20 8208 2853; Fax: Int.+44 [0]20 8452 6434; E-mail: rhino@dial.pipex.com; Web: www.DoBe.org).*

Neighborhood Innovations Program

BILL BERKOWITZ

I HELPED CREATE THIS NEIGHBORHOOD INNOVATIONS PROGRAM in my home town of Arlington, Massachusetts.

Run from Arlington's Department of Planning and Community Development, the program asks "Got an idea for your neighborhood?" It makes small awards of up to $1,000 to neighborhood groups for starting activities to improve neighborhood life. The budget is $5,000 a year.

Projects sponsored so far include neighborhood fairs, tool-lending libraries, skills exchanges, job clearing houses, and computer co-ops.

The Department will look for originality, feasibility, concrete neighborhood support, specific neighborhood benefit, and potential lasting value.

The leaflet distributed explains that in the letters of application, people have to "try to include a list of names and addresses of people in your neighborhood who support your idea. The Department will look for originality, feasibility, concrete neighborhood support, specific neighborhood benefit, and potential lasting value. Some preference will be given to applications from low- and moderate-income groups."

"Think about what you would like to see in your neighborhood," the leaflet urges. "Your imagination is the only limit. Maybe we can help make your idea come true."

→ *Bill Berkowitz, 12 Pelham Terrace, Arlington, MA 02174 (Phone: 617 646 6319).*

Neighborhood Salons

Summarized from *Utne Reader* and its website.

UTNE READER, A DIGEST OF THE BEST OF THE ALTERNATIVE PRESS, ran a story some years ago entitled "Salons: How to Revive the Endangered Art of

N

Conversation and Start a Revolution in Your Living Room." The story burgeoned into a national Neighborhood Salon program, with over 500 salons existing independently today. Inspired by the words of Margaret Mead — "Never doubt that a small group of thoughtful, committed citizens can change the world ... it is the only thing that ever has" — salons began primarily as places for conversation with like-minded *Utne* readers.

There has been a rapid and organic proliferation of salons throughout the country.

Today, some are dedicated to talking, possibly using an article from the *Utne Reader* as a springboard for discussion; others practice "devout listening" and speaking from the heart. Still others have become book clubs, writing circles, study circles, and creative play groups. The rapid and seemingly organic proliferation of salons throughout the country has meant that *Utne* has largely relinquished official charge of the salons; their anarchic zest makes them almost impossible to monitor. But the magazine still receives wedding snapshots of those who met at a neighborhood salon, or group snapshots celebrating a salon's anniversary — confirmation that salon life is indeed alive and well in America.

The Utne Reader Neighborhood Salon Association has also launched a global network of internet mailing lists designed to foster small-group dialog on hundreds of current and timeless issues. These e-mail salons, coordinated by the online Cafe Utne, are structured in the same way as face-to-face salons — participant numbers are purposefully limited to 25 so as to create a more relaxed atmosphere and to enable members to get to know one another.

→ *Neighborhood Salon Association, c/o* **Utne Reader**, *1624 Harmon Place, Minneapolis, MN 55403 (Phone: 612 338 5040; Web: www.utne.com).*

→ *See: Salons:* **The Joy of Conversation** *(New Society Publishers &* **Utne Reader**, *2001) available from either organization.*

Neighborly eating

NICHOLAS SAUNDERS

A SMALL-SCALE INNOVATIVE DANISH PRACTICE, which I liked and thought could act as a model elsewhere, involved a group of independent families who bought neighboring houses for sale. They also bought a workshop building, an old smithy. They decided to knock down the walls between the gardens — except for one family that wanted to keep its wall. With their own labor they converted the smithy into a communal dining hall. A communal meal was cooked each evening by one of the eight families on a rotational basis. Once every eight days, a family had to buy all the food and cook it — it was hard luck if there were a large number of people that day, but it tended to work out evenly in the long run. You had to say if you were going out. You could do swaps with other people if you did not want to cook that day. There was a charge for guests.

A kitchen and dining room that were open for membership to anyone who lived nearby — there were about 30 members. There was a rotational for who did the cooking, and the person cooking bought the food.

Somewhat similar was a scheme for mostly single people living in the same area of Copenhagen. They had got together a kitchen and dining room that were open for membership to anyone who lived nearby — there were about 30 members. Again there was a rotational for who did the cooking, and the person cooking bought the food. If someone did not have much money, he or she prepared something simple.

Such a scheme could appeal to people living alone who do not like to cook elaborate meals for themselves but would not mind a lot of effort once a month. It would probably depend on finding a neighborhood of like-minded people living fairly close to each other.

✦ *Nicholas Saunders died in a car accident in South Africa. Please send feedback to The Institute for Social Inventions, 20 Heber Road, London NW2 6AA, UK (Phone: Int.+44 [0]20 8208 2853; Fax: Int.+44 [0]20 8452 6434; E-mail: rhino@dial.pipex.com).*

Neo-tantric yoga

DAVID MISKIN

MANY COUPLES WHO WOULD OTHERWISE SPLIT UP, perhaps particularly those with children, could save their relationship and cement the bond between them if they adopted what I call "neo-tantric yoga." This consists of a ceremony or ritual of making love, with the male, as far as possible, avoiding orgasm. The ritual takes place at regular, predetermined times, preferably on a daily basis before getting up — however busy the couple are, however many children they have, they can manage at least ten thrusts or "strokes," and several hundred if not pressed for time, to set the tone for the day.

N

However busy the couple are, they can manage at least ten thrusts or "strokes", to set the tone for the day.

It needs to be seen not so much as a matter of sex but as a ceremony of commitment by both partners, a renewing of their pledge, for better or for worse, one that is undertaken whatever the state of the relationship (almost), however depressed or stressed or tired or sulky or rushed either partner feels — a ceremony that is beyond desire or even readiness (here lubricating creams are helpful). It can be seen, too, as a chance to talk, and because the physical connection is maintained, the relationship tends not to feel under threat, regardless of the topic being discussed. Within that contact all sorts of problems dissolve more readily, arguments and hurts can be aired and heard, with the other feeling less threatened; and even aggressions can be play-acted.

So many couples allow divisions to creep into their lives, bit by bit. Getting to the point of making love becomes a series of obstacle courses to be run, with the frequency diminishing as tensions build or as babies arrive. Neo-tantric yoga helps rid the relationship of sexual frustration without focusing on sex as such — and without, of course, preventing other kinds of lovemaking at other times.

Couples who become adept at this neo-tantric ceremony might even begin to study the actual (far more subtle) Eastern tantric rites.

A ritual without intercourse

At times when, for whatever reason, lovemaking is not appropriate, couples can fall back on other quick and simple rituals to start the day, such as one where they repeat together a shortened form of their marriage vows. Lying in bed, looking into each other's eyes and touching each other intimately, they can say together, for instance, "I (name) love and cherish you (name), now and forever, for better, for worse, in sickness and in health, so help us God."

Network of Hippocratic drop-in groups for doctors

The following is summarized from four sources: the Institute for the Study of Health and Illness website; a report entitled "Educating for Compassion" by Mark McCaffrey (on the web at <http://csf.colorado.edu/sine/sat/remen2.html>); an article entitled "Say where it hurts" by Jennifer Desai (at <www.mv-voice.com/morgue/2000/2000_03_31. forum31.html>); and an interview with Peter Warshall in the *Whole Earth Review.*

IN AUGUST 2000, THE INSTITUTE FOR THE STUDY OF HEALTH AND ILLNESS (ISHI) in Bolinas, California, launched a new outreach program for physicians who are interested in medicine as service and in finding deeper meaning in their work. Based on the physicians' discussion group model successfully piloted by Dr. Rachel Remen in San Francisco's Bay Area, this program is a way for physicians to create supportive collegial communities. The program is easy to initiate, costs little, and requires no institutional support. Expertise in group facilitation is not required.

The price of admission is a story
from each physician's personal or professional life.

To start a group, a physician simply invites several like-minded colleagues to meet one evening a month for two to three hours. The price of admission is a story from each physician's personal or professional life on a topic selected by the group, a related story or poem from world literature, a song or other artistic expression, or an exercise to enable the group to explore the topic at greater depth.

"When you know someone's story," says Dr. Remen, "you can connect to that person; he can never be an enemy. It's a form of connection."

Topics are selected at the previous month's meeting — topics explored by the Bay Area group include suffering, listening, dignity, mystery, forgiveness and mistakes, joy, love, loneliness, and fear.

The group organizer provides a place to meet; sends out reminders about the date, time, place, and topic; and initiates the discussion at the meeting by offering a story or poem. The organizer also manages time flow in the meeting to ensure that all have an opportunity to speak. The group grows by word of mouth. Several groups may run at various times within a local community, giving physicians a choice of options to fit their schedules.

Participants in the Bay Area group find these meetings extremely vital and relevant to their work in medicine, and their discussions are profound. Many have reported finding inspiration and renewed commitment to their work. This year Dr. Remen's group will explore the values of the Hippocratic Oath as a way to a deeply meaningful life in medicine, and the Institute for the Study of Health and Illness will prepare resource materials on these themes.

In an interview with Peter Warshall in *Whole Earth Review,* Dr. Remen describes this initiative as drop-in groups for doctors "who, like myself, are recovering from their training. Sometimes I think that medicine is like a disease: you have to recover from it. I'm a 'recovering doctor' ... I think we have made a trade between mastery and mystery, between information and wisdom ... I sometimes think that medicine is a front-row seat on mystery ... Once you get a group of doctors talking about mystery, it's often hard to get them to stop. So much of what we see just doesn't make sense."

ISHI hopes to launch more than 25 new groups this year in all parts of the US and Canada. They will provide materials, resources, and support to physicians interested in starting groups.

N

Restoring the Heart and Soul of Medicine

"Restoring the Heart and Soul of Medicine" is a course for practicing physicians developed by Dr. Rachel Remen within the Institute for the Study of Health and Illness and designed to have the same ethos as the Hippocratic drop-in groups for doctors. The course enables physicians to expand their ideas about what it means to be a physician, to begin to heal some of their wounds, and to explore the mysterious and sacred dimensions of their work.

An opportunity for honest and genuine dialog among peer physicians

---

The curriculum provides an opportunity for honest and genuine dialog among peer physicians. Their experiences with illness and death are unique and may not be understood by those who have not had medical training or felt the weight of its expectations. Engaging in supportive dialog with colleagues has the potential to strengthen physicians in their work and to rekindle the deep commitment that has drawn them to it.

"Restoring the Heart and Soul of Medicine" consists of three intensive workshops presented over a calendar year and repeated annually. Each workshop is a four-day retreat at Commonweal, the health-and-environmental-research institute located on a 60-acre site near Bolinas in the Point Reyes National Seashore, California.

Group size is kept small, with each workshop enrolling eight to ten physicians. The format is based on a discovery model: participants are encouraged to reflect upon and share their responses to innovative experiential exercises and materials as well as to share their professional and personal experiences, issues, and viewpoints. In addition to fostering dialog, the learning model draws on the theories and techniques of such diverse fields as humanistic and transpersonal psychology, theology, Eastern and Western spiritual traditions, imagery, the fine arts, and the great tradition of the art of medicine.

In addition to the more formal curriculum, each day begins with an hour and a half of yoga, and ample time is allowed for reflection, meditation, journal writing, and informal contact. Participants may also schedule a massage or Reiki treatment during the retreat.

The underlying philosophy

The way to heal a dominant culture, in Dr. Remen's view, is to form a subculture of credible people in the middle of the old culture. The subculture people have new values and reinforce and reward aspects that have been repressed in the past.

Objectivity can make people blind.

Dr. Remen believes that successful people tend to have the deepest wounds because they have been rewarded for "woundedness" and have been punished for wholeness. "Medical schools train rather than educate," she says, "with wholeness regarded as unprofessional and shameful. Students are trained to be objective — but more mistakes are made by objectivity than were ever made by knowing patients as whole people. Objectivity can make people blind. Students are also trained to be isolated, keeping truth at arm's length as if distance will keep one safe. Every culture imposes a 'shadow' on its people — encouraging them to repress parts of their wholeness in order to win approval."

Sample exercises

Among the exercises in the "Healer's Art" course (which Dr. Remen leads at the University of California, San Francisco, School of Medicine each year) are the following:

- The medical students are asked to close their eyes and visualize an image for the part of themselves that they are afraid may change in the process of becoming an expert. Then they draw a picture of this part of themselves and give a name to the quality at its core. Words such as compassion, wisdom, fidelity, trust of life tend to come up.
- The medical students are encouraged to keep a contemplative journal.
- A session may end with a five-minute period of "supportive community." You ask the person on your left to say his or her name aloud. And then, for about 45 seconds of absolute silence, everyone gives strength to that person. "For the first time," says Dr. Remen, "we come into right relationship with our fellow professionals."

Students reflect on what medicine could be, if they were to practice it according to their highest values.

- Students are invited to reflect on what medicine could be, if they were to practice it according to their highest values. They are then encouraged to ask for help in bringing more of this vision into their daily work, using the "language of help" — phrases such as "help me," "show me," "give me." Then, for about two hours, they all read out their material to each other.

N

→ *Mary Wade, Program Administrator, Institute for the Study of Health and Illness, Commonweal, PO Box 316, Bolinas, California CA 94924 (Phone: 415 868 2642; E-mail: ishi@igc.org; Web: www.commonweal.org/ishi.html). For details of the outreach program on Hippocratic values, see the ISHI website.*

→ *Dr. Remen is the author of* My Grandfather's Blessings: Stories of Strength, Refuge and Belonging *(published by Riverhead Books). Her previous bestseller was entitled* Kitchen Table Wisdom.

No local tax without a say in the allocation

NICHOLAS ALBERY

ONE WAY OF GETTING PEOPLE MORE INVOLVED in developing their neighborhoods would be to institute a mechanism whereby the allocation of at least a portion of the local tax money (for non-basic services?) could be decided not by the council but by each resident. An occasional newsletter would list which projects — community center, playground, and so on — needed money and how much they needed, and your tax money would be earmarked according to your order of preferences. If these were oversubscribed (or if you did not bother to select your preferences), the money would go towards the councillors' own preferences among undersubscribed projects.

Your tax money would be earmarked according to your order
of preferences.

Citizens would also be allowed to put projects needing money into the newsletter, if supported by the signatures of a certain number of local residents.

The main underlying principle would be: no taxation without a say in the allocation.

→ *Please send feedbace to The Institute for Social Inventions, 20 Heber Road, London NW2 6AA, UK (Phone: Int.+44 [0]20 8208 2853; Fax: Int.+44 [0]20 8452 6434; E-mail: rhino@dial.pipex.com).*

Non-pen friends

NICHOLAS CARR

NEARLY EVERY DISASTER HAS ITS POSITIVE SIDE, and the threat of AIDS has opened up the possibility of widespread acceptance for new codes of sexual behavior. Already it has become acceptable to discuss in public the intimate details of the ways we relate to each other sexually.

The following suggestion is a viable alternative to celibacy or using condoms with extramarital lovers — and has many positive virtues besides avoiding the risk of AIDS.

It is a mutual agreement to draw the line at penetration with new or casual sexual partners.

There is really nothing new to the idea itself — it is simply a mutual agreement to draw the line at penetration with new or casual sexual partners. Although this cuts out the possibility of having a "complete" sexual experience, I believe that it is a fair price to pay for avoiding the worries that so often spoil the fun: the fear of catching herpes, AIDS, or venereal diseases; worries about pregnancy and contraceptives; anxiety about sexual performance; the surfacing of deep-seated guilt feelings; and concern that aroused emotions may result in one or the other partner getting hurt.

I do not consider myself particularly promiscuous — in fact, my sex life has consisted of a series of monogamous relationships. But between these there have been periods when I have had many lovers, either for the excitement, the warmth, or in my search for a new long-term partner. Most of these casual sexual experiences have been disappointing, and even when they have been good, they have sometimes downgraded a relaxed friendship into an awkward relationship. There have also been emotional tragedies afterwards, when I have had painful longings that my partner has not shared, or vice versa.

A clean dirty weekend: we were able to relax and laugh a lot, it was continuously sexy, and it felt romantic and caring too.

Several years ago, after the ending of a serious relationship, I decided to avoid my usual pattern of casual sexual relationships. However, I discovered that celibacy was not the answer; it just made me tense. Then I got talking with a woman who was in the same situation, and we decided on fulfilling our needs (for warmth at least) by sleeping together but avoiding making love — which we carried on doing regularly until she found a new mate. Next I invited a woman (whom I had only known briefly when we talked about this) to spend a clean dirty weekend with me. We both had a wonderful time: we were able to relax and laugh a lot, it was continuously sexy because I avoided ejaculation, and it felt romantic and caring too. We both felt nurtured and warm inside after the weekend, yet the fact that we had not "made love" spelt out that we were not committed to one another. On another occasion I slept with a woman who had had many casual affairs since breaking up with her man. I insisted (rather against her choice) on a nonpenetration pact, and to her surprise she experienced the first orgasm of her promiscuous fling — due, she thought, to being relaxed enough to let go. Even as a "non-believer," she found that the restriction on penetration gave her more freedom to enjoy the experience.

> Withholding penetration and avoiding ejaculation actually heightens the experience, as is well established in many traditional practices, including tantra.

This might all sound like some sort of perversion that should not be applied to someone you regard as a potential spouse. In fact, it is a wonderful preparation for a good sexual relationship — to get relaxed together and enjoy the stimulation of one another's touch before going "all the way." Withholding penetration and avoiding ejaculation actually heightens the experience, as is well established in many traditional practices, including tantra.

There is, as I mentioned, nothing new or dramatic in having sex without penetration. What I am promoting here is the idea that it should be accepted as normal outside monogamous relationships. "Non-pen" sex is sexy, it is safe, and it is fun — and it will not leave you wishing you had never set eyes on each other.

O

Organic public swimming pool

Summarized from an article by Guy Dauncey in *Econews*.

IN THE TOWN OF BIBERSTEIN IN SWITZERLAND, an organic public swimming pool has just been opened with no chlorine, no tiles in outrageous shades of blue, and no ridiculous water slides. Its focus instead is on clear, clean water that brings simple joy back to the swimming experience.

> Dragonflies, reeds, water lilies, snails, and frogs have all been introduced into the pool.

Not only has artificiality been banned, but dragonflies, reeds, water lilies, snails, and frogs have all been introduced into the pool. The old pool on the site measured 80 by 40 feet, so two new ponds of the same size were added to aid the purification process. The new pool is, therefore, cleaner, purer, more natural, and, the builders hope, more enjoyable. Nature, it could be said, has come back full force into the lives of swimmers in Biberstein.

→ *Guy Dauncey, Sustainable Communities Consultancy, 395 Conway Road, Victoria, BC, V8X 3X1, Canada (Phone/Fax: 250 881 1304; E-mail: guydauncey@earthfuture.com; Web: www.earthfuture.com).*

P

Participants writing the minutes before the meeting

JOHN CARTER

From an e-mail to the Alternative Institutions discussion group on the internet. To subscribe to this online discussion group, send a request to <AltInst-request@cco.caltech.edu>.

MEETINGS ARE LONG SLOW THINGS OF LOW BANDWIDTH. I devised, implemented, and tested this variant:

The agenda of the meeting is placed on a central computer. (This could be done with RCS on any Linux system.)

The participants write in whatever they would have said
before the meeting happens.

The participants, in their own time, edit the agenda, writing in whatever they would have said in the meeting. In other words, everybody co-writes the minutes of the meeting before the meeting happens.

Before the meeting, the future minutes are printed and everybody reads them. The meeting can then simply approve 90 percent of the future minutes and briefly argue about any remaining controversial issues.

Pros: Fast. Simple. The minutes are far more accurate and complete. Quiet people can get their word in.

Cons: It doesn't work in the presence of Alpha personalities. They not only like to have their say, they like to be seen to have their say — and hence will verbally and at length go over everything again.

→ *John Carter (Phone: Int.+44 [0]27 12 808 077 74 ext. 194; Fax: Int.+44 [0]12 808 0338; E-mail: ece@dwaf-hri.pwv.gov.za; Web: www.geocities.com/SoHo/Cafe/5947).*

Pattern Language for community architects

NICHOLAS ALBERY

THE RIGHT TOOLS FOR "COMMUNITY ARCHITECTURE" are beginning to be recognized. *Pattern Language,* by architect Christopher Alexander (published by Oxford University Press), allows any group of people to take an informed part in the design of their own houses or neighborhood.

It is as simple as painting by numbers, with the book containing more than 250 patterns to choose from. The patterns put flesh on the bare bones of the principles for human-scale architecture.

Pattern Language allows any group of people to take an informed part in the design of their own houses or neighborhood.

For instance, the committee of the Frestonian Bramleys Housing Co-op in London, UK, when planning its new housing (see the entry on the "Free and Independent Republic of Frestonia," earlier in this book), circulated some 40 of the most relevant patterns and gave each a grading that indicated that pattern's importance for them. After further debate, the development took shape as a small cluster of low houses, along with flats, all with balconies, with overhanging roofs and decorated brickwork, surrounding a totally enclosed communal garden. As architects Pollard, Thomas, Edwards and Associates admitted (although one of their partners criticized *Pattern Language* for its "whimsicality"): "We would not have built such a particular solution without a specific client. We tend to be tamer."

→ *Please send feedback to The Institute for Social Inventions, 20 Heber Road, London NW2 6AA, UK (Phone: Int.+44 [0]20 8208 2853; Fax: Int.+44 [0]20 8452 6434; E-mail: rhino@dial.pipex.com).*

Poetry Challenge

NICHOLAS ALBERY

LEARNING A POEM EXERCISES THE BRAIN AND ELEVATES THE SPIRIT! On International Poetry Challenge Day, the first Sunday of October, people of all ages are urged to learn a poem by heart and to recite it to at least one other person, but preferably to a larger audience. Individuals ask relatives and friends to sponsor them, sending any money raised directly to the non-profit cause of your choice.

Inspired by the UK's Poetry Week, the Poetry Challenge has Andrew Motion, the UK Poet Laureate, as its patron and is also supported by Robert Pinsky, the United States Poet Laureate. "It's a wonderful project," says Pinsky.

For schools, the Poetry Challenge takes place anytime during the fall or spring term. It has worked well in the UK, where it has led to over 150,000 poems a year being learned by heart in schools. As the UK's Chief Inspector of Schools has said: "The poetry we learn as children stays with us for ever — a resource upon which to draw throughout our lives."

School participation is free and the guidelines for the challenge are simple:

- Agree as a school on what non-profit cause you want to raise money for.
- Get as many people as possible to take part — students, teachers, parents, friends.
- Get the free tips for teachers. Send an e-mail to <rhino@ dial.pipex.com>, stating that your school hopes to run a Poetry Challenge event and confirming that you will endeavor to send in a report if you do have an event, and you will be sent a free e-mail full of teachers' tips for a successful Poetry Challenge.
- Get all participants to agree to learn a poem by heart, one they have never learned before, and to recite it out loud to at least one person. (The poem can be any poem, old or new, or even one they have written themselves.) Shy people can recite their poem to just one person, braver folk can recite to an audience such as the whole class, and the bravest of the brave can recite to the whole school assembly.
- Have each person reciting ask to be sponsored for the school's chosen charity and raise at least five dollars from one or more friends.
- Send the money raised directly to the chosen cause.
- Have either the teacher or one or more of the students e-mail a report to the Poetry Challenge <rhino@dial.pipex.com>, saying how your school got on. There are awards and small money prizes for the best entries.

So, get training and exercise those brain cells! Do practice your poem on an audience of friends beforehand. It's amazing how every word you've remembered disappears from your memory as soon as you get up to recite.

School raises money for charity by reciting poems!
Elizabeth Howard sent in the following report:

Inspired by your brilliant idea of a Poetry Challenge, our school decided to have a "Poetry Happening." Every child in the school from age three to 13 (240 children) chose and recited a poem. We devoted a whole week to this project.

One class recited a poem all together. A group of teachers recited and mimed "Albert and the Lion."

The children recited their poems to other classes, and at our final assembly of the term, one child from each class recited a poem to the whole school — stage, lights, the works. A great success!

Parents and children all loved the whole project, said they enjoyed looking through poetry books, selecting their poem, and actually found it fun and pleasure to learn a poem by heart. Some children amazed us with the length of their poems. The teachers all participated with enthusiasm. We had a display of poetry books in the school entrance. Many of the children wrote out and illustrated their poems, which were also on display around the school. The older children organized the whole event, including collecting and counting the money! We raised the staggering sum of $3,500.

We intend to make this an annual event. We would like to include a reading by a poet and maybe have an evening to which the parents could be invited. The money will be divided between four good causes that we, as a school, support.

We also gave each child a certificate saying they had recited their poem successfully.

We all thank you for this wonderful idea, which was a total success in every way.

➔ *The Poetry Challenge, 20 Heber Road, London NW2 6AA, UK (Phone: Int.+44 [0]20 8208 2853; Fax: Int.+44 [0]20 8452 6434; E-mail: rhino@dial.pipex.com; Web: www.poetrychallenge.org).*

➔ *The Poetry Challenge is partly sponsored through the sale of the 486-page poetry anthology* A Poem A Day, *containing 366 poems, old and new, worth learning by heart (published by Steerforth Press).*

Poetry for trainee doctors on hospital rounds

Summarized from a paper by Harold W. Horowitz, MD, entitled "Poetry on rounds: A model for the integration of humanities into residency training," published in the *Lancet,* monitored by Dr. Marie-Louise Grennert.

DURING DAILY HOSPITAL ROUNDS, attending physicians and medical trainees interact and influence both each other and patients' care. However, the process of humanizing these rounds in order to create physicians who are more caring, and perhaps to alleviate the burnout that often occurs among overworked housestaff and awed medical students, has received little attention.

We would read and discuss a poem that was to be selected and brought in by team members on a rotational basis.

I decided to try a small experiment and use about 20 minutes of the 90 allotted to daily rounds to read and discuss a poem that was to be selected and brought in by team members on a rotational basis. Participants were encouraged to choose a poem from their country of origin whenever possible. To lessen anxiety, I brought in the first few poems.

In total we discussed 18 poems. Poems that were about illness and the nature of being a physician were most commonly chosen for presentation. But a love poem, "Comes the Dawn," created the liveliest discussion. This anonymous work was brought in by a resident from Haiti. It begins like this:

> After awhile you learn the subtle difference
> Between holding a hand and changing a soul.
> And you learn that love doesn't mean leaning
> and company doesn't mean security,
> and you begin to learn that kisses aren't contracts ...

The poem was the springboard for a discussion about the emotional demands of medicine on physicians' personal relationships.

This poem led to a conversation about the self-satisfaction required for a strong relationship. Furthermore, it was the springboard for a discussion about the effects of the emotional and physical demands of medicine on physicians' personal relationships. Issues such as the high divorce rate among physicians and drug dependency were also raised.

Whether the novelty of reading poetry on rounds was the main factor in the positive responses by team members is open to question. Reading poetry month after month could wear thin. However, perhaps a session or two a week would provide a moment of reflection and respite from didactic training.

It is my impression that the poetry discussions facilitated better interpersonal relationships among team members, as individuals became more aware of the feelings of both each other and the patients.

➔ *H.W. Horowitz, MD, Westchester County Medical Center, Division of Infectious Diseases, Room 209 Macy Pavilion, Valhalla, NY 10595.*

Police in wheelchairs

From an item in the *Examiner,* monitored by Roger Knights.

Half the members of the California Capitola
police department are in wheelchairs, acting as
parking enforcement officers.

HALF THE MEMBERS OF THE CALIFORNIA CAPITOLA POLICE DEPARTMENT are in wheelchairs, acting as parking enforcement officers. "We've been hiring the handicapped for parking enforcement for ten years, and it's worked well for us," says police captain Tom Hanna. "They're very hard workers, and grateful for the opportunity to be of service and to earn an income. They wear police uniforms and work right alongside the rest of us."

Danny, whose legs were paralyzed four years ago when he fell from a bridge, says that "placing tickets on cars is no problem. But if it's a big truck and I can't reach the windshield, I call one of the other parking enforcement officers who are mobile and they take care of it. We do get hassled occasionally, but we point out that if they disagree, they can take it to court. Once in a while we encounter someone who's had too much to drink and we have to call another officer, but that's a rarity."

Captain Hanna says that his seaside city's policy of hiring the handicapped would work well in other communities. "They've proven to us that they can get the job done."

Politicians' suits covered with sponsors' logos

PATRICK THERIEN
The following is summarized from an e-mail to the Global Ideas Bank.

The politicians would look much like racing car drivers,
sporting chevrons of all their sponsors.

I BELIEVE IT WOULD BE A GOOD IDEA FOR POLITICIANS TO WEAR (at least once a year) a ceremonial suit. On this suit would be patches and corporate logos of all their contributors. The politicians would look much like racing car drivers, sporting chevrons of all their sponsors.

The patches should be sized according to the percentage of contribution. For example, if a particular corporation contributes an amount that represents five percent of the politician's total campaign fund, then he or she would wear a patch for that corporation that covers five percent of the special suit.

At a glance we could all see who really pays for influence.

It may seem like a humorous idea, but think about it — once a year the media would have an opportunity to photograph this politician in his or her campaign finance suit. Anyone seeing the elected official covered with non-constituent donor patches would know what was going on. Long debates about campaign finance reform would immediately be put into perspective. At a glance we could all see who really pays for influence.

→ *Patrick J. Therien, 7403 NE 279th St, Battle Ground, WA 98604 (E-mail: mojosam@iname.com).*

Portfolio Life

Charles Handy

What I am trying to do is evolve a lifestyle for myself. I looked into my concerns and activities, and one thing I did was to resign my full-time, tenured professorship. I created what I call a "portfolio life," setting aside 100 days a year for making money, 100 days for writing, 50 days for what I consider good works, and 100 days for spending time with my wife.

I created what I call a "portfolio life," setting aside
100 days a year for making money, 100 days for writing,
50 days for what I consider good works, and 100 days
for spending time with my wife.

I mark these days out in my diary. When people phone and ask me to do something, I can then say, "I'm terribly sorry, that's my day with my wife." It is a freeing way of life. A hundred days a year for me is enough for making money; there is no point in making more, and I find I do as much work in 100 days as I used to in a year.

If somebody asks what you do, and you can reply in one
sentence, you're a failure. You should need half an hour.

I go to a lot of management courses and try to turn these managers into portfolio people — "Don't just be a systems manager for IBM, don't be a one-dimensional character, become a portfolio person now." I am trying to make such a lifestyle respectable for career people. If somebody asks what you do, and you can reply in one sentence, you're a failure. You should need half an hour.

Jobs are continually going to get shorter in years, smaller in hours. More people will be self-employed or will be offered bits of jobs rather than full-time, lifetime jobs. Most of us, at some time in our lives, are going to find that our jobs no longer dominate our lives. We shall need to find a new organizing principle.

If, rather than think of life as work and leisure, we think of it as a portfolio of activities — some of which we do for money, some for interest, some for pleasure, some for a cause — then, we do not have to look for the occupation that miraculously combines job satisfaction, financial reward, and pleasant friends all in one package. As with any portfolio, we get different returns from different parts, and if one fails, the whole is not ruined.

→ *Professor Charles Handy, 1 Fairhaven, 73 Putney Hill, London SW15 3NT, UK. See his book* The Empty Raincoat *(published by Hutchinson).*

Practice random kindness and senseless acts of beauty

With our news media constantly reporting random cruelties and senseless acts of violence, it is a relief to turn to the following item, which originated in *Glamour* magazine and was monitored by Chris Welch.

IT'S A CRISP WINTER DAY IN SAN FRANCISCO. A woman in a red Honda, Christmas presents piled in the back, drives up to the Bay Bridge tollbooth. "I'm paying for myself and for the six cars behind me," she says with a smile, handing over seven commuter tickets.

One after another, the next six drivers arrive at the tollbooth, dollars in hand, only to be told, "Some lady up ahead already paid your fare. Have a nice day."

The woman in the Honda, it turned out, had read something on an index card taped to a friend's refrigerator: "Practice random kindness and senseless acts of beauty." The phrase seemed to leap out at her, and she copied it down.

Judy Foreman spotted the same phrase spray-painted on a warehouse wall a hundred miles from her home. When it stayed on her mind for days, she gave up and drove all the way back to copy it down. "I thought it was incredibly beautiful," she said, explaining why she's taken to writing it at the bottom of all her letters, "like a message from above."

Her husband Frank liked the phrase so much that he put it up on the wall for his seventh graders, one of whom was the daughter of a local columnist. The columnist put it in the paper, admitting that though she liked it, she didn't know where it came from or what it really meant.

Two days later, she heard from Anne Herbert. Tall, blonde, and 40, Herbert lives in Marin, one of the country's ten richest counties, where she house-sits, takes odd jobs, and gets by. It was in a Sausalito restaurant that Herbert jotted the phrase down on a paper placemat, after turning it around in her mind for days.

"That's wonderful!" a man sitting nearby said, and copied it down carefully on his own placemat.

"Here's the idea," Herbert says. "Anything you think there should be more of, do it randomly."

Her own fantasies include breaking into depressing-looking schools to paint the classrooms, leaving hot meals on kitchen tables in the poor parts of town, slipping money into a proud old woman's purse.

Kindness can build on itself as much as violence can.

Says Herbert, "Kindness can build on itself as much as violence can."

Now the phrase is spreading, on bumper stickers, on walls, at the bottom of letters and business cards. And as it spreads, so does a vision of guerrilla goodness.

The phrase is spreading, on bumper stickers, on walls, at the bottom of letters and business cards. And as it spreads, so does a vision of guerrilla goodness.

In Portland, Oregon, a man might plunk a coin into a stranger's meter just in time. In Patterson, New Jersey, a dozen people with pails and mops and tulip bulbs might descend on a rundown house and clean it from top to bottom while the frail elderly owners look on, dazed and smiling. In Chicago, a teenage boy may be shoveling off the driveway when the impulse strikes. What the hell, nobody's looking, he thinks, and shovels the neighbor's driveway too.

It's positive anarchy, disorder, a sweet disturbance. A woman in Boston writes "Merry Christmas!" to the tellers on the back of her checks. A man in St Louis, whose car has just been rear-ended by a young woman, waves her away, saying, "It's a scratch. Don't worry."

Senseless acts of beauty spread: a man plants daffodils along the roadway, his shirt billowing in the breeze from passing cars. In Seattle, a man appoints himself a one-man vigilante sanitation service and roams the concrete hills, collecting litter in a supermarket cart. In Atlanta, a man scrubs graffiti from a green park bench.

They say you can't smile without cheering yourself up a little — likewise, you can't commit a random act of kindness without feeling as if your own troubles have been lightened, if only because the world has become a slightly better place.

Like all revolutions, guerrilla goodness begins slowly,
with a single act.

And you can't be a recipient without feeling a shock, a pleasant jolt. If you were one of those rush-hour drivers who found your bridge fare paid, who knows what you might have been inspired to do for someone else later? Wave someone on in the intersection? Smile at a tired clerk? Or something larger, greater? Like all revolutions, guerrilla goodness begins slowly, with a single act. Let it be yours.

✦ *Anne Herbert, PO Box 5408, Mill Valley, California 94942.*

✦ *Conari, the publisher of an anthology called* **Random Acts of Kindness,** *organizes National Random Acts of Kindness Days. For further details of books from Conari and of the progress of the Random Acts of Kindness movement, see <www.conari.com> or <www.actsofkindness.org>.*

Premarriage Compatibility Rating Test

There are complex premarriage questionnaires available. This simpler test was devised by Institute for Social Invention members in response to the engagement announcement of one of its workers. The word "marriage" is used here in the sense of any relationship likely to involve long-term responsibility in caring for offspring.

DECISIONS ABOUT WHO TO MARRY AND HAVE CHILDREN WITH are likely to have more effect on future happiness than any other decisions in life, so they are worth considering as soberly as possible, given that we can be so easily misled in the first flush of love. About half of the following questions derive from academic research about long-term success and failure in marriage and human relationships. If both you and your partner are trying this test, it might be diplomatic not to show your marks on individual items to your partner, but simply to discuss your final marks together.

Please give marks out of 10 to the following questions, with 10 being "Very True" and 0 "Not True At All"). Answer the questions as honestly as possible since you do not have to show the results to anybody else — there is nobody to deceive but yourself.

• There is very little conflict in our relationship.
• When there is conflict, we handle it very satisfactorily.
• I find myself agreeing with my partner far more often than disagreeing.
• If my partner ended up developing a similar character to his/her parents, or became like them in old age, I would be very happy about this.
• I feel that I can share all my feelings, good and bad, with my partner and that he/she does the same with me.

- My partner is very similar to me in cultural, social, intellectual, and economic background and probably in intelligence.
- We share similar philosophies of life or spiritual beliefs.
- We share the same sense of humor.
- My partner's health is good. I would describe him/her as basically a happy person and I don't think he/she is likely to suffer from depressions, obsessions, anorexia or other eating disorders, excessive anxieties, or other mental health problems.
- My partner is sensitive and kind and not selfish or self-obsessed.
- If I lived in a society where parents arranged marriages for their children, my partner is just the kind of person my parents might have chosen for me.
- We have a lot of conversational interests in common, I enjoy his/her conversation on a variety of topics, and I like his/her friends.
- Judging by track record to date, my partner is monogamous when in a serious relationship.
- We agree on the extent of freedom within marriage as regards other relationships, and I therefore don't think jealousy will be a problem for either of us.
- Our sexual relationship is extremely good.

Add up your totals. Take away 10 if you have lived together for less than six months. Divide your total by the maximum possible (150) and multiply by 100 for your Marriage Compatibility Percentage. If you are less than 70 percent compatible, you may well have to struggle hard to maintain a long-term relationship and might be well-advised to delay having children for several years until you are sure that the relationship will work out. Less than 50 percent compatibility could be a sign not to rush into marriage.

→ *We welcome suggestions for improvements for this test, as well as scores and comments from couples trying it out. Please send to Marriage compatibility test, c/o The Institute for Social Inventions, 20 Heber Road, London NW2 6AA, UK (Phone: Int.+44 [0]20 8208 2853; Fax: Int.+44 [0]20 8452 6434; E-mail: rhino@dial.pipex.com; Web: www.globalideasbank.org).*

Prisoners grouped by opposite tendencies to error

Adapted from Doug Wilson's website <www.island.net/~dpwilson/crime.html>. Doug Wilson lives on Gabriola Island, off the west coast of British Columbia, Canada, not far from Vancouver.

IF WE TREAT CRIME AS ERROR, then it is not too hard to see where it comes from. The people who commit most crimes are not well educated or informed, and they are usually surrounded by people who are similarly prone to many

forms of error. The abuse of alcohol and drugs is just one example of this —
there are no real benefits from alcohol or drugs, but there may be short-term
pleasure. Being seduced by this temporary pleasure is a mistake, an error, and
people are more likely to make this error if all their friends are doing it too.

**Putting people in prisons with thousands of other people who
have committed crimes is almost the exact opposite of what
we should be doing.**

Ultimately, people are affected by their friends. If your friends are criminals or associate with criminals, then you will likely make the same errors
and fall into a life of crime. Viewed in this way, the idea of putting people in
prisons with thousands of other people who have committed crimes and giving them an opportunity to meet all sorts of other criminals is ludicrous. I
think it is almost the exact opposite of what we should be doing.

There have been a few attempts in the right direction, particularly with
juvenile first offenders, where some programs have aimed at taking them out
of their social context and placing them in a stable family environment away
from the attractions of the big cities. The problem is, there are just not enough
people willing to expose themselves and their families to this kind of danger.

But there is another solution. All forms of error are not the same. Two
people who both have severe tendencies to make mistakes can actually have
a positive and corrective influence on one another if they tend to make the
opposite kinds of error.

I have a long and rather technical analysis that explains all this in terms
of personality theory and error-covariance analysis, but the important point
is this: we can solve the problems of prisoners being a bad influence on one
another by very carefully arranging them in small groups, so that the only
people they meet are those who have very different tendencies towards error.

To do this, we need to use a lot of psychological testing, and then we need
to divide the prison population into non-interacting clusters so as to minimize
the amount of overall error-covariance in each group. Whether each set of prisoners actually meets as a group in the standard pop-psychology group situation
is not important. But the other people a prisoner eats with, works with, or does
recreation with must not share his or her specific error-tendencies.

**If we use careful testing to match prisoners,
two people can in fact be good influences on one another**

If two (or more) prisoners share a cell, the same idea applies but is even
more important. If we use careful testing to match prisoners, two people in

a cell can in fact be good influences on one another, even if both are criminals. As a result, their time together will result in each one teaching and improving the other, and if they see each other after being released, they can continue to be positive influences on one another.

Does this sound too optimistic? Probably. But it is an idea with a lot of thought behind it, and it should work. I think it should be tried.

If anyone out there knows of any similar ideas or anything like this that has already been tried, please let me know.

➤ *Doug Wilson (E-mail: dpwilson@island.net). There are many other "social technology" ideas on Douglas P. Wilson's website <www.island.net/~dpwilson/index.html>.*

➤ *For more on Doug Wilson's ideas on how people could be better matched in terms of their spouses, their jobs, and their neighborhoods, and so be less likely to commit crimes, see the item "Web search engines to find compatible partners" in the present volume.*

Project Gutenberg

MICHAEL HART AND COLLEAGUES

The following are summaries of a website entitled "History and philosophy of Project Gutenberg" (http://promo.net/pg), monitored by Roger Knights. Hundreds of electronic texts of complete books can be accessed at this website. Michael Hart has been working for decades now on this electronic library. A Benedictine university in Lisle, Illinois, helped him by naming him an "adjunct professor of electronic text" and giving him a small annual salary and living expenses. Here are adapted extracts from the story of how Project Gutenberg developed.

PROJECT GUTENBERG BEGAN IN 1971 when Michael Hart was given an operator's account with $100,000,000 of computer time on the Xerox Sigma V mainframe at the Materials Research Lab at the University of Illinois. He proceeded to type in the Declaration of Independence.

Michael Hart based Project Gutenberg on the premise that anything that can be entered into a computer can be reproduced indefinitely. Hart termed this "Replicator Technology." The concept of Replicator Technology is simply that once a book or any other item (including pictures, sounds, and even 3-D items) can be stored in a computer, then any number of copies can and will be available.

Electronic texts are made available in the easiest-to-use form available: Plain Vanilla ASCII.

Project Gutenberg's Electronic Texts (etexts) are made available in the simplest, easiest-to-use form available: "Plain Vanilla ASCII." ASCII is used because 99 percent of the hardware and software a person is likely to come across can read and search these files.

Hart and his colleagues choose etexts they hope extremely large parts of the audience will want and use frequently. They are constantly asked to prepare etext from out-of-print editions of esoteric materials, but this does not provide for usage by the audience they have targeted: 99 percent of the general public.

Similarly, Project Gutenberg has avoided requests, demands, and pressures to create "authoritative editions." It does not cater to the reader who cares whether a certain phrase in Shakespeare has a colon or semi-colon between its clauses, but sets its sights on the goal of releasing etexts that are 99.9 percent accurate in the eyes of the general reader.

During 2002, Hart and colleagues are scheduled to complete 10,000 books in the Project Gutenberg Electronic Public Library.

During 2002, Hart and colleagues are scheduled to complete 10,000 books in the Project Gutenberg Electronic Public Library.

When the project started, the files had to be very small as a normal 300-page book took 1 megabyte of space, which generally, in 1971 no one could be expected to have. This is why doing the US Declaration of Independence (5 kilobytes) seemed the best place to start. This was followed by the Bill of Rights, and then the whole US Constitution, which took lots of space (at least by the standards of 1973). Then came the Bible, as individual books of the Bible were not that large; then Shakespeare (one play at a time); and then general works in the areas of light and heavy literature and references.

By the time Project Gutenberg became famous, the standard was 360-kilobyte disks, so we did books such as *Alice in Wonderland* or *Peter Pan* because they could fit on one disk. Now 1.44 is the standard disk and ZIP is the standard compression; the practical file size is about three million characters, more than enough for the average book.

Once an etext is created in Plain Vanilla ASCII, it is the basis for any future editions. Anyone desiring an etext edition matching, or not matching, a particular paper edition can readily input the changes they wish without having to prepare the whole book again. They can use the Project Gutenberg etext as a foundation and then build in any direction they like.

The major point is that years from now, Project Gutenberg etexts are still going to be viable, but program after program, and operating system after operating system, will have gone the way of the dinosaur, as will all those pieces of hardware running them.

There are three portions of the Project Gutenberg Library:

- Light Literature, such as *Alice in Wonderland, Through the Looking-Glass, Peter Pan, Aesop's Fables,* etc.
- Heavy Literature, such as the Bible or other religious documents, Shakespeare, *Moby Dick, Paradise Lost,* etc.
- References, such as *Roget's Thesaurus,* almanacs, encyclopedias, dictionaries, etc.

The Light Literature collection is designed to get people to the computer in the first place, whether the person is a preschooler or a great-grandparent. Project Gutenberg workers love it when they hear about kids or grandparents taking each other to an etext of *Peter Pan* when they come back from watching *Hook* at the movies, or reading *Alice in Wonderland* after seeing it on TV.

Project Gutenberg is there so people are able to look up quotations they heard in conversation, movies, music, and other books. With Plain Vanilla ASCII, you will be easily able to search an entire library, without any program more sophisticated than a plain search program.

→ *Michael Hart, Project Gutenberg, 405 West Elm Street, Urbana, IL 61801-3231 (E-mail: hart@pobox.com; Web: http://promo.net/pg). The project needs volunteers who can prepare etexts.*

Projects and Ideas Exchange (PIE)

AN INSTITUTE FOR SOCIAL INVENTIONS' AFTERNOON MEETING was used as an experiment for a new way to structure meetings. Projects and Ideas Exchange (PIE) was proposed by Dr. David Chapman and modeled on the cards that ladies used to have at balls so they could book gentlemen for particular dances. PIE was like a structured cocktail party. Booking forms allowed for 23 "brief encounters" (quarter-hour mini-meetings) within the space of two and a half hours — it was generally agreed to have been a most stimulating afternoon. Topics that won their way through to the final 23 from the many proposed in the initial voting circle (each person could volunteer three topics) ranged from the nature of the self (is it discontinuous?) to male liberation (why are men so repressed and depressed?) to language and behavior (people saying one thing and meaning another) to shanty towns for the UK (how to enable them) to money and credit cards (what future do they have?) to death (how to prepare for it).

Modeled on the cards that ladies used to have at balls

PIE may be the answer for your potentially dull conference or party. Often at ordinary gatherings there is no easy way people can find others who are interested in the same things, or can get to talk about what is really important to them.

Dr. David Chapman has now streamlined the PIE procedure, having written a computer program in both Microsoft and BBC BASIC to optimize the arrangements. Here is how Computerized PIE operates for a group of 20 or so in practice:

The group sits in a circle, and after the introductions, each person briefly describes up to three topics (projects, ideas, problems — anything) that he or she wants to discuss with others. Each topic has a number. Participants note down the number and beside it they record the extent to which they feel like discussing that topic by giving it a mark from one to nine. At the end, these scores are marked up on a master sheet, with the participants being identified by number. During the meal break, these details are fed into a computer, which is also given the number of rooms available and their seating capacity. It then comes up with the optimum arrangement of sessions so that participants can attend as many of the sessions they're interested in as possible. The schedule printout is posted for all to see.

Dr. Chapman's software is designed at present for meetings of up to 100 people, but could readily be extended to a larger number.

→ *Dr. David Chapman, Democracy Design Forum, Coles Centre, Buxhall, Stowmarket, Suffolk IP14 3EB, UK (Phone: Int.+44 [0]1449 736 223).*

Proper energy behavior — A social skill learned in kindergarten

The following is developed from an item entitled "Schoolchildren save energy in Stjördal," which appeared in the Norwegian Ideas Bank. The material on which it is based was sent to the Global Ideas Bank by Per Hilmo.

PROPER ENERGY BEHAVIOR IS A SOCIAL SKILL that has to be developed in the early years of life. Nursery schools in Norway are set to become a counterweight to the throwaway society surrounding them.

A project entitled "Energy Monitoring in Schools and Kindergartens," financed by the Norwegian government and the electricity supply companies, aims to involve more than 3,000 schools and kindergartens in Norway over the next few years.

The man behind the project is Per Hilmo, who has a doctorate in thermodynamics and was formerly a consultant on energy efficiency for the Stjördal municipality in central Norway, where the project was first tried out.

Each student is given an Energy Diary in which to keep tabs on home electricity consumption.

Nursery school staff undergo special training. The children check on actual energy use, reading meters each week at school (with the caretaker) — and at home. Each student is given an Energy Diary in which to keep tabs on home electricity consumption. Parents are informed and each family receives a folder entitled "The school and the energy company can help you reduce your electricity bill."

Per Hilmo's involvement with preschool teachers also resulted in a book, *Veronicas virkelighet,* the two key chapters of which have been translated under the title *Veronica's Veracity.* In addition to being a love story, the book is also about how to use energy reasonably and with common sense. Per Hilmo regards the hundreds of thousands of nursery and primary school students as the best champions of energy efficiency. He wants to raise awareness of energy as a resource. The simplest and most important message — that proper energy behavior is necessary and possible for everyone — has yielded positive results.

Measures taken include turning out lights when not needed; closing doors and windows when they should be shut; keeping the temperature at a not-too-high level; heating the nursery school only when in use; running the dishwasher only when full; turning off the heat in the drying room when the clothes are dry; and several other suggestions. Added together, these measures would reduce energy use by as much as 25 percent. If all Norwegian schools were to take part, energy savings would equal one-third of the production of the Alta power plant, which opened amidst violent protest and remains the most controversial power station in the history of Norway.

Anne-Lise Holmvik, the director at Tussilago nursery school, cannot understand why people even raise the question about how long her school is going to continue the program. No one asks the municipal officials, she retorts, how long they are going to keep on separating household garbage.

Both Holmvik and Hilmo know that the children take home with them what they have learned in nursery school. Confronting their parents with questions and attitudes about nature, the environment, and the future also results in energy conservation at home. What the students learn thus has a double effect.

➜ *Per Hilmo, Ofe As [the Information Centre for Energy Efficiency], Postbox 6734 Rodelökka, 0503 Oslo, Norway (Phone: Int.+47 [0]22 80 50 00; Fax: Int.+47 [0]22 80 50 50; E-mail: post@ofem.no).*

➜*See also Stiftelsen Idebanken, PO Box 2126 Grünnerlokka, Norway (Phone: Int.+47 [0] 2203 4010; Fax: Int.+47 [0]2236 4060; E-mail: idebanken@online.no; Web: www.idebanken.no).*

Q

Q

Quality of Life — A deathbed perspective

MEREDITH THRING

Professor Meredith Thring is the author of *Man, Machines and Tomorrow* (published by Routledge & Kegan Paul), chairman of the charity Poweraid, and a Fellow of the UK's Royal Academy of Engineering. The following is summarized from a paper in the *Future Generations Journal* entitled "A decent world for our descendants" and a paper in *World Futures* entitled "Necessary conditions for a permanent civilization."

THE QUALITY OF LIFE (Q) OF A PERSON REFERS TO HIS OR HER GUT FEELING that life is worthwhile. When I lie on my deathbed, will I feel that my life has been entirely useless, or will I be able to feel that it has been of some value to other people, living and future? Will I have caused more harm than good to the Ecosphere, to Gaia?

When I lie on my deathbed, will I feel that my life has been of some value to other people?

In the rich countries there are clear statistical signs of a falling Quality of Life:
- Opting out by suicide, alcoholism, and drugs
- Psychosomatic illnesses and illnesses affected by stress
- Crime, violence, and vandalism

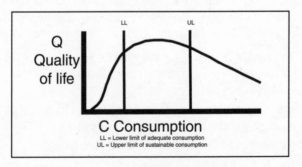

Since the Quality of Life (Q) must be very low when people are starving, it follows that there is an optimum level of consumption (C) which enables a maximum Q, and the relation between Q and C must be as shown in the figure. I have shown in my book *The Engineer's Conscience* that this optimum level of consumption is one which the Earth could supply to many billions of people on a permanent basis.

I conclude that the only hope for our descendants having a decent life is that, within the next two decades, the basic paradigm of society shifts in such a way that people juege their own success (and that of others around them) by their Quality of Life rather than by their wealth. This is not a new idea and indeed many people already make this judgment, but it must become so widely accepted that decisions are taken on this basis in order to enable all people to have the opportunity of a higher Quality of Life in addition to access to all the physical necessities.

The only hope for our descendants is that the judgment of success becomes Quality of Life rather than wealth.

It is obvious that the average Quality of Life is low when the standard of living is so low that people are starving or desperately scratching a bare living. But a study of the rich societies shows clearly that Q is falling due to the loss of all life purpose other than the desire to acquire luxuries and wealth.

Ambitious people are never satisfied with their wealth and power and elbow others out of the way to get more, often either coming a cropper or reaching the end of their lives with a nagging feeling of guilt. Defense lawyers become the highest paid people. Apart from experiencing the fundamental distress of feeling that they are useless, the unemployed are subjected to the stigma that this is their own fault. Many people are terrified by the risk of losing their jobs. Thus the Equilibrium Society must be based on the principle that everyone puts at least as much into the system as he or she takes out.

This change of paradigm will probably come about when a disaster looms so clearly that people are genuinely frightened, just as we accepted rationing when we were frightened of Hitler.

The other civilizations that lived in equilibrium with the ecosphere for thousands of years, such as the North American First Nations, the Kalahari Bushmen, and the Australian Aborigines, were basically nomadic, with very few people living on a given area of land. Our problem is to produce a stable system with perhaps some eight billion people on earth, and to make available to them all the real benefits of the industrial revolution, but without the harmful effects outlined above.

Equilibrium Engineering

If we adopted an Equilibrium Engineering approach, the total world consumption of fossil fuel would have to be reduced to a third of the present figure. For instance, there could be no private cars in towns, only bicycles, public transport, and some taxis. Very economical (200 miles per gallon) and long-lasting (one million miles) cars would be available for hire for longer journeys. They would be powered by methanol/air fuel cells or by agricultural substitutes for diesel or gasoline.

Trains also would have to be powered by renewable energy.

Air travel would be at 300 to 400 miles per hour, at which speeds turboprop engines can give very much reduced fuel consumption per ton-mile. Public transport in and between towns would be frequent, comfortable, and convenient. Ultimately trains also would have to be powered by renewable energy, e.g., by wind, tidal, and/or solar electric power (photovoltaic or steam concentrators, also producing hot water or steam). Methanol fuel cells or diesel engines would be available for calm periods.

I am hopeful that my great-great-grandchildren will live in the Equilibrium Society, because I believe that rich people will accept the rationing of resources that is essential when their conscience is sufficiently aroused, and that this will happen before it is too late.

→ *Professor Meredith Thring, Poweraid, Bell Farm, Brundish, Suffolk IP13 8BL, UK (Phone: Int.+44 [0]1379 384 296). See also web items by or about Professor Thring: "Investing for our grandchildren" <www.globalideasbank.org/reinv/RIS-47.HTML> and "The engineer's conscience" <www.globalideasbank.org/socinv/SIC-97.HTML>.*

R

Ratio of praise to blame predicts happiness in love

Summarized from a story by Jerome Burne in the *London Guardian*.

WHAT COUNTS IN THE SURVIVAL OF A RELATIONSHIP is the proportion of praise to blame, according to Professor Gottman of the University of Washington in Seattle. Having recorded numerous couples arguing in his laboratory, Gottman reckons he can predict with 90 percent accuracy which of them will still be together five years hence.

Couples who say five positive things to each other
for every negative one should be OK.

According to his findings, what counts is not how much in love they say they are, or the number of fights they have, but the balance of positive to negative exchanges. "Couples who say five positive things to each other for every negative one should be OK. If the ratio drops to one in two, they're in trouble."

Rehearsing for old age

A WORKSHOP FOR NURSES AT VICTORIA HOSPITAL, Accrington, Lancashire, UK, gave nurses an insight into the feelings of elderly patients. Frances Biley reported in the *Nursing Times:* "Participants were asked to tie their legs together, place cotton wool plugs in their ears, and wear spectacles with the lenses obscured. Music was played, a TV turned on, and I was pulled out of my chair, led about the room, and introduced to people. I was left to wander aimlessly about, painfully bumping into furniture, before being pushed into a chair. All sense of time was lost, my feelings became introverted, and I began to resent any intrusion into my own safe world."

Participants were asked to tie their legs together,
place cotton wool plugs in their ears,
and wear spectacles with the lenses obscured.

After the half-hour exercise, Biley and her colleagues realized the need for change in their approach to the care of their elderly patients.

Restaurant reviews to include decibel ratings

Summarized from a letter by Alison Munro to the London Times.

RESTAURANT CRITICS SHOULD INCLUDE IN THEIR REVIEW A NOTE ON THE AVERAGE DECIBEL LEVELS in a restaurant in their review. A note on the presence and type of background music could also be helpful in enabling discerning diners to make a more informed choice about what is a suitable eatery for them.

Restaurants have long been judged on the standard of food, the service, and the amount of cigarette smoke (or lack thereof), but for the frequent restaurant diner, quietness is now a priority.

Restaurant in complete darkness to educate about blindness

Summarized from an article by Stephen Moss in the London Guardian entitled "Blind Date", and from an article by Allan Hall in the Financial Times entitled "Taste of luxury in the first hotel for disabled".

FINDING WORK IF YOU ARE BLIND IS NEVER AN EASY MATTER, particularly when the vast majority of the world has no idea what it is like to be unable to see. These two issues were at the forefront of Jorge Spielmann's mind when he set up the Blindekuh (Blind Cow) restaurant in Zürich. It is a restaurant staffed by blind waiters, where everybody eats in complete darkness in order to provide work for blind people and to give sighted people a brief experience of blindness. As Adrian Schaffner, the restaurant's (sighted) manager, explains, "We hope to make people more sensitive to the problems of the blind. It's a new experience for diners: you take one sense away, so you have to use all the others much more."

The Blindekuh is named after the Swiss equivalent of the party game blindman's buff, and it has its own rules to follow. Bags and coats are left in lockers for safety reasons, cell phones and luminous watches are removed, and diners are led to their seats by placing their hands on the shoulders of a waiter or waitress. Try as they might, it's impossible to make out even the slightest shapes, so absolute is the darkness. Waiters then take orders by memorizing them (the menu is limited to a number of options), relying on a dictaphone for exceptionally large orders.

The emphasis is on what you say rather than on
what you wear and how you look.

Apart from it being a totally new eating experience, it is also a new social experience for sighted customers. Conversation without gesture, facial expression, and eye contact places the emphasis on what you say rather than on what you wear and how you look. Schaffner puts it more bluntly: "If you don't talk, you don't exist." Significantly, the restaurant has become a popular venue for blind dates, as couples can gauge how well they get on without the immediate distraction of esthetics. There is undoubtedly a liberating, even transgressive element to the experience as well: no one knows if you're downing your wine at an anti-social rate or licking your pudding bowl. Whether it makes you savor the food more is debatable, but the mixture of blind eating and blind education is an excellent one. And the public agrees — there's a four-month waiting list to get in, and restaurateurs from America, Ireland, and Britain have already expressed an interest in franchising the idea. Jorge Spielmann may be blind, but he shows no lack of foresight.

Reward scheme for workers who recruit and nurture new employees

Summarized from an article by Julekha Dash in *Computer World* entitled "Filling slots with inside referrals," monitored by Roger Knights.

REWARDING EMPLOYEES WHO RECRUIT NEW PEOPLE to a company could be the way to avoid costly recruitment fees and worker short-termism.

Employees who refer workers receive $2,000 when the person is hired.

At Minneapolis-based Carlson Co., employees who refer workers receive $2,000 when the person is hired, and a further $1,000 every year for four years, providing both employees stay with the company. This not only encourages employees to refer friends or acquaintances but also encourages them to look after their referrals once they have got the job.

As a result of the combination of a lump sum and a deferred payment tied to both employees remaining with the company, Carlson's scheme has been a great success. More than one-fifth of newly hired employees have been from employee referrals in the first half of this year. Furthermore, as Lynne Carroll, a recruiter with the firm, points out, the scheme "keeps everybody involved in making sure that people are happy with their jobs."

The idea works for everyone: the company saves on recruitment fees and ensures greater loyalty to the company; the original employee has a chance to make some relatively easy money; and the person being hired immediately feels more at home at a company where he knows people. Internal recruitment could bring a whole new meaning to job satisfaction.

River blindness — 30 million saved

MARK EDWARDS
Mark Edwards runs Still Pictures, an environmental photo agency.

I RECENTLY RETURNED FROM A TRIP TAKING PHOTOGRAPHS to celebrate the virtual elimination of river blindness in Africa thanks to a long-term program coordinated by the World Health Authority and others. This program is now being handed back to national governments, which will caretake it for the future.

---

30 million people are protected from river blindness by Ivermectin, donated free of charge by the manufacturers.

Onchocerciasis, also known as "river blindness," is a parasitic disease found primarily in tropical Africa that is endemic in fertile river valleys. Severe infections will eventually lead to blindness and may cause whole communities to migrate from their villages to live in the desert.

At the present time, 30 million people are protected from the disease by a drug called Ivermectin, which only has to be taken twice a year. The drug is donated free of charge by the manufacturers, which presumably make sufficient profit on it from sale in Europe and America, where it is used by vets. This idea could be extended: for example, each condom purchased in Europe or America would pay for a free condom being made available for distribution in Africa and parts of South America, where many people cannot afford to buy them.

Editorial comment

The company that has provided more than 100 million tablets for this program in both Equatorial Africa and areas of Central and South America deserves to be named: it is Merck Sharp & Dohme, and the brand name for their Ivermectin tablets is Mectizan.

Up to 15 percent of the population of African villages were blind. This forced entire communities to abandon fertile riverside lands.

Onchocerciasis has caused blindness or severe visual impairment in more than one million people. Up to 15 percent of the population of African villages were blind when the disease was prevalent. Millions more suffered severe itching and disfiguring skin changes.

The disease is spread by a tiny blackfly that breeds in fast-flowing rivers near where victims live — thus the name "river blindness." It has forced entire communities to abandon fertile riverside lands and to resettle on less fertile land.

In 1995 a seven-foot sculpture named "The Gift of Sight" was unveiled at Merck's New Jersey offices. The statue depicts a young boy leading a blind man along a path in an African village — a once common scene that is now beginning to disappear as a result of the Ivermectin distribution.

→ Mark Edwards, Still Pictures, 199a Shooters Hill Road, London SE3, UK (Phone: Int.+44 [0]20 8858 8307).

→ For information about community-based river-blindness treatment programs, contact Mectizan Donation Program, 750 Commerce Drive, Suite 400, Decatur, GA 30030. The details above were supplied by Merck Sharp & Dohme, Hertford Road, Hodeston, Herts EN11 9BU, UK (Phone: Int.+44 [0]1992 467272; in the USA call Maggie Bute, Phone: 908 423 5655).

Rights of Nature

ROBERT MCPARLAND

Summarized from Robert McParland's review of *The Rights of Nature* by Roderick Frazier Nash (published by University of Wisconsin Press). The review appeared in *Breakthrough* magazine.

AS ENVIRONMENTALISM EVOLVES AS A SOCIAL MOVEMENT, the idea of liberating nature from human persecution emerges more frequently and forcefully. When Thomas Jefferson wrote that all men are created equal, he and his colleagues (and his country) apparently were not thinking of women or racial minorities, nor about the idea of extending ethical treatment to animals, plants, and rivers. But modern US federal law provides legal protection for endangered species and habitats.

> When Thomas Jefferson wrote that all men are created equal, he was not thinking of women or racial minorities, nor about the idea of extending ethical treatment to animals, plants, and rivers.

Today the field is prepared for mass participation in ethically impelled environmentalism. The Rights of Nature now concern lawmakers, theologians, scientists, and the many individuals who seek to secure the inviolable worth of the natural world for future generations. Nash believes that serious confrontations could arise between advocates of the Rights of Nature and those now profiting from nature's exploitation.

A Declaration of the Rights of Nature

1. Nature — animate or inanimate — has a right to existence; that is, to preservation and development.

> Nature has a right to the protection of its ecosystems, species and populations, in all their interconnectedness.

2. Nature has a right to the protection of its ecosystems, species, and populations in all their interconnectedness.
3. Animate nature has a right to the preservation and development of its genetic inheritance.
4. Organisms have a right to a life fit for their species, including procreation within their appropriate ecosystems.
5. Disturbances of nature require a justification. They are only permissible, firstly, when the presuppositions of the disturbance are determined in a democratically legitimate process and with respect

R

for the rights of nature; secondly, when the interests of the disturbance outweigh the interests of a complete protection of the rights
of nature; and thirdly, when the disturbance is not inordinate.
Damaged nature is to be restored wherever possible.

6. Rare ecosystems and, above all, those with an abundance of species
are to be placed under absolute protection. The driving of species
to extinction is forbidden.

✦ From **Rights of Future Generations, Rights of Nature,** *edited by Lukas
Vischer (published by the World Alliance of Reformed Churches), monitored by
one of the booklet's contributors, Professor Peter Saladin, Forrerstr. 26, CH-
3006, Bern, Switzerland (Phone: Int.+41 [0]31 44 8006).*

S

Save the World Club

DES KAY
From Des Kay's *Save The World Club Newsletter.*

PEOPLE ARE NOW JOINING THE SAVE THE WORLD CLUB (STWC) at an unprecedented rate and getting involved with all sorts of affiliated organizations —
Greenpeace, Friends of the Earth, etc. This is very encouraging.

**I am a member of STWC,
and today I will do all I can to help save the world.**

Remember that you can still take advantage of free membership — the
only requirement being a pledge to say "I am a member of STWC, and today
I will do all I can to help save the world" every day when you wake up.

✦ *Des Kay, Crescent Road, Kingston, KT2 7QR, UK
(Phone: Int.+44 [0]20 8547 0335).*

Saving islands from the devastations of tourism

NICHOLAS ALBERY

THE BEAUTIFUL GREEK ISLAND OF SKYROS HAS LESSONS to teach islands everywhere. Skyros is one of the few tourist islands that has survived tourism relatively intact, and in my view the following factors have helped (and could to some extent be adopted by islands elsewhere):

- A local Skyros activist named Panos brought together all business and other interests to keep the island relatively unspoilt. Panos ran a taverna in the high street and a gift shop, and started a tourist organization that brought together the shops, the restaurants, the renters of rooms, etc. His association fought off a Thompson Holidays plan to build a large hotel and to bring in package holidays. Some of the other initiatives Panos and his friends organized were also laudable: e.g., equipping one person living near each forest or beach with a phone, so that any fires can be immediately reported before they get out of control.

Tourists have to stay in the homes of residents, who move out of their bedrooms in the summer to make some money

---

- There are virtually no hotels, so tourists have to stay in the homes of residents, who move out of their bedrooms in the summer to make some money. These are really charming local houses with beautiful china plates and brass pots hanging on the wall. As a result, tourism money goes straight into local pockets, and visitors get a more intimate contact with local people than they would otherwise.
- Buildings are allowed to be a maximum of three stories tall.
- Rubbish is collected quite efficiently and compacted in the center of the island (though there was a fire from methane gas recently).

Skyros is also protected by two geographical factors:

- The island is relatively hard to get to. There is only one tiny plane twice a week from Athens, able to take about 20 people. Otherwise it is quite a journey from Athens, requiring three buses and two ferries.
- The main town physically prevents the entry of cars and motorbikes because of its steps and narrowness.

→ *The Institute for Social Inventions, 20 Heber Road, London NW2 6AA, UK (Phone: Int.+44 [0]20 8208 2853; Fax: Int.+44 [0]20 8452 6434; E-mail: rhino@dial.pipex.com). See also the article "Skyros Year 2050" on the web (www.globalideasbank.org/inspir/INS-175.HTML).*

→ *The Small Islands Information Network is on the web at <www.upei.ca/~siin/>.*

Saving the planet with gravel dust

GRAVEL DUST, OFTEN AVAILABLE FREE FROM THE SILT PONDS AT GRAVEL PITS and rich in minerals and trace elements, should be added to your garden according to the Soil Remineralization movement. This movement is most active to date in Austria, Germany, and the USA. Robert Schindele, for instance, writes: "I discovered the phenomenon of gravel dust by accident. While building a 1.5-mile-long road through my forest property near Melk, Austria, a lot of gravel dust developed. In areas where this dust settled, within a few months all the sick fir trees became healthy again and have grown very strongly since."

> In areas where the gravel dust settled, within a few months
> all the sick fir trees became healthy again.

Don Weaver, in his book with John Hamaker on the subject of gravel and rock dust (*The Survival of Civilisation*, published by Hamaker-Weaver Publications), writes: "By adding gravel screenings from industry gravel pits east of San Francisco bay to my average organic garden at rates of two to four lbs per square foot, I was able to increase crop yields two to four times in quantity with unmistakable flavor enrichment. Pole beans climbing out of prolific zucchini and tomato beds went to 18 feet before being turned back by the weight of heavy beans at the top." Hamaker's mineralized corn crop turned out to have 57 percent more phosphorus, 90 percent more potassium, 47 percent more calcium, and 60 percent more magnesium than chemically grown crops from the same seed. On Lanzerotte in the Canary Islands, vines have flourished in soil rich in volcanic rock. And now in the UK, interesting results are beginning to show from the experiments at Springhill Farm near Aylesbury. Working in conjunction with the Department of Chemistry at Surrey University, the farmers are growing wheat in soil to which granite dust from a nearby quarry has been added.

> During an ice age, as glaciers grind rock to a
> fine dust over millennia, a fertile soil is created.

The movement in the US has an almost messianic note. Joanna Campe, president of Remineralize the Earth, believes that "the ultimate poverty is poverty of soil. The fate of the earth hangs in the balance." Remineralization will help avert a new ice age: "During an ice age, as glaciers grind rock to a fine dust over millennia, a fertile soil is created. Adding finely ground gravel dust nourishes the micro-organisms in the soil, whose protoplasm is the basis of all life. Remineralization can save the dying forests in the temperate latitudes. Otherwise, as forests begin to die off worldwide, giving off carbon dioxide, the climate of the earth is altered, triggering the transition from the warm interglacial to an ice age."

Robert Schindele is even more extreme. He eats gravel dust, two teaspoons a day, and markets it in parts of Europe as a "mineral dietary supplement" under the name Superbiomin — despite heavy opposition from the German and Austrian pharmaceutical industry. "For years my hair was as white as snow," he says, "but since I have been taking gravel dust, it is almost black again. Chronic diseases, especially gout, disappeared."

He further claims that Superbiomin acts against radioactivity, "breaking down the high oscillation rates of ionized particles, as confirmed by the Institute for Atomic Physics in the Ukraine." Apparently after the Chernobyl accident, the Russians picked up 4,400 pounds of Superbiomin with a military truck.

The indications of the movement's growing acceptance in the mainstream, claims Joanna Campe, include various research projects and conferences on the subject sponsored by the United States Department of Agriculture: "Eight universities in the US are carrying out research into the area, not to mention many projects being conducted in the country's high schools."

→ *For further information and sources of research, see <www.geocities.com/HotSprings/Sauna/1432/ links.htm>.*

→ *Philip Madeley has compiled an extensive list of resources on the subject of soil remineralization (including links, organizations, books, and videos) that you can find on the web at <www.geocities.com/HotSprings/Sauna/1432/SRInfo.htm>. His dissertation on this topic is at <www.geocities.com/HotSprings/Sauna/1432/SoilRemineralization1.htm>.*

→ *See also the Remineralize the Earth website <www.Remineralize-the-Earth.org>.*

School for Social Entrepreneurs

MICHAEL YOUNG

Adapted from an article originally published in the *London Guardian* under the title "Do-gooder inc." Michael Young is the founder and chair of the School for Social Entrepreneurs.

WHEN PEOPLE ASK ME WHAT I DO FOR A LIVING, I'm often stuck for an answer. When I look back at my life, it seems I've spent it helping to create a succession of useful, but not particularly glamorous, institutions: the Open University, the Consumers' Association and *Which?* magazine, and the Open College of the Arts. I suppose if I had to come up with a job title I'd describe myself as a "social entrepreneur" — someone with the heart of a do-gooder but the mind of a businessman.

Everyone, at one time or another, has an idea about how to make things better. Most of these ideas aren't much good, but a few of them are really worthwhile. Unfortunately, the vast majority of these good ideas are never acted upon because their originators lack the skills to put them into practice. So these people end up being dismissed as eccentrics, as people who don't live in the real world, and their ideas never see the light of day.

To provide do-gooders with the training to make their ideas a reality

---

In 1997 I set up the School for Social Entrepreneurs (SSE) as an attempt to provide do-gooders, including people in the public sector and in business, with the training to make their ideas a reality.

If you think you have an idea that might work — from a way to improve your neighborhood to a scheme for reducing unemployment in your region — you should apply to the SSE. If you've got a good one and there's a real chance it might work, we'll do what we can to help you turn it into a reality.

The term "social entrepreneur" brings together two old words in a new combination. As ordinarily understood, an "entrepreneur" is a man or woman of business who has a new idea and makes it work. Add "social," and the person described also has a new idea and acts on it, but the purpose is different: to meet a social need. Unfortunately, do-gooders will seldom do good unless they have some key entrepreneurial qualities.

The school's students who have gone, or are going through, the mill have demonstrated some of the qualities that are required. These are energy, talent, persistence, flexibility, resilience, a capacity for thinking up and winning support for creative compromises — and a keen sense about how to raise money for a cause other than themselves.

There has to be a market, an unmet need, as well as an innovation to meet it.

The school can foster such talents and equip students with practical skills in an atmosphere of mutual support. Of all the qualities in demand, perhaps the most important is an ability to pick winners. Being governed by the market, a social entrepreneur needs to be like any other entrepreneur.

There has to be a market, an unmet need, as well as an innovation to meet it. The need may be an old one that can be satisfied in new ways, or a new need that is revealed by what the entrepreneur does.

When I started the Consumers' Association, it satisfied a need for impartial information about the value of goods and services to counter self-interested advertising. When I helped launch the Open University, it met a new need that, it turned out, many people had without realizing it — namely, to study for a degree without going near an ordinary university. A new opportunity can create a new demand as well as the other way round.

The students have been well aware — or made aware if they weren't beforehand — that their efforts have to be market-led. I will give a few examples of what they have done, or are doing, in just two fields: training and disability.

Newham Wise is a training organization in east London with an excellent record for getting its young trainees into jobs, but they had a problem with funding. Bert Leslie was an experienced businessman who sold his construction company in order to join the voluntary sector. During his placement at Newham Wise, he contributed to raising half a million pounds in grants.

Tessa Dugmore is a young woman working with Providence Row housing association to create a community center on the ground floor of a disused school in London. The top floors will provide living accommodation for homeless young people, on condition that they train for jobs.

Fabien Bunani came to the UK as a refugee from Rwanda. He is a highly skilled man and was previously an auditor for the African Continental Bank, but the qualifications of many Third World refugees aren't always recognized in Britain. He has set up a training scheme that will help other skilled refugees find employment in Britain.

Ann Cotton is founder of Camfed in Cambridge, which supports the education of girls in Africa. It has helped 1,860 girls in Zimbabwe and Ghana to stay on at school, and 240 have completed their secondary education. They are now agents of change in their communities. Ann has come to the school in order to get help in planning further expansion of the organization in other parts of Africa.

We've also had several students at the school who've been convinced that, given the right kind of encouragement, disabled people can do far more than is usually thought possible. Our students have persuaded employers to take on people suffering from autism; set up a day center for people from ethnic minorities with mental health problems; started an organization for the prevention of young people committing suicides; and developed a business whereby people with learning difficulties provide cleaning and other services for football clubs.

The school cannot create entrepreneurs, but it can certainly foster people's talents, equip them with practical skills, and give them a chance to test out their ideas in an atmosphere of mutual support.

"The range of experience and contacts my fellow students bring is a treasure trove in itself," says Tessa Dugmore, "especially for someone like me who is still at the start of her career. The students and staff are tremendously well-connected, and if you're ever stuck, a suggestion or name will be forthcoming. I also think the school has helped me become a bit more 'hard-headed' by sticking to the practicalities of innovation."

We must add to our heritage or lose it, we must grow greater or grow less, we must go forward or backward.

The reason I founded the school is that I believe that without a constant flow of new ideas, our society will never realize its full potential. I'm reminded of a passage from "The Lion and the Unicorn," George Orwell's essay on the nature of Englishness: "Nothing ever stands still. We must add to our heritage or lose it, we must grow greater or grow less, we must go forward or backward."

→ *The School for Social Entrepreneurs, 18 Victoria Park Square, Bethnal Green, London E2 9PF, UK (Phone: Int.+44 (0) 20 8981 0300; Fax: Int.+44 (0)20 8983 4655; E-mail: sandra.wynter@sse.org.uk; Web: www.sse.org.uk/). SSE's first social entrepreneurs program outside London is based in inner-city Salford. It is funded by the Manchester, Salford, and Trafford Health Action Zone and delivered in partnership with Salford Community Health Council. SSE supports the local organization through a package of services including advice and consultancy on setting up the school, recruiting students, and delivering the program; training for the local staff; and an electronic communications infrastructure to serve the network and support dispersed learning. SSE is also delivering a Millennium Awards Scheme to support community entrepreneurs in ten disadvantaged areas around the UK.*

School Social Invention Workshops

SINCE THE 1980s, THE INSTITUTE FOR SOCIAL INVENTIONS has been running social invention workshops in state schools in the UK. The formula is very simple: a class (of any ages from 7 to 18) is allocated a budget of up to £50 ($80) to spend on a project of its own devising that will benefit either the school or the local community, with the project to be completed within one term of weekly two-hour sessions.

In the first session, students look at problems in their school, their neighborhood, and their own personal lives, selecting one or two problems to focus on. In the second session they are taught brainstorming as a way of coming up with ways of tackling these problems that are as imaginative as possible. In the third session they draw up an action and evaluation plan so that they will know at the end of the term to what extent they have succeeded, according to their own criteria. Thereafter, the students carry out their plan, sometimes working hard between sessions, and often ending up with striking projects. Here are descriptions of some of the workshops:

Pooper Scooper Action Squad

A class of 23 seven- and eight-year-olds at Essendine Primary School, London, were asked to think up a list of neighborhood problems. The one that they decided to brainstorm about was dog's mess, since the streets around the school were particularly fouled.

They made colorful placards with pictures and messages such as "I hate dog's mess," and they laboriously prepared and sent out a press release announcing the formation of a Children's Pooper Scooper Action Squad — for it was the Parisian technological solution of Pooper Scooper motorbikes that appealed to them. These motorbikes, with vacuum cleaners on the back, go up on the pavement to vacuum up the mess.

With the *Daily Telegraph, Paddington Mercury,* and LBC radio in attendance, the children visited Richard Branson's barge near their school with a petition suggesting that he spend some of his clean-up millions — he was then in charge of the government's environmental program — on buying some of these Pooper Scooper motorbikes.

The children also wrote to the Westminster Council, which responded by bringing over from Paris one of the Pooper Scooper motorbikes, the first to be tried in the UK.

To fulfill their Action Squad image, the children used plastic gloves and seaside spades to collect demonstration amounts of dog's mess for the newspaper photographers. The children also wrote to the Westminster Council, which responded by bringing over from Paris one of the Pooper Scooper motorbikes, the first to be tried in the UK.

The class teacher, Isla Robertson, was delighted with the workshop, as the Westminster Council subsequently made a special effort to clean up around the school. "You can't imagine what a disaster it is," she pointed out, "when you have 20 young children out on an expedition and one of them falls in dog's mess — there's no way to get them clean."

Video of trouble with the police

KAREN CHESSELL

Ten non-academic 14-year-olds in my social invention workshop at Raines Foundation School, Bethnal Green, London, were encouraged to brainstorm on problems to do with school, the community, and their personal lives. Two major problem areas were identified: experiencing school as a "prison" and getting into trouble, especially with the police. Further brainstorming for solutions to these problems produced the idea of going out of the school and making a drama documentary film that could be used to teach younger children how not to get into trouble.

Under my guidance and that of their teacher Carolyn Hallohan, the students set about outlining a film script and enlisting information and help from relevant sources. A video camera was organized by one of the students. Welfare Education Officer Mr. Waters gave valuable preliminary information on legal aspects of juvenile crime and also accepted an acting role as a social worker. Sergeant Jackie Hunt and Constable Russell Taylor from the Bethnal Green Police Station not only agreed to come to talk to the class but also took part in the dramatized "arrest" scene, complete with police van and its flashing lights. Furthermore, they arranged for the use of the Arbours Street Magistrates Court so that scenes could be shot in the charge room, courts, and cells.

Students filmed a dramatized arrest scene
complete with police van and its flashing lights.

Five of the students proved themselves to be "naturals" as actors, doing justice to the work the whole class put into ideas for plot, location-hunting, music, and artwork. The film is scheduled to be screened to other classes, with money from donations going to a local detention center.

⇢ Social Invention Workshops — A manual Designed for Teachers or Other Group Leaders *is available for £2.50 from the Institute for Social Inventions, 20 Heber Road, London NW2 6AA, UK (Phone: Int.+44 [0]20 8208 2853; Fax: Int.+44 [0]20 8452 6434; E-mail: rhino@dial.pipex.com; Web: www.globalideasbank.org).*

Self-help groups for philanthropists

THERE ARE SEVERAL ORGANIZATIONS AROUND THE WORLD THAT ACT as self-help groups for rich people who aspire to use their resources to make the world a better place. In the UK, for instance, the Network for Social Change was founded in 1985 and now has about 60 members, but it is always on the lookout for more. The projects that the Network members fund collectively are all sought out by members themselves. Unsolicited applications are not considered.

One member says, "It is a deeply unfair society in which we live, and if you have money in a world where it is unequally distributed, you are in a powerful position. However, the responsibility can become too much, and you can get really paralyzed by the guilt."

The twice-yearly conferences of the whole membership encourage a sharing at many levels and challenge directly the isolation of those with money.

One new member commented, "My husband and I became involved in Network about seven months after we received the money from the sale of our business, and it helped us to get things into perspective." She also asked, "Where else can you talk about your money and not worry about people looking at you sideways?'"

Projects the network has funded range from an education center set up by miners' wives in Yorkshire to a tree nursery in the Cape Verde Islands developing species suitable for drought-stricken Africa, to an Indian project producing artificial limbs that are suited to local cultural conditions.

We grapple with questions such as how to make giving satisfying.

In the United States the main organizations doing this work include the following:

- The Threshold Foundation, based in San Francisco. It is for members with financial capability and a personal commitment to philanthropic endeavors. It seeks "to build a more just, caring, and sustainable world, a legacy for all."

- More than Money, based in Arlington, Massachusetts. This is a similar organization, but it also provides a journal, counseling, and special outreach to inheritors in their 20s. "People with wealth supposedly have it all," they say. "Targets of envy and resentment, we rarely have a safe forum for addressing the unique challenges and opportunities that come with having surplus while deeply caring about others who have too little. We grapple with questions such as how to make giving satisfying, whether or not to set up a trust fund for children, and how to deal with money issues in relationships."

➔ *The Administrator, The Network for Social Change, BM 2063, London WC1N 3XX, UK.*

➔ *The Threshold Foundation, PO Box 29903, San Francisco, CA 94129, USA (Phone: 415 561 6400; Fax: 415 561 6401).*

✦ *More than Money, 226 Massachusetts Avenue, Suite 4, Arlington, MA 02474 (Phone: 781 648 0776; Fax: 781 648 6606; E-mail: info@morethan money.org; Web: www.morethanmoney.org).*

✦ *Further resources for philanthropists can be found at <www.chardonpress.com/titles/ip_resources.html>.*

Self-taught computer literacy for kids in Delhi slum

Summarized from an interview by Thane Peterson, edited by Paul Judge, in *Business Week Online* entitled "A lesson in computer literacy from India's poorest kids." This item was originally monitored by Clive Semmens.

USING A POLICY OF WHAT HE TERMS "MINIMALLY INVASIVE EDUCATION," Sugata Mitra, the head of the Research and Development wing of NIIT, India's premier software and education company, has opened up the astounding prospect of helping 500 million Indian children achieve basic computer literacy over the next five years.

Plugging a high-powered PC into a wall that separates his company's grounds from waste land

---

Mitra's "hole-in-the-wall" experiment consisted of plugging a high-powered Pentium PC with a high-speed data connection into a wall that separates his company's grounds from waste land which poor people use as their toilet. He connected the PC to the internet, left it on, and allowed any passerby to tinker around with it. Mitra monitored the activity on the PC using a remote computer and a video camera mounted in an adjacent tree.

Within a matter of a few days, slum children had learned how to browse the internet.

Sugata Mitra discovered that within a matter of a few days, slum children between the ages of six and 12 (the most frequent users of the machine), despite their lack of education and any knowledge of English, had learned how to draw on the computer and how to browse the internet. Attainment of basic level computer literacy — the ability to use the mouse, to drag, to copy, to point, to drop, and to surf the net — was almost instantaneous. The most popular features for the slum children were Microsoft Paint and Disney.com, the latter because of the games and the former because every child loves to draw, but these children did not have easy access to paint and paper.

Mitra came up with the idea of providing slum kids with access to the internet after listening to almost every parent he knew. They would admit that when their children were provided with a computer, the children's knowledge of it soon far outstripped their parents'. From this, Mitra deduced that it was not something exceptional in the children that he was encountering, but simply adult incomprehension and their underestimation of a child's ability to use the computer.

This led him to the idea that methods of teaching adults were not really suitable for use on children. Through his "hole-in-the-wall" experiment, he realized that curious children, working together as groups, can attain basic computer literacy without outside help. In other words, if children are interested in something or view it as worth learning, no formal infrastructure is necessary to teach them. Therefore, any kind of funding for formal education of children in subjects they are interested in is a waste of money, time, and resources — all of which would be better employed teaching aspects that children cannot master on their own.

To illustrate this further, Mitra once played a digital-music file, MP3, for the slum children. They were astonished to hear music come out of the computer. When they asked him whether it worked like a TV or radio, Mitra, in keeping with his policy of minimal invasion, replied, "Well, I know how to get there, but I don't know how it works." Then he left them to it. A week later, true to Mitra's hunches, these children knew more about MP3 than he did. Not only had they discovered what MP3 was, but they had also managed to download free players, had discovered Hindi music websites, and were playing all their favorite film songs.

Even more astonishing is the fact that these children did not know the terms and terminology connected with the technology they had managed to use. They did not know what a computer was, but they managed to overcome the language barrier that presented itself to them since most of the information on the internet is in English. By inventing their own terminology for what was going on, they bypassed the language barrier. For example, they did not know the terms for the mouse or the pointer. But they called the pointer of the mouse "sui," the Hindi word for needle. The hourglass that appears when an operation is taking place they termed "damru," after an hourglass-shaped drum that the god Shiva holds in his hand. They could tell that the "sui" became a "damru" when the "thing" — the computer — was doing something. So Mitra suggests that it is not the terminology which matters but the metaphor. As long as the children have an idea of the function, does it matter whether or not they know that a mouse is called a mouse?

That language is no barrier to these children is borne out by the fact that when Mitra provided them with a Hindi interface with links for connecting to websites in their own language, they shut it down and went back to the

Internet Explorer browser software. They did not have a semantic understanding of the word "file," but they certainly developed an operational understanding of it, realizing that within "file" were options for saving and opening up files.

He gave them a computer terminal and two hours to find the answers.

To give yet another example of how the internet is revolutionizing the acquisition of knowledge, Mitra conducted another experiment. He chose four ninth-graders, two boys and two girls, from a middle-class school and found out from their physics teacher that viscosity was the topic he would teach these children the same time next year. He asked the teacher to write down possible exam questions on the subject. He then presented the questions to the four children, who, of course, did not understand them at all. He gave them a computer terminal and two hours to find the answers. In two hours they had answered all the questions correctly, and to prove that they had learned something significant about the subject, they conversed intelligently with their physics teacher on the topic. The teacher remarked that they certainly did not know everything about viscosity or everything he would eventually teach them next year, but that they did know a substantial amount — plus a couple of things that he did not know. This drove home Mitra's point that if you can make the children curious enough, a mass of content, knowledge, and information is available on the net for them to access.

Sugata Mitra asserts that if he is given the resources and funding to conduct this experiment for five years, with 100,000 kiosks, then 500 million Indian children will make themselves computer literate. He reckons that this would cost about $2 billion, but that it would cost twice as much using traditional methods of teaching children computer technology.

Mitra says that the original experiment continues to progress very well. He and his team have also started another experiment of the same kind in a village approximately 300 miles from Delhi. The results of that experiment, Sugata says, are "almost identical to those obtained in Delhi."

→ *Sugata Mitra, Centre for Research in Cognitive Systems, NIIT, Synergy Building, IIT Campus, New Delhi 110 016, India (Phone: 91 (11) 658 1002; Fax: 91(11)620 3333; E-mail: sugatam@niit.com; Web: www.geocities.com/SoHo/1718/).*

Sewage marshes as nature sanctuaries

Summarized from an article by Doug Stewart in the *Smithsonian,* monitored by Roger Knights.

THE ARCATA MARSH AND WILDLIFE SANCTUARY IS A 154-ACRE WETLANDS PARK about 280 miles up the coast from San Francisco. This quiet and perfectly pleasant-smelling park has turned Arcata into a tourist stop and bird-watching mecca. It also enables the town to meet California's strict sewage-discharge standards.

Sewage has been meandering through the park's chain of artificial marshes.

Since 1986, partially treated sewage from the town's conventional primary treatment plant has been meandering through the park's chain of artificial marshes. After a two-month odyssey, it's piped into Humboldt Bay. The discharged marsh water is generally clearer and cleaner than the water already in the bay.

The system's low-key simplicity won the city a $100,000 grant from the Ford Foundation's Innovations in Government program and has set off a flood of inquiries from mayors and town engineers throughout the US.

Bob Gearheart, a professor of environmental engineering at the local college, Humboldt State University, had helped set up crop-irrigation systems using wastewater in several Third World communities. In developing countries, he found that high-quality fresh water was often unavailable and chlorine unaffordable.

The design he helped produce for Arcata involved digging out ponds from 32 acres of desolate waterfront land where a series of abandoned and decrepit lumber mills stood, dominated by an old county dump. Each marsh has a balance of open water and marsh plants. The shapes of the marshes are pleasantly irregular, and small human-made islands punctuate their surfaces. "What really does the work here are the micro-organisms that grow around the roots and stems of these cattails," Gearheart explains. The stems of the cattails are slippery, evidence of underwater bacteria and fungi that have latched onto them to feed on the organic nutrients in the water flowing past — tiny biological filters, in effect.

The wetlands flora attracts astounding numbers of waterfowl.

Duckweed, cattails, pennywort, and hard-stem bulrushes flourish in this nutrient-rich swamp water. The wetlands flora, in turn, attracts astounding numbers of waterfowl: ducks, coots, egrets, herons, hawks, avocets, pelicans, and peregrine falcons. Joggers huff down the redwood-chip trails, and office workers on their lunch breaks sit reading in parked cars. A visitors' center is being planned for the park, and there's talk of posting signs inside the toilet stalls that will read "Thank you for your contribution."

↪ Bob Gearheart, Professor of Environmental Engineering, Humboldt State University, Arcata, Northern California.

Sharing your gifts

GAIL RAPPAPORT

MOST OF US, DURING THE COURSE OF GROWING UP, were asked the question "What do you want to be when you grow up?" in one form or another, at one time or another.

Wouldn't it be wonderful if the question asked of our children was more like "What gifts of yours would you like to share with the world?" or "How would you like to contribute to making the world a better place?"

Remember: Language is Powerful.

Sign language for babies

Summarized from the Sign With Your Baby website <www.sign2me.com>, monitored by Roger Knights.

SIGNING WITH BABIES WAS BORN FROM AN EXPERIENCE Joseph Garcia had while visiting the family of a deaf friend. There he saw a baby, around ten months old, communicating with his parents in a much more sophisticated way than he had seen with hearing children of hearing parents the same age. The child was using American Sign Language.

Signing children tended to have a
better grasp of grammar and syntax.

Joseph was so impressed that he decided to make it the focus of his research and ultimately of the thesis for his masters degree. During his research, he discovered that hearing children began replicating signs as early as eight months, with some exceptional children doing it as early as six months, far earlier than they could articulate the same words verbally. Additionally, once the signing children began speaking, they tended to have a better grasp of grammar and syntax, past and present tenses, and of language in general. He was so convinced of the importance of his discovery that he wrote a book on the subject, *Toddler Talk*, and has since helped compile a pack entitled the *Sign with Your Baby Complete Learning Kit* (available from Stratton Kehl Publications Inc).

Using Joseph Garcia's method, babies can tell you such things as "I'm hungry," "I'm thirsty," or "I have an earache" many months before they speak.

Babies have control over their hands long before they develop the fine motor skills required for speech. Parents and caregivers who recognize the benefits of this early communication are teaching their infants to sign, starting the process as early as seven months.

Dr. Burton White, the director of the Center for Parent Education and author of *The First Three Years of Life* and *Raising a Happy Unspoiled Child,* found that one of the greatest advantages to signing comes when the child is between 17 and 20 months of age. "What it boils down to is that in our experience, children are least able to tolerate frustration during that three-month period," says Dr. White. "And one of the major reasons is, they can't easily say what's on their minds. A child who has a reasonably extensive signing vocabulary is much better off in that respect."

Parents start slowly by teaching their babies some easy American Sign Language signs that represent simple ideas babies can understand, like "more," "eat," and "milk." When babies are able to replace some of the screaming, whining, and crying with a few simple hand gestures, it can dramatically improve their relationships with their caregivers. Parents who use Garcia's system report reduced frustration for them and their baby, a stronger parent-child bond, and in many cases an accelerated verbal language skill development.

Parents who are communicating with their babies may be less likely to neglect or abuse them. It is possible that parents who get into the habit of communicating with their babies through signs may develop into parents who listen more to their speaking children and adolescents.

By age three, children exposed to signing had language skills approaching those expected of four-year-olds.

In recent studies funded by the National Institutes of Child Health and Human Development, Dr. Linda Acredolo and Dr. Susan Goodwyn wrote that signing children outperformed non-signing children in comparison after comparison, including language development and IQ. Acredolo and Goodwyn recently revisited those same children (now seven and eight years old) to compare the original signing babies to their control group. The results indicated that as a group, children who signed as babies had a mean IQ of 114 compared to 102 for non-signers. In their study they discovered that not only do signing children tend to learn to speak sooner, but by age three, children exposed to signing had language skills approaching those expected of four-year-olds.

✦ *Additional research in this area is continuing today at Ohio State University. See the website <www.newswise.com/articles/1999/1/SIGNLANG.OSU.html>.*

Sleep in the street before house buying

KEN CAMPBELL

I SUGGEST THAT BEFORE BUYING A HOUSE IN ROUGHER PARTS OF CITIES, people should park a van in the street on a Saturday and sleep in the van overnight. How a neighborhood behaves at its worst on a Saturday night could put you off buying and so save you much heartache later.

✦ *Ken Campbell, 74 Watermint Quay, Craven Walk, London N16 6BT, UK.*

Slow food —
Worldwide movement to protect the two-hour lunch

Summarized from the American Airlines magazine *American Way,* quoted in *Utne Reader;* from <www.slowfood.it/>; and from "PremioSlowFood" by Andrew Finkel in *Time Europe.*

AT THE BEGINNING IT WAS JUST A PLAYFUL TWEAKING, a good-humored philosophical shot at the ubiquitous burger, symbol of a minute-made and minute-mad world. McDonald's was poised to invade Rome's beautiful Piazza di Spagna at the base of the famed Spanish steps. Just the thought of it gave indigestion to food-and-wine writer Carlo Petrini and his fellow members of Arcigola, the Italian gastronomical society.

What better weapon to battle fast food than "slow food"?

What better weapon, they thought, to battle fast food than "slow food"? So Petrini's pack formed the International Movement for the Defense of and the Right to Pleasure and issued a "Slow Food Manifesto" — the first salvo in the Slow Food War. "In our century, born and nurtured under the sign of Industrialization, the machine was invented and then turned into the role model of life. Speed became our shackles," the manifesto began. "We fall prey to the same virus: 'The Fast Life' that fractures our customs, assails us even in our own homes, cages us and feeds us fast food." The remedy? An "adequate portion of sure sensual pleasures, to be taken with slow and prolonged enjoyment" — beginning in the kitchen with the preparation of an elaborate meal, and ending at the table with fine wine and rambling conversation.

"It was just a game at first," says Petrini, a chance to remind people that food is a perishable art, as pleasurable in its way as a sculpture by

Michelangelo or a painting by Titian. Not mere nourishment to be wolfed down, but culture to be savored. The time had come, the group proclaimed, to get back to the two-hour lunch and the four-hour dinner.

But, ho hum, McDonald's paid little heed, opening its restaurant in spite of the slow eaters' pleas in late 1986. With no competition nearby, it became one of the corporation's ten highest-volume locations worldwide. Nevertheless, Petrini discovered that his slow food idea was catching. Calls poured in asking about the "movement." There was obviously an eager and growing following for the eat-a-lot-slowly philosophy.

"Slow food," says Petrini, "was in the air. We in Arcigola only made the idea concrete."

Members meet for marathon meals and talk food, wine, culture, and philosophy.

Formally founded at a Paris gathering in 1989, the Arcigola Slow Food Movement has become an international rallying point for the inevitable back-lash against societal velocity and homogenized, industrial grub. Members meet for marathon meals and talk food, wine, culture, and philosophy. They organize wine tastings and classes about traditional cuisine. And they disdain the stressful fast life.

"Fast food is killing off the social aspect of food," Petrini says. "It strips people of their food wealth and culture."

The non-profit movement now boasts 65,000 members in 45 countries organized into 560 local convivia. These convivia, or chapters, as they are sometimes called, are the linchpins of the Slow Food Movement, interpret-ing and representing its philosophy at a local level. Convivia members meet informally to learn about culinary traditions and culture, to arrange tastings, and of course to enjoy together the pleasures of slow eating and drinking. But they are also instrumental in the promotion of small, local producers. The USA office opened in New York in 2000. The snail, Slow Food's logo — slow, but delectable — moves faster than one might imagine.

Petrini has never heard any reaction to the movement from McDonald's or any other of the stopwatch chains. He says a McDonald's representative failed to show up for a debate arranged by a Paris radio station. Brad Trask, spokesman at McDonald's worldwide headquarters in Oak Brook, Illinois, says he is not familiar with the slow food movement. "But," he adds, "I don't think we'd want to go into any location and take away their food culture. We don't exactly go where we're not wanted."

Slow food is primarily a state of mind.

Slow food, however, is primarily a state of mind, and Petrini is careful to point out that members are not gastronomic elitists. "Even eating a sandwich," Petrini says, "can be a slow-food experience." Besides, "you can be rich and eat badly ... and you don't have to eat luxury foods every day."

But the Slow Food Movement is about more than eating, though, to be sure, its members do plenty of that. It organizes numerous gastronomic events around the world every year as part of its global offensive, the most famous of these being the annual Salone del Gusto, staged in recent years in Turin. It is a remarkable taste extravaganza and the largest market exhibition of quality food and wine. At the last of these, every inch of floor space in Turin's former Fiat factory was crowded with cheeses, wines, and truffle-scented chocolates. Food workshops, tastings, and seminars attest to the seriousness with which the gourmet world approaches the business of taste education.

A section of the hall is reserved for products from the Arc of Taste, a symbolic ship loaded with foods threatened by industrial standardization and hyperhygienist legislation. These products, among them such delicacies as mullet roe and Moselle red peaches, Corbara plum tomatoes and violino di capra, are victims of a modern agrofood industry that produces cheap food at high cost to the environment. This, then, is the confluence of the movement's stakes in food appreciation, environmental consciousness, and the protection of those artisans using traditional manufacturing techniques — yet another threatened species. Slow Food desires not only to salvage almost obsolete flavors from the relentless flood of synthetic, homogenized food stuffs, but also to promote the small-scale specialist food producers — the natural stewards of biodiversity. And it achieves all this through the tastebuds.

**A jury panel selects specialist producers
deemed to have preserved or rediscovered
ancient tastes and production methods.**

The success of these festivals is certainly a victory for distinctive regional cuisine and traditions, but the movement also recognizes and rewards the individual. A distinguished jury panel of some 400 cooks, writers, and food activists from around the world is invited to select five winners from a short-list of specialist producers deemed to have preserved or rediscovered ancient tastes and production methods. This has rapidly become the Nobel Prize of the gastronomic world. One popular winner, Turkish beekeeper Veli Gulas, makes his distinctive honey in the trunks of trees in a remote forest above the Black Sea. Before the Slow Food festival, he had never left his homeland, and, he had to walk for more than a day from his village to get a passport.

A further mark of the movement's resistance to the increasingly aggressive advance of food and cultural standardization is its commitment to educating children in the pleasures of the table. There are tasting sessions for children at every Slow Food festival, while Slow Food has collaborated with teachers in schools to educate children on the importance of the senses as a tool of knowledge. Slow Food is also planning two new adult education projects: the Master of Food and the European Academy of Taste, part of the Pollenzo Agency project. The Master of Food, or the Popular University of Taste, as it is known, proposes a study syllabus that covers subjects ranging from wines to cooking techniques, from cheese to olive oil. The courses will take place throughout Italy in conjunction with the network of convivia. Despite its name, it is clear that the Slow Food Movement's growth continues apace.

→ *The Slow Food Movement can be contacted by snail mail at Slow Food, Via della Mendicita Istruita, 14, 12042 Bra (CN) Italy (Phone: Int.+39[0]172 41 96 11; Fax: Int.+44 [0]172 42 12 93; E-mail: international@slowfood.com; Web: www.slowfood.it/).*

Small prisons are calmer

JOHN PAPWORTH
Summarized from a letter in the *London Times*.

THE *LONDON TIMES* REPORTED THAT 24 PRISONERS IN THE CELLS of a Doncaster police station were serving their sentences "in an atmosphere free of the tension and the harsh conditions of a conventional prison," prisoners and officers were on first-name terms, and officials visiting the unit were "astonished by the transformation of attitude and the peaceful mixing of what would normally [sic!] become a critical mass." The *Times* report concluded that it would have been impossible to apply these conditions to the 1,600 locked in Strangeways prison when the place exploded in violence.

They were quickly able to restore conditions not by appealing to the goodwill of the prisoners but by cutting their groups into smaller and more manageable units.

Well, of course. But why then is Strangeways being rebuilt? Do we really learn from history that we learn nothing from history? More than 30 years ago Professor Leopold Kohr, in his book *The Breakdown of Nations* (published by Green Books), pointed out that after years of trouble in the overcrowded Korean prison camps, it began to dawn on the authorities that "the cause of difficulty was not the incorrigible nature of the communists but the size [my emphasis] of the compounds containing them. Once this was recognized, they were quickly able to restore conditions, not by appealing to the goodwill of the prisoners but by cutting their groups into smaller and more manageable units."

Of course small units cost more to run, but we surely need to ask ourselves whether we want prisoners released back into society after serving a sentence during which they have been treated with humanity, or after years of brutalization in such hellholes as Strangeways? It is surely rather late in the day to discover that far from serving the purpose for which our prisons exist, they are defeating it.

→ *John Papworth, Editor,* **Fourth World Review,** *The Close, 26 High St, Purton, Wiltshire SN5 4AE, UK (Phone: Int.+44 [0]1793 77221; Fax: 01793 772521).*

The example of the Dutch
Summarized from an article in the *Economist* entitled "Keeping sex offenders safe."

The Dutch experience none of the problems with violence and discontent associated with overcrowded, massive prisons in the UK and the United States. They lock up a third as many people, relative to population, as Britain, and keep them in small units of 12 to 20 people. Each unit has its own staff, which gets to know a group of inmates and can tell when tension is rising.

The costs of this kind of arrangement are inevitably high, but the indications are that money spent here is saved in other areas of penal finance. For instance, the Home Office has recently complained about the high cost of "Rule 43" provisions, which segregate sex offenders into parallel facilities for their own protection. In the Dutch system, there is no need for such arrangements as tensions between prisoners can be so well-monitored in their units.

This kind of integration in smaller units has been shown to work in at least one UK prison, Littlehey, where morale — unusually for a British jail — is reported to be high.

Smart Cars —
A proposal for a radically new transport system
NICHOLAS SAUNDERS

NEARLY EVERYONE NOW AGREES THAT PRIVATE CARS ARE NOT THE ANSWER to transport needs of the future because they are extravagant on fuel, cause enormous pollution, and are dangerous. Instead, it is being suggested, we should use buses and trains.

First, I want to convince the reader that people will not switch to buses and trains, whether monorail or "bullet." The reason is that people are basically selfish and will only change to something that suits them better. Private cars take some beating — always ready to take you anywhere, whenever you want, right from your door to your destination, with your personal comforts, such as sounds and privacy and almost complete security from the outside world. It is clear that most people who can afford a car will not give it up voluntarily in favor of efficient and cheap public transport, as can be seen in countries such as France. Forcing people to give up their cars, or taxing them off the roads, will never be politically popular, although such measures may have to be adopted in the short term. The long-term answer is to provide something better — not as perceived by the worthy few, but by ordinary, selfish people.

A pollution-free and noise-free transport system that is within our reach.

Second, I want to show that there are alternatives to buses and trains. For instance, a friend suggested converting surplus cruise missiles to person carriers — they can already take off and find their way to the destination, avoiding other aircraft and obstacles, so all they need to be taught is how to land! I won't stick my neck out to promote that, but at least it moves us in the right direction: forward. In fact, technology has opened up the way to enormous untapped choices for future transport systems that have so far been largely ignored. Sadly, few people have the imagination to visualize anything other than a modification of what they have already experienced, and fewer still have the ability to assess which fantasies are practical.

Thirdly, I am going to describe my own realizable vision. This is not an invention, as it is based on bits of existing technology; nor is it a system ready to be built, as it would take a great deal of development. It is merely an example of a pollution-free and noise-free transport system that is within our reach.

The system would consist of a network of tubes about 6.5 feet (two meters) in diameter in which the cars, about the size of the back of a London taxi, would run underground or aboveground (depending on whether the increased cost would be justified by the environmental savings). Links up to about 200 miles per hour could follow ground tracks like roads and railways, but very high-speed links would require specially straight tracks, probably suspended aboveground like a suspension bridge. Windows in the tubes would allow the traveler to see out. The speed would be controlled by the track; it would be decided by the designers and fixed for every point on the track, enabling cars to run very close together without bumping into each other. This raises a safety issue in traditional engineering terms: the stopping distance between cars in an emergency. The answer is that you don't need a stopping distance between cars any more than you do between the carriages of a train, because each car is magnetically locked into a slot, like being hooked onto a moving chain. But what if the current fails? The cars fit the tube closely so that the air between them moves at the same speed and would act like springs preventing them from crashing together. This is proven safety technology from lifts.

The cars would be suspended by magnetism, providing a smooth and silent ride.

The cars would have no engines or even wheels — instead the track would provide the propulsion, using electricity, by means of built-in linear induction and linear synchronous motors. The cars would be suspended by magnetism, providing a smooth and silent ride. The overall effect would be to make the cars cheap but the track expensive. (The Germans and Japanese have trial high-speed trains using similar technology.)

I envisage stations being at about the same spacing as bus stops are at present, though as prosperity grew, people might afford their own. And I hope that each station would be operated by staff able to offer assistance if required; to deliver mail and goods to homes; and to hire out trolleys and low-speed electric cars. In fact, I have a much broader vision in which these stations become the new local social centers because everyone passes through them, and they could also become the base units of the political system.

The car would be routed through the network in much the same way as a telephone call.

To make a journey, passengers would go to the nearest station, where there would always be at least one car waiting. The passenger would get in, insert a credit-type card, dial the destination, and the car would be routed through the network in much the same way as a telephone call. Once on a journey, the traveler could stop at a service area just like on a highway.

At junctions, tracks would run adjacent and at the same speed, analogous to on-ramps on a highway. Between the two running tracks there would be an intermediate transfer track. Cars changing track would transfer straight across if there were a slot available immediately adjacent, or accelerate on the transfer track to an empty slot. With correct programming there would always be a slot reserved, because congestion would be predicted and cars diverted, just as happens with telephone calls. As a further fail-safe feature, each track would form a complete loop, so that if a car did not leave a track for any reason, it would be able to carry on round.

At each station, which would have its own loop of track, cars would come up like lifts to a small shop-front-style station at street level. They would pass through a detector that would check them for weight and damage (and possibly even scan them for explosives) before they were allowed to leave the station's loop and return to the main track. Anyone finding a car dirty or vandalized would dial in a code that would send it to a depot — where it could be repaired and the previous user traced via the fare card. Additional detectors would check cars running on the tracks and divert those that were untrackworthy. Similarly, specially equipped cars would constantly monitor the state of the track.

In country areas, where the nearest station may be several miles away, people would still use road cars.

In country areas, where the nearest station may be several miles away, people would still use road cars to get to the station and to make local journeys. However, as these journeys would be short, I envisage that it would eventually be acceptable to allow only battery-driven electric cars — slow, safe, and unable to travel far without recharging.

Empty cars would return to the track. While every station would have at least one waiting, there would be more diverted to particular areas to deal with rush hours, etc. Like any system, this one would have limited capacity too, but that could be increased by adding new tracks, stations, and high-speed links.

Goods would be carried in much the same way. A goods car would carry a normal forklift pallet load up to about a ton. Special cars could be called for longer loads, and some (such as tankers) would be privately owned. Every factory and warehouse would have its own station, and the staff at public stations would be able to deliver goods locally. Although this would require far more vehicles to carry the same goods as a truck does now, the environmental impact would be less than at present because a high-speed six-foot tube could carry more than a 12-foot highway lane. There would be an enormous economic advantage for business, as both people and goods could be expected to arrive within an hour or so of being dispatched. Not only would the saving of time spent traveling save money, but there would also be a vast saving in distribution depots, warehousing, and handling of goods. For example, a manufacturer of cookies could dispatch direct to each supermarket, while a washing machine chosen from a showroom could be delivered direct from the factory by the time the customer got home.

The invaluable saving in road accidents and casualties is another major advantage of the system.

The environmental advantages of such a system over road transport would be vast. Apart from the fuel and pollution aspects, very little land would be required as one six-foot tube track could carry the same amount of traffic as about 30 highway lanes, at 200 miles per hour (more at higher speeds). This compares very favorably with high-speed trains. The invaluable saving in road accidents and casualties is another major advantage of the system.

The development costs of this new system would be high, but thereafter the capital and running costs should be lower than for new highways or for aboveground or underground railway lines: the tunnels required are narrow; the cars are engineless, small, and cheap; and electricity can be produced from any energy source.

The problem with any new and potentially international system is how you begin. Suitable model trials could include extensions to existing tube lines — such as in south London — replacing suburban bus services. As more of these Smart Car tubes were built, they could be joined by fast links so as to form an independent system.

Editorial comment

Very similar concepts have been explored in Germany, France, Japan, and the US since the 1970s, with this type of personal monorail going under the name of Personal Rapid Transit (PRT).

With the advances in computer technology, highly flexible systems have been developed running small four-seaters for personal use. Each "car" allows its user to select a destination and be taken there directly, without the need to stop at other stations along the way. With only very small distances between the cars, which pull off the track when they stop at a station, allowing others to pass, PRT could, according to its proponents, easily match the carrying capacity of rail, while also attracting car users who prefer their own private space.

A PRT network is planned for Rosemont, the airport suburb of Chicago, and one test track is operating in woods outside Marlborough, Massachusetts. The latter was designed by the Raytheon Corporation, which, coincidentally, also builds Patriot missiles (see Nicholas Saunders' comment about cruise missiles above).

Michael le Page mounted the argument against PRT in the pages of *New Scientist*, where he argued that the cost of building an infrastructure for the PRT guideways would be immense. Also, the PRT threat to the dominance of cars would lead to a stern resistance from all those with a stake in maintaining the status quo, such as private car owners, car manufacturers, and multinationals.

The dual mode system, exemplified by the Danish RUF system, might point a way forward out of this dilemma. This system, devised by Palle Jensen, resembles PRT but with a major difference: vehicles have wheels as well as slots that allow them to travel on monorail, so they can ply both rails and normal roads.

Such a dual system would offer commuters the chance to drive onto a fast network of guideways in busy city-center areas and then to let the monorail take over as they are chauffeured into the city. This system would grow organically, unlike the PRT, and might even win the support of car manufacturers, who could easily switch to producing dual-mode vehicles. It will also have the added advantage of dramatically reducing road accidents, which are predicted to become the third biggest cause of death and disability by 2020.

→ *Nicholas Saunders died in a car accident in South Africa. Please send feedback to The Institute for Social Inventions, 20 Heber Road, London NW2 6AA, UK (Phone: Int.+44 [0]20 8208 2853; Fax: Int.+44 [0]20 8452 6434; E-mail: rhino@dial.pipex.com).*

→ *Jerry Schneider, professor of civil engineering and urban planning at the University of Washington, has an Innovative Transportation Technology website at <http://faculty.washington.edu/~jbs/itrans/>.*

→ *A proposal for a Non-Switch Rapid-Transit Vehicular System from Dong Yi in China can be viewed at <www.fortunecity.com/tattooine/sturgeon/281/>.*

Smart Urban Transport website

ROBERT ALCOCK

I'VE SPENT TIME IN CITIES DOMINATED BY PRIVATE AUTOMOBILES (Los Angeles) and cities where public transportation works acceptably (San Francisco, London, Dublin, Bilbao). For quality of life, I would choose the second group every time.

Unfortunately, no matter whether you're using trains, buses, trams, or funiculars, urban transport systems are generally incomprehensible, unreliable, disjointed, unresponsive, and, in a word, stupid.

What if every city had an independent website devoted to making public transport more intelligent?

Timetables for all the modes of transport linked to a database of postal addresses

---

Features would include the following:
- One-stop timetable consultation, with timetables for all the modes of transport linked to a database of postal addresses. Put in where you are and where you want to go, and you'll be told the easiest route, along with directions for getting to and from the bus or train stops at either end.
- Fully integrated information for disabled users.

- Statistics on the reliability of different routes so you would be able to calculate the likely delay on any route.
- Information about special conditions due to repairs, weather, strikes, etc.
- Message boards for travelers.

A section of the website would be devoted to organizing public transport users to lobby for improvements. It would include the following features:
- Mechanisms by which to submit and vote on suggestions for improvements.
- Polls on the best and worst services in areas such as punctuality, cleanliness, and safety.
- Results of polls sent to those in charge of public transport, with their replies.
- Links to other organizations working to improve public transport.

I'd emphasize the independent or at least autonomous nature of the proposed website, because otherwise you would tend to get the information provided in a piecemeal way that reflects organizational divisions between transport modes and companies, and without effective feedback mechanisms (since companies and governments aren't very keen on funding people to put pressure on them to improve their services!).

For instance, in Bilbao (where I live) the city government is starting to do this, with interactive maps of the city bus services available in public info kiosks.

They are also installing a tracking system for the buses (so they know where they really are, instead of where they should be!). But that's only one out of the six transport systems in this city of just one million people (metro, tram, two local bus companies, plus at least three national train systems). And naturally the systems for feedback are near to useless.

A private company should build a generic system that could be adapted to fit any city. The large number of potential users would provide advertising revenue to fund the operation of the system.

The key to smarter transport is putting all the information together in one easily accessible site.

Although many companies are working on different applications of intelligent technology for urban transport, I think the key to smarter transport is putting all the information together in one easily accessible site.

Social Enterprise Zones —
Relaxing rules for social innovations

Summarized from an article by David Robinson in the *London Guardian* entitled "Money isn't everything,"

DAVID ROBINSON PROPOSES A RELAXATION OF REGULATIONS in a specified community to allow the testing of innovative social, economic, and political arrangements. His idea has a community, self-help, no-cost focus.

> ## Zones to allow the testing of innovative social, economic, and political arrangements

Local authorities, Robinson says, should be permitted to operate Social Enterprise Zones similar to the existing Business Enterprise Zones. Rules would be relaxed to assist socially beneficial undertakings. One example he gives is that of enabling the unemployed to start up businesses using their underused skills in areas such as car maintenance by allowing them to remain on benefit until the business generates sufficient income to be a realistic proposition. Income from the business could be held in trust to form a capital fund to support its continued existence. He sees room for similar experiments in areas such as housing, schools, training, and health.

↦ *David Robinson is director of a social action center in the East End of London. He can be contacted at 105 Barking Road, London E16 4HQ, UK.*

Songs as a way of reaching a patient with Alzheimer's

Summarized from a story by John Carter in the *Wall Street Journal* entitled "Singing with Mom," monitored by Roger Knights.

JOURNALIST JOHN CARTER, LOOKING ON IN DESPERATION as his 87-year-old mother's memory seemed to disappear altogether, made the mutually consoling discovery that her ability to recall music had remained intact.

After his father died, his mother had gone into a steady decline, growing vaguer and vaguer until her short-term memory deserted her almost entirely and she no longer recognized her own son. Carter attempted to stir her memory with familiar anecdotes. Nothing seemed to work. She sensed her son's distress and then became agitated, too.

> ## To my astonishment, Mom began to sing along, singing from memory.

S

Then one day, in desperation, he brought in an old songbook that had graced his mother's piano for many years. He could remember her singing "Loch Lomond" to him as a child, and hesitantly he tried singing it now. "To my astonishment," he writes, "Mom began to sing along, reading the words above my finger, then singing from memory. Mom was ecstatic as we sang, and so was I."

During visits after that, they devoted themselves to making music, his mother singing and he playing the recorder, working through a repertoire of melodies his mother had known since she was a child.

For both mother and son, the fact that they could at least still share music was a source of deep consolation. "She'd clap her hands as we finished a song," Carter writes, "and once took my hands in hers, looked into my eyes, and said, 'I never knew there could be so much sweetness in a human relationship.'"

Speaking Circles for practicing public speaking

NICHOLAS ALBERY

A review of *Be Heard Now! How to Compel Rapt Attention Every Time You Speak* by Lee Glickstein (published by Leeway Press.)

LEE GLICKSTEIN HAS LAUNCHED A MOVEMENT CALLED SPEAKING CIRCLES to help people practice becoming public speakers, and has led over 2,000 such groups himself. He believes that any group, whether of friends, family, or business colleagues, can use the formula to create a Speaking Circle of its own.

To allow each member five minutes on stage,
with the audience giving only positive feedback afterwards,
thus creating a feeling of safety

The essence of a Speaking Circle is to limit the number of members to a maximum of ten and to allow each member five minutes on stage, with the audience giving only positive feedback afterwards, thus creating a feeling of safety and gradually repairing the damage from any earlier public traumas in life.

Here is how Speaking Circles work:

- The Circle lasts no more than two and a half hours, starting with tea or coffee.

- There is a brief introduction from whoever is facilitator, reminding participants of the ground rules. Everyone then stands up, one by one, for three minutes each, to introduce themselves and to "check in," with no feedback from others.

- Each person then gives a five-minute talk on stage.
- The facilitator raises his or her finger when 30 seconds are left.
- The audience gives the person speaking unconditional support and positive acceptance — silently during the person's talk and with only positive comments during feedback time.
- The audience members do not talk among themselves during or between speakers (laughter is of course allowed). No notes are taken. No comments are made on the content of people's talks.
- The content of talks is confidential, not to be discussed outside the Circle without specific permission.
- Feedback is limited to 30 seconds per person and should be entirely positive, describing the listener's feelings and responses, without referring to the speaker's life; without evaluating or comparing this talk with a previous talk; without turning people's attention back to the listener; and without coaching, analyzing, or advising. Here are some examples of forbidden feedback:
"That's the best talk you've ever done"
    — (comparing with a previous talk).
"You really opened up today; I finally see who you really are"
    — (again comparing with previous efforts).
"That could be a professional talk, especially if you'd ..."
    — (giving advice).
- The speaker makes no comments in response to feedback beyond saying "thank you."

All participants bring their own tape, which is used to record their talk.

- If possible, the meeting is videotaped. All participants bring their own tape, which is used to record their talk and which they can take away and appraise at home.
- The facilitator wraps up the meeting with a few words. There can then be a time for socializing.

How to be a compelling speaker

How do you find what to talk about in your five minutes? In a Speaking Circle it is perfectly permissible to remain silent for your five minutes on stage. The idea is to be yourself. If you are a nervous wreck, do not seek to hide this. But Glickstein tells his readers that meditating beforehand on the following questions may help you find a suitable subject matter:
- What has life taught you?

- What have been the turning points in your life? In what directions have you turned at these points? What have you learned?
- What secrets have you discovered?
- Who are the people who have inspired you in your life?
- When you comfort or counsel friends, what do you usually wind up talking about?
- Into which areas of life do you have particularly clear insight?
- What are you good at?
- Where do you seem to have a unique perspective?
- What obstacles have you overcome? What did you do to overcome them?

There is no list of techniques you can apply in order to be yourself on stage, but here, nevertheless, are some of Glickstein's helpful suggestions:

- Silently receive your listeners for at least a few seconds before you speak.

**Speak as if to individuals, lingering with
each person for five to ten seconds.**

- Speak as if to individuals in the audience, lingering with each person for five to ten seconds before moving on.
- Speak in short sentences, pausing frequently to connect with individuals.
- Leave longer silences between important points.
- Stand relatively still and move slightly towards individuals as you speak to them.
- Use humor based on your own experiences if you use humor at all.

**Receive applause "into your heart" rather than walking off
modestly while people are clapping.**

- Stand still and receive applause "into your heart" at the end of your talk, rather than walking off modestly while people are clapping. (In films of President Kennedy's speeches, according to Glickstein, "you can see him pausing graciously to let the crowd's love wash over him").

Glickstein also gives advice for longer speech-making in daily life, much of which is relevant to Speaking Circles too. He recommends opening your speech with a short true story from your own life — an experience that you learned from and that connects with the topic of your speech (take up to three minutes on this). Then outline in three or four sentences the major points you will cover. Now promise people in one sentence what they will get out of your talk. Make sure, either by asking or through non-verbal signals, that this prospectus is acceptable to your audience, and then launch into the body of the talk.

Open your speech with a short true story from your own life.

The talk can be designed to follow Glickstein's ARC, which stands for Awareness, Reframing, and Commitment. In the Awareness section you need to address the following questions:
- What is the problem about which you are passionate?
- Why does the problem exist?
- What efforts have been made to fix it?
- Why have these efforts failed?

Present a way of solving the problem in a new and dynamic way.

In the Reframing section you present a way of solving the problem in a new and dynamic way.

In the part on Commitment you tell the audience what specific things they can do right away to help tackle this problem in their own lives.

Each part of the ARC is best introduced with a relevant personal story.

Close the talk by telling the audience what it has been like to spend this time with them, by inviting them to contact you, or with an inspirational quotation or more of your personal story. "Your ending," writes Glickstein, "can be an opening to their relationship with your solutions and a lifetime relationship with you."

This book — and its socially innovative Speaking Circles — is not only a must for anxious public speakers, but could also help people relax and be themselves in ordinary day-to-day encounters.

➔ *Lee Glickstein can be contacted at the Center for Transformational Speaking, 450 Taraval Street #218, San Francisco CA 94116 (Phone: 800 610 0169; Web: www.usa-web.com/speakers/glickstein). A videotape,* How to Conduct Your

Own Speaking Circle, *is available for $23.38 incl. shipping and California sales tax. The book is also available from this address for $18.88 inclusive.*

→ *See also <www.speakingcircles.com/circle.htm> and <www.nsanc.org/speakers/speakerlist/glickstein.html>.*

Speed dating — Seven minutes to converse before the next

Summarized from an article by Janet I. Tu in the *Seattle Times* entitled "Hurry Up and Date," monitored by Roger Knights.

SPEED DATING, A MEETING AND CHOOSING SYSTEM, could help promote marriage while also providing those too busy to date and mingle with a way to meet people.

The speed-dating system works by giving men and women seven minutes to converse. The man then has to move to another woman. After each conversation, those taking part write a note indicating if they would like to see that person again. If each of them decides they want to see the other again, they are given each other's phone number, with the man encouraged to call the woman first.

The system is promoted and run by Jewish organizations that are keen to foster links between Jewish people wherever possible, especially as one-faith communities have continued to disappear. Speed dating, as one of its organizers, Danny Moskkowitz, says, "gives them an interesting way to meet people who happen to be Jewish, which is in the back of their minds for most Jewish kids, if not their mothers."

Each participant pays $20, and the events are organized by ten-year age groups (such as 22 to 32, and 30- to 40-year-olds). Most of those involved seem enthusiastic about the way the idea works, despite the slightly frenetic atmosphere generated by the organizers ringing a bell and shouting "Get ready! Get set! Date!" at the beginning of the evening. There is a brief half-time snippet of wisdom from the organizing rabbi, but the dating soon begins in earnest. One of the men taking part at an event in Seattle admitted that he was a bit tired by the end of it all, but he found it better than "competing with the rest of all that chatter at a party." One of the women he'd been talking to also said that the experience was more of a marathon than a sprint, but found it a simple, fun way to meet like-minded people.

Get ready! Get set! Date!

If one thinks of the system not so much as speed dating, perhaps, but as a focused dating agency with less pitfalls and no blind dates, the attraction becomes more apparent. That thousands of people have now tried it in cities all over America and in five other countries, including England and Australia, certainly seems to endorse that view.

→ *See also <http://aish.com/speeddating/default.asp> and the similar 10-minute dating at <www.meetinggame.com>.*

State Dowry — Relieving population pressure

GUY YEOMAN

Summarized from the book *Africa's Mountains of the Moon* by the late Guy Yeoman (published by Hamish Hamilton/Elm Tree Books).

THE CURRENT BENEFITS OF WESTERN FINANCIAL AID TO KENYA are largely illusory, since any increase in national wealth benefits only a small proportion of the population, while for the majority of people it is canceled by the high birthrate. Paying aid funds directly to women of childbearing age in the form of a State Dowry, as an incentive to restrict family size, is the only practicable way of *rapidly* stabilizing the population. Such a system could have substantial welfare benefits for women and children as well as enhancing women's liberation, and it is the essential first step towards a sustainable agriculture and fundamental environmental conservation.

The proposal is to be regarded as an emergency measure in the face of a crisis, to make possible the other necessary long-term measures of education and poverty reduction.

Biological cataclysm

In 1925 Norway had almost exactly the same population as Kenya. Sixty years later, Norway's population has scarcely increased by half; it is now virtually stable and Norwegians enjoy a degree of social well-being that is hardly surpassed elsewhere in the world. In the same period, Kenya's population has multiplied ten times, and in spite of all the commendable efforts of the Kenyans, no substantial impact has been made on the widespread poverty, while the country has suffered enormous environmental deterioration. Kenya and many other countries in the Third World are heading for biological cataclysm.

Pay aid funds directly to women of childbearing age.

The attempts to transplant Western birth control tactics to Africa have so far largely failed. The reason for this is the widely different ethos of African society. In a situation where the male's machismo demands children, family restriction advice addressed to men is unlikely to be heeded. If it is addressed to women, it is only likely to be effective in a form that is going to put the women in a stronger position in the face of male dominance. The problem thus becomes a question of what can be done for African women, not just to provide them with a contraceptive option but also to provide an incentive to take up this option that is stronger than the strong male pressure to ignore it.

The dowry

At present, throughout Africa, a dowry or bride-price is paid by the parents of a young man to those of a girl whom they wish their son to marry. Consequently there is great pressure to marry a girl off as early as possible, and for her to justify her "price" by becoming pregnant as soon as possible.

There is only one time in an African woman's life when she is in a position to call the shots. This is in the premarital period, when the dowry is under negotiation. I suggest that she should be offered some form of personal wealth that could, on the one hand, give her negotiating power in the choice of a husband or, on the other, finance the option of delaying or refusing marriage. The extent of such wealth and the manner of its provision would be dictated by what was found to be necessary to outweigh the existing social pressure for her to marry early.

Every woman, on reaching the age of, say, 16
without becoming pregnant, would become
eligible for a regular cash allowance.

I propose that the state, riding in a sense on the back of the traditional dowry system, should introduce a State Dowry. Under this system, every woman, on reaching the age of, say, 16 without becoming pregnant, would become eligible for a regular cash allowance. The payments would cease as soon as it was established that she was pregnant, but would resume again after a further period of non-pregnancy. There would thus be a strong incentive for her and her parents to delay marriage, and after marriage, for her and her husband to delay conception.

Uplifting the village economy

Would such a system be unacceptably expensive? One way of answering this is to say that it would effectively cost nothing. All we would be doing is altering the direction of the flow of money. At present, money flows from the West to governments or agencies, and thence through the hands of ministries and departments to contractors and managers who are all too often incompetent or corrupt, with little benefit to rural communities. This procedure, whereby multibillion-dollar sums are poured away, must be regarded as unacceptably expensive, wasteful, and demoralizing. Under the State Dowry system, the same volume of cash would go directly to peasant families through post office accounts or cooperative women's groups. For the first time, the African agriculturalist (and women are the primary agriculturalists) would be free to decide for herself how she wished to be "developed." Whether more or less wisely saved or spent (and my belief is that rural women would spend it wisely, provided they could keep it in their own hands), the money would find its way into uplifting the village economy, which is something most aid schemes signally fail to do.

For the first time, the African agriculturalist would be free to decide for herself how she wished to be developed.

No money would be wasted. Cash would only be paid out where it was successfully persuading a woman to limit her family; where the scheme failed to do this, money would not be paid out.

Dr. Raymond Crotty, of the School of Systems and Data Studies at Trinity College, Dublin, has called my attention to the similar proposal in his book *Ireland in Crisis.* His computations show that, on the basis of the current annual Western aid to the Third World, adequate funding would be available to halve the present birthrate. This would, for example, meet the recent plea of President Moi of Kenya to reduce the average Kenyan family from eight to four children.

Practicalities

Though in the early days of such a system women might find it difficult to ensure absolute control over dowry payments, the very existence of the scheme could act as a stimulus to the advance of female power and the development of women's organizations. These would eventually lead to recipients achieving a large measure of control over funds paid in their name. A possible outcome of this could be a moderation of the present oppression of women and a hardening of their attitude to such institutions as child marriage, polygamy, and female circumcision.

A system of state dowries could lead to a hardening of women's attitude to such institutions as child marriage, polygamy, and female circumcision.

Such an idea would obviously take off slowly, and cash requirements in the early days would be small. The concept could of course be pilot-tested on a scale as small as desired in order to find out the best administrative system. It is easy to point out difficulties — the solutions must be found by trial and error. A pilot scheme could also determine the size of monthly payments needed to offset the present social pressures on women to start a family early in life and to have many babies.

We would in effect be creating a child allowance system without the incentive to have children that such a system entails. The funds paid to discourage women from starting a pregnancy would in fact enhance the welfare of any existing child, or of children to come in the future. The chances of the survival of such well-spaced and well-provisioned children would be much greater than is commonly the case at present. One may note that while all societies accept the concept of paying people to do things, we in the West increasingly pay people *not* to do things. The principle has been widely used for controlling agricultural production and for encouraging conservation policies. In the final analysis we would simply be reinforcing every woman's inalienable right to say no.

The actual logistics of providing the necessary family planning services are sometimes spoken of as a stumbling block, but I do not share this view. We should get away from the idea that sophisticated clinics with highly trained staff are necessary. Village shops, free dispensing machines, and barefoot advisors could provide a service at the very simplest level. In the early days, we should not feel required to provide the near 100 percent guarantee against conception that is the norm in the West. In the early stages the widespread adoption of the male condom would be unlikely, but the recent prototype development of a female condom points the way to future possibilities.

AIDS

Any discussion of future population trends in Africa would be unrealistic if it did not take into consideration the dark shadow of AIDS that stretches across the continent as a heterosexually transmitted disease. My proposals for the dowry system should be looked at against this background. The future effect of AIDS is difficult to assess, but a recent attempt by researchers at Imperial College, London, and Princeton University concludes that it is unlikely to make any major difference to current African population forecasts for several decades to come. There is to my mind one hopeful chink of light. The only measures that can be anticipated to control the AIDS pandemic are largely the same as those that will be necessary to bring about population stabilization. AIDS will be controlled in the end by the polarization of society according to behavior patterns. On the one hand, a subculture will emerge that, because it adopts a preventive approach to sex, will be virtually "immune" to this avoidable condition. At the other pole, the disease will run its tragic course.

AIDS will be controlled in the end by the polarization of society according to behavior patterns.

It should be noted that eligibility for the State Dowry would be universal, for town dwellers as well as country folk. It could be expected that it would become a major factor in promoting safe sex and the use of the male and female condom as well as in reducing prostitution and promiscuity. African urban prostitution is a response to urban poverty, male mobility, and the widespread abandonment of wives and partners that has become a feature of the unstable new urban societies. If such women are provided with an alternative source of finance, I believe fewer of them will be forced into prostitution.

The State Dowry would become a major factor in promoting safe sex and the use of the male and female condom as well as in reducing prostitution and promiscuity.

Conclusion

All attempts to conserve the animal and plant ecosystems of Kenya will prove fruitless and the existing structure of reserves and parks will collapse, unless a sustainable agriculture and forestry (fuel supply) can be attained. The essential precursor to this is to stabilize the human and livestock populations. All agencies, whether governmental or non-governmental and whether concerned with social, agricultural, or wildlife problems, should therefore concentrate their resources and energies on this vital primary objective.

➔ *Guy Yeoman, veterinary surgeon and explorer, died on August 3, 1998, aged 78.*

➔ *The State Dowry concept received a Social Inventions Award for the best proposal to assist developing countries. This money was used to initiate a small feasibility study in Kenya.*

➔ *In the UK, Mrs. Jo Hanson has been promoting the initiative through leaflets and other work and is involved with a Gambian feasibility study. Jo Hanson, Field End, Little Street, Yoxford, Suffolk IP17 3JQ, UK (Phone: Int.+44 [0]1728 668 309).*

➔ *Raymond Crotty, School of Systems and Data Studies, University of Dublin, Trinity College, Dublin 2, Ireland (Phone: Int.+353 [0]1772941). Crotty's piece on population stabilization appears in his book* **Ireland in Crisis** *(published by Brandon).*

Stopping smoking by betting with a friend

ERIC SCIGLIANO

Here is a good way to stop smoking. Summarized from "Still living without Camels" by Eric Scigliano, published in the *Seattle Weekly*, monitored by Roger Knights.

I NEEDED SOME IRRESISTIBLE INDUCEMENT, NOT TO QUIT SMOKING but to refuse any chance to smoke. The inspiration hit as my father and I drove back from a movie. "I'll bet you $300 you smoke again before I do," I blurted out. He understood immediately and agreed. We've been clean ever since — I don't expect to ever meet a cigarette worth $300.

Straw bale dwellings

Summarized from an article by Becky Kemery entitled "Christina's House: Earthship and Straw Bale in Taos, New Mexico," in *Alternatives for Cultural Creativity* (on the web at <www.alternativesmagazine.com/16/kemery.html>).

THE CONSTRUCTION OF STRAW BALE HOUSING MAY NOT BE A NEW CONCEPT — the techniques were used well over a century ago by early settlers, whose lack of conventional building materials led them to improvise shelters from immediately available resources. After the 1930s such houses were rarely built, but the surprisingly durable structures — 14 of the originals still stand — provided inspiration in the 1970s for a worldwide resurgence of interest in the approach.

> The construction and the operation of buildings
> consume more materials and energy than
> any other activity in the United States.

In the 1990s the Navajo Nation initiated a program of straw bale construction to address housing shortages on a reservation, and it has gained new acceptance in the American southwest. At a time when, according to the Center for Resourceful Building Technology, the construction and the operation of buildings consume more materials and energy than any other single activity in the United States, the need for sustainable, energy-efficient dwellings has never been more pressing.

> Earth-filled tires make up the exterior walls, while water-
> encased pop cans and glass bottles are used the interior walls.

Christina Sporrong, a 26-year-old who moved from Seattle to Taos, New Mexico, went to work for local architect and builder Mike Reynolds, whose buildings, known as Earthships, combine tires and pop cans to stunning effect. Earth-filled tires make up the exterior walls, while mortar-encased pop cans and glass bottles are used for interior walls.

Christina purchased a quarter acre for $500 and began to design a house she could build in one summer with the help of friends, one that combined the Earthship design with straw bale construction. First, in early spring she staked out her house and then collected tires from a local land-fill. Each tire had to be filled with earth and then stamped down with a sledgehammer — an arduous, labor-intensive job. Christina took a job wait-ressing so that she could continue building during the day, but still depend-ed on assistance from friends. Between them they poured eight yards of con-crete in one day to form the footings for the straw bale walls; then she gath-ered material for the posts and beams, including posts recycled from an old feed store. Only when the tire walls were completed could she focus in earnest on the straw bale construction.

The straw she purchased from a feed store. "You only want to buy the bales when you're ready to put them up so you don't risk getting moisture on them," Christina points out. The bales were stacked in offset rows like huge bricks inside the post-and-beam framework of the house. Rebar was driven down through the walls and then covered in chicken wire. "My bales were so uneven that, after the initial plastering, my place looked like a smurf house," she laughs.

Using only a quarter of the straw available each year in North America, we could build over 3 million houses.

Alternative construction may be more labor-intensive, but Christina believes it's worth it: "Sustainable building expresses a different set of values, using materials that at some level are friendly to the environment." Both tires and straw meet this standard, the latter available in abundance. Indeed, the authors of *Build it with Bales* provide an ambitious perspective: "Using only one quarter of the straw available each year in North America, we could build over 3 million houses with an interior square footage of 1,500 square feet."

➔ *An information pack on straw bale building and on workshops can be obtained for £1 from Barbara Jones, Amazon Nails, 554 Burnley Road, Todmorden, OL14 8JF, UK (Phone: Int.+44 [0]1706 814696).*

➔ *See* Straw Bale Building: How to Plan, Design, & Build with Straw, *(New Society Publishers, 2000).*

➔ *The Straw Bale Association of Texas, 3102 Breeze Terrace, Austin, Texas TX 78722 (Phone: 512 499 0526, voice mail).*

↳ On the web, see <www.greeenbuilder.com/sourcebook/strawbale.html>; for workshops, lectures, and seminars on straw bale building, see <www.ironstraw.com>; and for details of the first straw bale building in the UK, check out <www.globalideasnabk.org/diyfut/DIY-36.HTML>.

Subtitling TV songs for mass literacy

BRIJ KOTHARI
The following is adapted from an e-mail to the Global Ideas Bank.

SAME LANGUAGE SUBTITLING (SLS) OF FILM SONGS is an extremely simple and ridiculously economical concept that capitalizes on the powerful conjunction of music and television to infuse everyday entertainment with reading practice. In Same Language Subtitling, the lyrics of songs shown on television appear as subtitles in the same language as the audio.

This simplest of additions to popularly watched song programs in every state and every language could contribute to colossal gains in the literacy levels of millions of Indians. Even those we consider literate have abysmally low literacy levels presently. Yet television increasingly commands an overwhelming share of media presence in the average Indian household. The dominance of television is matched in programming only by the insatiable appetite for film-based entertainment.

Gujarat Experience

Same Language Subtitling is more than just an idea with potential. Gujarat is the first and so far only state where it has become a reality, thanks to the efforts of three collaborating institutions in Ahmedabad: the Indian Institute of Management (Ravi J. Matthai Centre for Educational Innovation or RJM-CEI), ISRO (Development and Educational Communication Unit or DECU), and Doordarshan Kendra (State TV for Gujarat).

Since May 1999, the weekly telecasts of *Chitrageet* — a program of Gujarati film songs — have been subtitled in Gujarati. The subtitled words change color to exactly match the audio, making it easy for neo-literates to follow along with the song. Over 2,000 postcards received from literate and neo-literate viewers alike have almost unanimously been in favor of subtitling. Generally, people enjoy Same Language Subtitling because it helps them to sing along, to get to know the song lyrics and even to write down parts of the song. Due to the complementary effect of sound and subtitles, many claim to "hear" the songs better. "A partially deaf member in my family started dancing while watching this program," wrote Rameshbhai Naik, a painter from Kadi village in Mehsana district.

The subtitled words change color to exactly match the audio.

The power of Same Language Subtitling lies in the fact that it is covertly educational. On the surface it enhances the entertainment value of popular song programs and simultaneously makes reading practice an incidental, automatic, and subconscious process. Same Language Subtitling weaves life-long literacy transactions in a home environment at a ridiculously low cost per person, compared with what the National Literacy Mission and individual states are spending on literacy.

Currently in Gujarat the combined Centre and state expenditure is approximately US $2 per neo-literate per annum. Less than five percent of the neo-literate population is covered. With Same Language Subtitling of one weekly episode of *Chitrageet*, at least 25 percent of the neo-literates (3.5 million people) can get 30 minutes of reading practice per week for one year. For Gujarat, the yearly cost of Same Language Subtitling comes to less than one cent per person.

The economics of Same Language Subtitling become even more attractive in states with larger populations. In the Hindi belt (Bihar, Madhya Pradesh, Rajasthan, Uttar Pradesh, and Himachal Pradesh), which accounts for almost half of the country's illiterates and neo-literates, Same Language Subtitling of one weekly episode of *Chitrahaar* would give weekly reading practice to over 120 million neo-literates at a lowly US $ 0.0001 per person per annum.

Same Language Subtitling's everyday presence on television makes it a lifelong strategy with a regular and incremental impact on the reading skills of millions, without compromising entertainment.

Same Language Subtitling — Popular and effective

Indications of the enormous potential of Same Language Subtitling for promoting state and national reading skill improvements were obtained from a sustained three-month experiment with children in a government primary school in Ahmedabad. Reading improvement was measured and found to be greater among children who saw subtitled song programs than among those who saw the same programs without subtitles.

The target viewership of Same Language Subtitling on television is broad. It includes school-going children who can get out-of-school reinforcement, school drop-outs who can relearn eroded skills, and millions of adults who enthusiastically pick up basic skills under the literacy campaigns but have had few opportunities or perhaps lacked personal motivation to engage in regular practice. A major advantage of Same Language Subtitling is that it invites reading without depending on personal motivation for literacy practice.

> Same Language Subtitling is dependent on an
> interest in film songs — and here the passion of
> one billion Indians is unquestionable.

If Same Language Subtitling is dependent on anything, then on an interest in film songs — and here the passion of one billion Indians is unquestionable. Now it is up to media and education policy makers in different states, and at the Centre, to allow this simple and low-cost tool to succeed.

Same Language Subtitling can use the idiot box to improve the quality of life of millions of neo-literates.

→ *Brij Kothari, professor, Indian Institute of Management, Ravi J. Matthai Centre for Educational Innovation, Wing 14, Vastrapur, Ahmedabad-380015, Gujarat, India (Phone: Int.+91 [0]79 6307241, ext 4938; Fax: Int.+91 [0]79 6306896; E-mail: brij@iimahd.ernet.in and brijkot@hotmail.com).*

Sunken walls round jails

Nicholas Saunders

A modern high-security jail in Denmark (near Ringe in Fun) has a sunken wall in a ditch (further protected electronically), which allows the prisoners to see out into open countryside and so not feel as enclosed. The prisoners are divided into small mixed households (although there are ten times as many men as women). Each household does its own cooking and washing up and does its shopping from its own budget in the prison supermarket. The prison has its own factory.

Is it not time for other prison services to move into the 21st century?

→ *Nicholas Saunders died in a car accident in South Africa. Please send feedback to The Institute for Social Inventions, 20 Heber Road, London NW2 6AA, UK (Phone: Int.+44 [0]20 8208 2853; Fax: Int.+44 [0]20 8452 6434; E-mail: rhino@dial.pipex.com).*

T

Ten commandments for extra-planetary travelers

Nicholas Albery

What an unsavory character Christopher Columbus was, at least as described by Kirkpatrick Sale in *The Conquest of Paradise: Christopher Columbus and the Columbian Legacy* (published by Hodder and Stoughton). And the Europe from which he came was itself "petty, racist, morbid, disillusioned, violent and arrogant."

Columbus landed on an island in the Antilles inhabited by the Taino people and proceeded to enslave them, with "unchecked Spanish ruffians embarking on daily raids of rape, pillage, robbery and murder." In 1500 a second expedition arrived and, seeing the ravages Columbus had allowed, sent him home in chains. The devastation continued, however. Within a generation the Taino were driven from their islands; within a century they were almost extinct.

And yet these were the people Columbus had described on his first landfall as "so affectionate, they have so little greed ... and there is in my opinion no better people and no better land in the world. They love their neighbors as themselves, and their way of speaking is the sweetest in the world, always gentle and smiling. Both men and women go naked as their mothers bore them; but ... their behavior to one another is very good and their king keeps marvellous state, yet with a certain kind of modesty that is a pleasure to behold, as is everything else here."

During the next century the Spanish from the Old World were responsible for the deaths of upwards of 15 million of the New Worlders. Paradise had been expelled.

What lessons can be learned from Columbus's errors?

This tragic incursion set me thinking. One day our race, if it survives, may feel its destiny is to leave the solar system before our sun expires and to go in search of other habitable solar systems. What lessons can be learned from Columbus's errors? For the crew setting off for Alpha Centauri, what Ten Commandments would be appropriate? Here is my version:

For the crew setting off for Alpha Centauri, what Ten Commandments would be appropriate?

1. Thou shalt not travel beyond thine own solar system without first studying the history of previous explorers and of their tragic impact on the beings they encountered.
2. Thou shalt not assume that human culture is superior or treat intelligent beings from other solar systems as less than human, for that way lies genocide.
3. Thou shalt eat as low down the IQ chain as possible, in case thou ever needst a moral argument to persuade more intelligent beings from other planets not to eat thyself.
4. Thou shalt approach other species as if thou wert a mass of infections and a bearer of plagues.
5. Thou shalt have ecologists who respect ecological diversity in charge of thine explorations.
6. Thou shalt take minimal action on arrival, simply observing the ways and rituals of the inhabitants and staying permanently hidden if there is any danger of thy culture overwhelming theirs.
7. Thou shalt have no sexual intercourse with other species.
8. Thou shalt leave any planet visited in at least as good a condition as when thou hast arrived.

Thou shalt leave any planet visited in at least as good a condition as when thou hast arrived.

---

9. Thou shalt take up as small and unobtrusive a space as possible on any planet where thou stayst long-term, and thou shalt go away if not made welcome, whether at the outset or at any time thereafter.
10. Thou shalt not take advantage of the innocence or naivety of any extra-terrestrial beings.

→*Please send feedback to The Institute for Social Inventions, 20 Heber Road, London NW2 6AA, UK (Phone: Int.+44 [0]20 8208 853; Fax: Int.+44 [0]20 8452 6434, E-mail: rhino@dial.pipex.com).*

→ The Conquest of Paradise – Christopher Columbus and the Columbian Legacy, *by Kirkpatrick Sale (published by Hodder and Stoughton).*

Ten principles of scale

NICHOLAS ALBERY

MANY PEOPLE ARE PESSIMISTIC ABOUT THE FUTURE, believing that the established "political-industrial-military complex" cannot and will not allow the radical decentralization and ecological transformations required. The reasoning is hard to fault, and there may well be only an outside chance of peaceful change happening in time. It is as if a miracle were needed. And yet it is not irrational to expect a miracle: today's society would seem magically (if insanely) transformed to a past citizen dragged instantly 200, 100, or even 50 years forward into our present. The future is almost bound to be weirder than we can imagine, rather than being a straightforward continuation of present trends — and today's seemingly puny David-versus-Goliath-style efforts may well turn out to have had a catalytic and positive effect.

One such effort is that of the Fourth World movement for "small nations, small communities, and a human scale," whose long-term strategy for change seems not only desirable but also just conceivably feasible.

A long-term strategy for change

(A) There would need to be a widespread and well-funded education and publicity campaign by the Greens, the Fourth World movement, and others to show how Schumacher's "Small is Beautiful" ideas can be applied to the political system — for instance, making sure that no politician or student of politics is unaware of the ten Principles of Scale drawn up by Professor Leopold Kohr and Kirkpatrick Sale. I would like to see these principles published as a poster. They read as follows:

The Principles of Scale

1. *The Beanstalk Principle:* For every animal, object, institution, or system, there is an optimal limit beyond which it ought not to grow.

2. *The Law of Peripheral Neglect:* Governmental concern, like marital fidelity or gravitational pull, diminishes with the square of the distance.

The Law of Peripheral Neglect: Governmental concern,
like marital fidelity or gravitational pull,
diminishes with the square of the distance.

---

3. *The Law of Government Size:* Ethnic and social misery increases in direct proportion to the size and power of the central government of a nation or state.

4. *Lucca's Law:* Other things being equal, territories will be richer when small and independent than when large and dependent.

5. *The Principle of Limits:* Social problems tend to grow at a geometric rate, while the ability of humans to deal with them, if it can be extended at all, grows only at an arithmetic rate.

6. *The Population Principle:* As the size of a population doubles, its complexity — the amount of information exchanged and decisions required — quadruples, with consequent increases in stress and dislocation and mechanisms of social control.

7. *The Velocity Theory of Population* ("Slow is Beautiful"): The mass of a population increases not only numerically, through birth, but through increases in the velocity with which it moves.

8. *The Self-Reliance Principle:* Highly self-reliant local communities are less likely to get involved in large-scale violence than those whose existence depends on worldwide systems of trade.

9. *The Principles of Warfare:* (a) The severity of war always increases with an increase in state power; (b) War centralizes the state by providing an excuse for an increased state power and the means by which to achieve it.

10. *The Law of Critical Power:* Critical power is the volume of power that gives a country's leaders reason to believe that they cannot be checked by the power available to any antagonist or combination of antagonists. Its accumulation is the inevitable cause of war.

To which I suppose could be added an eleventh principle, modestly entitled: *Albery's Law of Inevitability:* High-technology superpowers are inherently unstable and their fragmentation is inevitable within a relatively short time span. The main variable is the violence with which this transformation occurs. (Thus a return to a human scale is guaranteed, even if, at worst, it is a nightmare world of radiated tribes eking out a post-nuclear existence.)

The breakdown of nations

The education campaign would also focus on two main practical policies for achieving a politics of the human scale, both derived from Leopold Kohr's work:

- No nation or federation should have more than about 12 million inhabitants.
- Within the nation there needs to be a Swiss-style non-centralized structure, with villages and neighborhoods having as much autonomy as possible within a federation of cantons or counties.

The neighborhood

(B) Greens or others with policies of this nature would need not only to present them at national election time but also, as is already beginning to happen, to focus on putting human-scale ideas into practice at the local neighborhood, municipality, and county levels — in movements for creating smaller schools, locally controlled banks and credit unions, barter currencies, and the like, so that if and when a break-up of the centralized nation state occurs, local people are as experienced as possible in running their own affairs.

National elections

(C) In the UK, for instance, Greens and others could campaign at national elections on a platform of dividing the UK into half a dozen independent nation states. It took the Labour Party less than 50 years from its founding to be elected, despite the UK's lack of proportional representation. It may well take a Greenish party less time, as civilization continues its downward rush with more events of Chernobylian proportions. And given that their first act on being elected would be to honor their manifesto commitment to divide the UK into independent nations, the obstructive power of civil servants to carry on the same old policies would be much reduced.

Multinationals

(D) Taxation would need to be altered to make it advantageous for multinational and large companies to divide gradually into independently run units, with incentives for companies to become as small in size as their particular industry allows.

Superpower size reductions

(E) At the international level, there would have to be negotiations for multilateral and balanced reductions in bloc size — with Russia, China, India, and other megastates giving independence to their constituent parts at the same rate as the USA gives independence to its states and the EC to its member countries.

Russia, China, India, and other megastates would give
independence to their constituent parts.

The first step

But the first step would have to be a widespread educational debate and campaign, on the lines of the influential campaign for a Swiss-style constitution in South Africa run by the Groundswell group there. Human-scale policies would be implemented readily enough once the underlying Kohr philosophy were taken to heart. As Kohr put it:

'The young people of today have yet to grasp that the unprecedented change that has overtaken our time concerns not the *nature* of our social difficulties, but their *scale*.

As in a uranium bomb, our very compactness
will lead to the explosion we try to avert.

The real conflict of today is between Man and Mass, the Individual and Society, the Citizen and the State, the Big and the Small Community, between David and Goliath ... And the more united we become, the closer we get to the critical mass and density at which, as in a uranium bomb, our very compactness will lead to the explosion we try to avert.

➔ *Please send feedback to The Institute for Social Inventions, 20 Heber Road, London NW2 6AA, UK (Phone: Int.+44 [0]20 8208 2853; Fax: Int.+44 [0]20 8452 6434, E-mail: rhino@dial.pipex.com).*

➔ *Human Scale by Kirkpatrick Sale is a 559-page book (published by Secker and Warburg).*

➔ *A subscription to the* Fourth World Review, *which covers these issues, costs £20 from* Fourth World Review, *The Close, 26 High St, Purton, Wiltshire SN5 4AE, UK (Phone: Int.+44 [0]1793 77221; Fax: 01793 772521).*

Three ideas each for every meeting

Summarized from an article by Martin Edelston in the American magazine *Boardroom Reports* entitled "What business schools should have been teaching all along," monitored by Charles Clarke.

PETER DRUCKER ASKED, WHEN WE WERE TOGETHER A FEW YEARS AGO, "How are the meetings at your company?"

"Frankly," I answered, "they're pretty bad — but meetings at all companies are."

Have everyone who comes to the meeting prepared
to give two ideas for making their own work or
their department's work more productive.

"Try this," he suggested. "Have everyone who comes to the meeting prepared to give two ideas for making their own work or their department's work more productive — or ideas for helping the company as a whole."

We started out simply, even a little clumsily, right after my meeting with Dr. Drucker. When I sent out the agenda for a meeting that I would chair, I put down as item number one: "Three ideas from each person about improving work, saving money, or making money."

Dr. Drucker had suggested two, but the drive for continuing improvement provided a quick 50 percent productivity increase.

I had a big gong and a huge hunter's horn to salute the ideas as they were put forward.

I expected most of our team at the first few meetings to be wary, unsure, or shy about their suggestions. So I turned up at the meetings with a stack of dollar bills and handfuls of candy to hand out. And I had a big gong and a huge hunter's horn to salute the ideas as they were put forward. One strike of the gong was for a $1 idea, two strikes tolled for a $2 idea. Honks of the hunter's horn were for weak ideas — which were rewarded with candy. The honking didn't work because it raised negative feelings, so now I use the gong and horn interchangeably. I also award at least $1 for each idea. That modest amount helps to create a bright, positive atmosphere.

As it became clear to all that ideas were welcomed with enthusiasm, the sterility of the typical meeting format disappeared. We still had our presentations, reports, and comments, too — and it all gave way to an extraordinary flow of accomplishments.

Boardroom is now saving hundreds of thousands of dollars as a result of ideas generated by the people who work here. And the company has laid the foundation of much, much greater growth in the future.

To keep improvement a continuous process here at *Boardroom,* we pay a great deal of attention to details.

First, we take all ideas seriously and don't lose track of them. Department heads are requested to ask for ideas at their own meetings. And we hold special lunches with groups of team members regularly, where the only subject on the agenda is coming up with ideas to improve a particular publication or company function. At every meeting, someone is assigned to take down each specific idea. We've also put a big top hat, marked I-Power, at a central spot in our main office, where people can drop in their suggestions.

We put every idea from every source on yellow post-its. That keeps the idea focused and the words simple. It also enables us to put six post-it ideas on a sheet of paper and to photocopy it. Each Friday, I take a folder of such sheets home, review each idea, and rank them with an A, B, or C. (Or I jot down a question, ask for more information, or note that the idea doesn't seem appropriate to work on right now.)

The essential second part of the I-Power program is feedback and reward. Everyone who submits an idea gets a response.

The team members who submit ideas that will not be acted on right away get handwritten notes of thanks for making a contribution. Some action is taken on every feasible idea.

Each week we issue a report to all on the many suggestions that have been integrated into our operations. No idea is lost. We carefully keep a "Pending File" with notes on who is working on the idea, what progress is being made, what obstacles are turning up — until the idea becomes an accomplishment. Each month we distribute a report listing all the ideas accepted that month and the name of the person who submitted them.

- Every A idea earns $10.
- The person with the highest number of A ideas in a month gets an additional $50.
- The best idea each month, selected by a committee of three managers, earns the winner two tickets to a show or concert.
- In the case of a big money-saver idea, we also make a special cash award.

It now takes us about 220 hours a week just to keep track of this flow of creative ideas and sound thinking about the work we do here at *Boardroom*, with no sign that the flow is drying up.

→ *Martin Edelston, I-Power seminars, 55 Railroad Avenue, Greenwich, Connecticut 06836, (Phone: 203 625 5920).*

Toddlers rewarded with stickers and caps for good eating

Summarized from an article by Sharon Maxwell Magnus in the *London Guardian* entitled "Hey dude! Eat up your food."

PROFESSOR FERGUS LOWE AND COLLEAGUES AT THE UNIVERSITY OF BANGOR, in a six-year program with 100 children, have found a method that has young children (aged two to seven) asking for fruit and vegetables in preference to sweets.

A video showing the Food Dudes (slightly older children) fighting the evil Junk Food Junta and gobbling down their fruit and vegetables had little effect on its own. But when the children were rewarded with Food Dude stickers and caps for trying "good" foods, the consumption of fruit and vegetables rose by 100 percent.

The researchers found that the key was getting the children to taste the food. The more often the children tried a particular food, the better the chance of it becoming part of their regular diet.

The researchers also believe that this program removes pressure on parents, who are often the ones trying to instill good eating habits, only to find themselves drawn into tense and long-term battles.

Touch for Health Month

Nicholas Albery

The non-profit participatory events website <www.DoBe.org> is promoting May as Touch for Health Month throughout the world.

The idea behind this is that it would work like a touch chain letter: (1) touch three men and three women (in a social, non-sexual way) who you wouldn't normally touch, and (2) get them to touch six others, while passing on these two instructions. It can be a barely perceptible touch on the shoulder, for instance.

When this month was first piloted in the UK in 1982, a random survey afterwards indicated that as many as two million people had touched more that month as a result. The UK seems to be particularly touch-starved. A research project reported that in a Paris cafe there were 110 incidents of touching per hour, as against 0 in a London cafe.

A great deal of scientific research has shown that touch is vital to our health and to our social lives. In the United States in foundling hospitals as late as the second decade of the 20th century, before fondling was introduced, the death rate for infants under one year of age was nearly 100 percent, despite the cleanest of material conditions. Later in life, our self-esteem is, as evidence shows, related to how much we touch others. And whether we are touched or not can color our feelings about virtually any social encounter. In one library research project, for instance, those who were touched almost imperceptibly by the librarian as the books were handed out assessed the librarian (and some even the library as a whole) more positively than those who weren't.

→ For summaries of the research on touching, see "Touching: The Promotion of Touching in Casual Social Encounters" at <www.globalideasbank.org/touching.html>.

ToughLove

The interview below comes from the book Local Heroes: The Rebirth of Heroism in America by Bill Berkowitz (published by Lexington Books).

Phyllis and David York got involved in community work that arose from personal trauma. One of their three daughters was arrested for robbing a cocaine dealer, the capping point of a history of troubles. They'd tried everything they knew to help her (and they were family therapists themselves in Philadelphia). A threshold had been crossed: they couldn't bring themselves to bail their daughter out of jail.

Instead they turned to their friends for help. They asked for community support, and they got it. Out of that incident, ToughLove was born.

ToughLove is an approach for parents who have trouble raising their teenage children or whose teenagers are getting into trouble, or (usually) both. The approach typically involves parent self-help groups that meet regularly to support each other, to change family behavior, and to set limits, or "bottom lines." More than a thousand such groups meet in the US and Canada, with another 75 groups in New Zealand.

The "tough" part of ToughLove means enforcing standards, calmly but unfailingly, up to and including, if necessary, committing the teenager to treatment.

The "love" part of ToughLove includes setting reasonable and fair behavioral standards so that teenagers can grow to be responsible and caring adults. The "tough" part means enforcing those standards, calmly but unfailingly, up to and including, if necessary, committing the teenager to treatment, refusing to appear in court, or evicting the older teenager from the house. Other ToughLove parents, if needed, can temporarily take your place.

The Yorks believe that the community has a responsibility with parents for raising kids. If kids go wrong, it's partly because community standards have been poorly defined or poorly taught. The community has to take care of its own. In that respect, ToughLove is an intentional model for community involvement.

The Yorks started ToughLove mainly for themselves and for the people around them, not thinking in larger terms until a local magazine story appeared, got spread around, and touched a national nerve. Now ToughLove is an international non-profit organization.

Interviewer: How did things move from calling up a friend and getting support for your daughter to broadening the network?

David: Someone we knew in this local community called us up and said they were having trouble with their son, who was 17. He'd taken off. He'd taken his father's camel hair coat and his whisky and done a whole number on him. And now the father says, "Now what do I do? I don't know where the kid is, he's somewhere around, but we don't know where he's living."

So we said, "Call up the people in your community; call up your friends, your neighbors, and get everybody together, because we know your son's living somewhere in this … vicinity. Let's see if we can track him down and cut off his resources." And so they got 30 folks together, and that was our first ToughLove group …

We became like the leaders of this group. That was okay for a while, but after about seven or eight months, it got to be really tiring to go every week to this meeting. And we began to put a manual together …

Time magazine interviewed us. And the gal that interviewed us had a hard job getting it published; they didn't want to publish it. They thought it was too radical a movement.

Phyllis: Kicking the kids out.

David: Yeah, it runs against the common trend of the poor kids, you know, suffering from terrible parents.

Phyllis: Then when Ann Landers put it in, we got 1,500 letters a day for I don't know how long. Ten days, we got 15,000 letters. Over 2,000 phone calls in a week. At this little office in Sellersville, with one person, one maniac person, working.

→ *ToughLove, PO Box 1069, Doylestown, PA 18901 (Phone: 215 348 7090). ToughLove has spawned books, a newsletter, and a movement, and nowadays there are also "kids' groups" running parallel to the parents' groups, where the children tackle problems with the assistance of a trained counselor. There are no registered groups in the UK yet, but the book* **ToughLove** *by Phyllis and David York and Ted Wachte (published by Bantam Books) is available from ToughLove for $4.*

→ *Bill Berkowitz, the author of* **Local Heroes**, *is at 12 Pelham Terrace, Arlington, MA 02174 (Phone: 617 646 6319).*

Tree-house eco-resort

DAVID GREENBERG

The following could perhaps be imitated by other ecotourist developments. It is adapted from an e-mail to the Institute and from the websites listed below.

DAVID GREENBERG BUILT his first tree house in Maui, Hawaii, three miles from the town of Hana at the edge of the jungle. This, he wrote at the time, is "a magical romantic getaway, with an ocean view overlooking a flower farm." The tree house was ten feet above ground, spanning African tulip trees. Although, as Greenberg warns, his tree houses are not for those seeking the sanitized, controlled environment of a condo — they purvey the feeling of camping out with a roof — most nonetheless possess the dimensions and even many of the amenities of terrestrial living, including bathrooms with toilet and hot shower, and covered camp-style kitchens, complete with barbecue pit and propane stove.

The Hawaiian Hale Hotel Tree House, set in old tamarind trees

---

Greenberg says, "I used to be an architect urban designer. I am now an anti-architect rural designer." His enthusiasm for alternative high-rise accommodation has led to the development of a small tree-house eco-resort in

Hawaii. Greenberg's tree houses are much in demand; he recently completed four houses for vacation rental on the island of Hainan, near Sanya on the South China Sea, including the Hawaiian Hale Hotel Tree House, accommodating up to 20 people in seven separate spaces over three levels. These are set in old tamarind trees at the edge of the 5,000-acre Sanya Nanshan Buddhist and ecological theme park, a site of outstanding beauty boasting botanical gardens, temples, and pagodas. Two further resorts in Hue Province, Vietnam, have also recently been completed.

→ *David Greenberg, Box 389, Hana, Maui, Hawaii 96713*
(Phone: 808 248 7241; Fax: 808 248 7066; E-mail: hanalani@maui.net;
Web: www.maui.net/~hanalani).

→ *Tree houses on Hainan Island (E-mail: chinatreehouses@yahoo.com;*
Web: www.treehousesofhawaii.com).

→ *See also* **Tree Houses: The Art and Craft of Living Out On a Limb** *by Peter Nelson (published by Houghton Mifflin). Peter Nelson runs workshops on tree-house construction and can be reached at Treehouse workshop, PO Box 1136, Fall City, Washington 98024 (Phone: 425 222 4739; E-mail: treehouse@accessone.com; Web: www.treehouseworkshop.com).*

Transforming Third World begging

JEFF GREENWALD
Summarized from *New Age Journal*, monitored by Roger Knights.

Doling out sugar candies and coins turns kids into beggars.

I HAVE WITNESSED CASE AFTER CASE OF WELL-MEANING WESTERNERS blowing into far-flung villages, attracting local children, and doling out handfuls of sugar candies and coins. This kind of behavior turns kids into beggars faster than you can say "Hello, mister," as future travelers to those areas quickly learn. Even a humble Bic pen is a rich prize to a kid whose family earns 40 cents a day, and it takes no time before anyone wearing Ray Bans or rip-stop nylon is viewed as a potential mark. Generosity is not a habit we want to cure ourselves of. Despite our sometimes better judgment, we will give things away. But is it possible to do this without transforming the places we visit into shark dens?

I think it is. There are dozens of ways to express good will and geniality without cultivating greed and dependency. With imagination and a little advance planning, it's possible to make the process of gift-giving one of the most pleasurable parts of a trip or trek — and one of the best opportunities for engagement with local children and adults.

First off, though, I want to emphasize that gift-giving does not always have to entail giving away things. Sharing a bit of one's self, a part of one's life or personal history, is often enough. During my career as a travel writer, for instance, I've discovered that adults and children all over the world — from Bali to the Bronx — have something in common. They all want to know about your family and about the place that you come from.

Assailed by a cadre of ten-year-old beggars, I pulled out a cheap inflatable globe.

Among the most useful items a person can pack on a trip to the Third World, I've found, are family snapshots and postcards of one's home town. Recently, assailed by a cadre of ten-year-old beggars in northern India, I sat down and pulled out a cheap inflatable globe that I sometimes carry around. What had begun as a feeding frenzy transformed instantly into a geography lesson. The boys, who could barely read, threw themselves into the session with devotion. They immediately began matching the bits of news they had been hearing on the radio — about Germany, the United States, and Russia — to the appropriate countries and argued heatedly about why India and Russia were pink, while Pakistan and the United States were green. True, they finally demanded the globe itself; but my firm refusal, on the grounds that I required it for future such encounters, was met with agreeable wags of the head.

When trekking above 8,000 feet, my bag of tricks includes other, equally entertaining props. A simple magnifying glass, powerful enough to burn a tiny hole in a dry leaf, seems miraculous to people who see it for the first time. The same can be said for a small kaleidoscope, or even a telephoto lens. When I stop for an extended break — and find myself surrounded by local kids — I'll often pull out a set of colored pencils and let them take turns drawing in my journal. Some have turned out to be quite good artists, and their uninhibited sketches of animals, flowers, and beefy Westerners in blimplike parkas are among my most prized souvenirs.

Although I'll frequently stop, chat, and spend time demonstrating a prism or kaleidoscope, I very rarely give anything away to people along the trail. Often, though, after a memorable stay at a cozy lodge, I'll have developed a warm relationship with the owners and decide to give a small gift to them and/or their kids.

For these situations I offer two rules of thumb. First of all, it's unwise to distribute money or candy. There are countless other gifts that are less dubious and genuinely expressive of one's personality. Picture postcards, mentioned before, are light and cheap. They make excellent tokens and are usually displayed and cherished by the people who receive them. Incense, good matches, a reliable pen, or a disposable lighter are also much appreciated.

Avoid giving children gifts directly. Hand the present over to a parent.

Kids are much easier. I recommend balloons, plastic rings and magnifying glasses, prisms, tops (stock up on those little plastic Hanukkah dreidels before your trip), colored pencils, pens, crayons, little plastic animals or dinosaurs, or even those cheap foil hologram stickers that are sold by the dozen in many toy stores. All of the above make fun and educational presents that kids can share and that can help them unlock a few secrets of the universe to boot. My second rule is to avoid giving children gifts directly. Hand the present over to a parent or an older brother or sister, and let them make the actual presentation. Such a gesture is a sign of respect and reinforces the endangered notion that family members — rather than wealthy Western tourists — are the ones to turn to for gifts and rewards.

One very poignant situation, which I encounter more and more, is children and villagers along trekking routes begging for basic medical supplies. Simple first-aid items such as bandages, iodine, aspirin, or Tums are hard to refuse, especially when the person doing the asking substantiates the request by clutching his or her head, doubling over, or displaying a gaping wound.

My personal feeling is that one should help however one can, short of dispensing drugs. I will not, needless to say, leap to the aid of anyone with a scrape or splinter, but if the situation looks potentially threatening I usually try to deal with it. Sometimes it's even a good idea to find out where the nearest health post is and, in extreme cases, to give a relative or porter enough money to take the sick or injured person there.

The bottom line, though, is that begging has become a kind of game and a genuine nuisance — one that Westerners have helped to create and perpetuate. Unless we make an effort to deal mindfully with the situation, what is now an irritating habit will become, for many Third World villagers and their children, a way of life.

→ *Jeff Greenwald, PO Box 5883, Berkeley, CA 94705 (Phone/Fax: 510 653 6911).*

Travel passes compulsory for university students

Summarized from an article by Peyton Whitely in the *Seattle Times*, monitored by Roger Knights.

IT HAS BEEN PROPOSED TO THE UNIVERSITY OF WASHINGTON that every student, whether or not they would individually benefit, should pay about $22 to $50 every quarter for a "Universal Transportation Pass," entitling them to unlimited travel on the metro and buses. The university's present problem is that more than 35,000 people go to classes daily, but there are only 12,300 parking spaces.

> More than 35,000 people go to classes daily,
> but there are only 12,300 parking spaces.

In the debate on this issue it was pointed out that the 8,000 students who walk to university would get a poor deal, but one person spoke up to say that she would happily pay for the pass even though she would never use it — on public transport it would take her three hours' commuting each day to make her journey.

Compulsory travel pass scheme
Roy Simpson

Public transport has a great deal of spare capacity, but not everywhere and not at all times. This is a resource running to waste. When this spare capacity is made available — e.g., to a pensioner with an off-peak travel pass — it has a real money value for the recipient, and since it comes from a resource otherwise running to waste, the cost to the community is very small — an arrangement that is satisfactory to both sides.

The concept of a compulsory public transport travel pass for drivers (extending the concept behind the university scheme outlined above) would maximize the service public transport can give to the country and reduce the pressure on public transportation companies, but without overburdening the system by allowing unlimited free travel.

As a general principle, local off-peak travel would be unrestricted, but longer journeys would (using computerized accounting) be restricted, to a limited number per month, varying according to length of journey, place visited, and so on. At peak hours, commuters might be restricted to a specified journey.

> Drivers would automatically pay for their
> travel pass along with the car tax.

In the UK, for instance, drivers could automatically pay for their pass along with the car tax (and perhaps for their family also). The licence badge on the windscreen would show the type of pass issued. Drivers wishing to enter a city center or other congested area would be free to do so subject to car parking charges and provided that they had paid for a pass entitling them to enter the area by public transport.

These measures would greatly reduce the traffic flow while using minimum compulsion. Children, senior citizens, the low paid, etc., would get their passes via the social security system. "One-off" journeys not covered by a pass would of course be paid for by the individual.

→ *Roy Simpson, Chacewater, 13 Dalmore Avenue, Claygate, Surrey KT10 OHQ, UK (Phone: Int.+44 [0]1372 65073)*

U

Uncovering buried city streams

Summarized from an item by Mark Overbay in YES! *A Journal of Positive Futures* entitled "Bringing streams to light."

COMMUNITIES IN THE SAN FRANCISCO BAY AREA ARE OPENING UP STREAMS that were buried when buildings and streets took over. Using shovels, picks, and, on occasion, heavy equipment, workers open up a portion of a creek and replant exposed areas with vegetation — thus encouraging the return of insects, birds, amphibians, and snakes. The waterflows also please local residents by bringing nature and agriculture back into an urban habitat.

Volunteers use the shapes of animals and insects
to mark the underground creek location.

The first step advised in a creek restoration project is a "creek stenciling" program, with volunteers using the shapes of animals and insects to mark the underground creek location and to begin building up community awareness and support.

→ *Bar Area Citizens for Creek Restoration, c/o Aquatic Outreach Institute, 1327 South 46th Street, #155 Richmond Field Station, Richmond, CA 94804 (Phone: 510 236 9558).*

Unofficial Community Cafe

PATRICK GRAHAM, A PROFESSIONAL SOUND RECORDIST, knew very few of his neighbors living in Numbers 1 to 244 Inverness Place, Cardiff. So he converted a real estate agent's For Sale sign to read "Unofficial Community Cafe. Open and free to all local residents as long as the sign is up," and persuaded a local firm to let him run off a hundred copies of a newsletter about it.

> A young mother up the road even borrowed
> the sign to host the cafe herself for a time.

Graham had a trickle of visitors after that, almost all women, coming in for a cup of tea. "Nearly everyone on the block would say hello to me," says Graham, "and a young mother up the road even borrowed the sign to host the cafe for a time."

"There were no official opening times," he adds, "just up with the sign and kettle full when you wanted visitors, take it in or pass it on when you didn't." He vetted people at the door and had no trouble. And his experiment in neighborliness cost him nothing, with visitors bringing gifts of tea and coffee.

→ *Patrick Graham, 217 Mackintosh Place, Roath Park, Cardiff CF2 4RP, Wales (Phone: Int.+44 [0]29 20491127). The project is dormant now that he no longer lives in Inverness Place.*

V

Village control of right to hunt elephants

Summarized from an article by Kar Hess Jr. entitled "Wild Success," published in *Reason* magazine, monitored by Roger Knights.

WHITE COLONIALISTS FORBADE THE NATIVE AFRICANS TO HUNT WILDLIFE. The result was that elephants and other species were seen as marauding pests with no economic or social worth (except on the black market). Africans resorted to poaching to stop the wildlife destruction of their crops and to provide meat, skins, and ivory for their families.

Campfire, a program of the Zimbabwe Department of National Parks and Wildlife, has as its goal the allocation of rights over communal resources (especially big game) to small rural communities — which could then sell those rights, mainly in the form of licences for trophy hunts.

> Whereas a poached elephant is only worth about
> $500 in meat and ivory, a trophy elephant is
> worth as much as $20,000.

The revenue earned — several thousand dollars for a buffalo and many times more for an elephant — has given villagers money for local development and strong incentives to protect elephants and other money-earning wildlife. Whereas a poached elephant is only worth about $500 in meat and ivory, a lawfully marketed trophy elephant is worth as much as $20,000. Thanks to Campfire, poaching has declined and elephant numbers in Zimbabwe have soared from 46,000 to 66,000.

Campfire works best where district councils allow a complete devolution of property rights in big game from the state to self-governing village bodies.

Campfire advocate Brian Child writes that the project is "like the communist system in that it is based on community rather than private ownership, but resembles the capitalist system in that it uses the market to allocate resources."

The Campfire approach is spreading throughout Southern Africa, supported by the World Wildlife Fund and others, but its success is threatened by animal rights groups such as the Humane Society of the United States. The society lobbies the United States government to use its Endangered Species Act to outlaw all trophy hunting.

Community conservation
Summarized from an article by Paul Saloper entitled "African Wildlife's Last Hope," published in the *Seattle Times,* monitored by Roger Knights.

Environmental organizations have started up projects of "community conservation" in the jungles and villages of Uganda, using them as a sort of testing ground for a controversial theory. The idea at the heart of community conservation is a simple one: in order to save the wildlife of Africa, the Africans must be given back the animals. If the local villagers are invited into wildlife parks, the theory is, they will have a renewed sense of connection with protected species and areas.

The massive scale of the community conservation effort has been compared to an ecological Marshall Plan.

Many different approaches are being tried. Through ecotourism, economic links between the people and the animals are being strengthened, reinforcing the relationship of dependency between the two. Other schemes, such as the piping of water to villagers from inside a gorilla park, are aimed at making the local villagers anything but indifferent to the wildlife around them. The massive scale of the community conservation effort, backed by organizations as diverse as the European Union, the World Bank, CARE, and the Dutch government, has been compared to an ecological Marshall Plan. Its supporters believe it is the only way that Africa's wildlife will survive.

Virtual play for ill children

Summarized from an item by Don Clark in the *Wall Street Journal*,
monitored by Roger Knights.

STEVEN SPIELBERG'S STARBRIGHT FOUNDATION and four technology companies
have formed a partnership to electronically link bedridden children in hospitals around the world.

Therapeutic for chemotherapy patients or others whose illnesses affect the way they look

---

The idea is to reduce the isolation of severely ill children by letting them
see and talk to family members and other patients using computer video-
conferencing technology. They can also create "avatars" (animated characters)
to represent themselves and play with avatars of kids in other hospitals. This
may be especially therapeutic for chemotherapy patients or others whose illnesses affect the way they look.

Some early studies suggest that such electronic diversions may sharply
reduce the need for pain-killing drugs.

Vitamin T — The tribal vitamin

NICHOLAS ALBERY

THE QUESTIONNAIRE THAT FOLLOWS IS DESIGNED TO HELP PEOPLE take note of the
extent to which they are detribalized and rootless and determine whether or
not they are getting their Recommended Daily Allowance (RDA) of what I
term Vitamin T, the tribal vitamin. My rating today, as I type this, adds up to
69 — so I am getting a mere 69 percent of the Vitamin T RDA, although I
suspect I am getting a good deal more than the average person.

Most people do not seem to realize that they have near-starvation levels
of Vitamin T. I know that I'm deprived of Vitamin T simply because I was
lucky enough as a young man in the 1960s and 1970s to experience feeling
part of a tribe as an active participant in community-based organizations in
London's Notting Hill, so I feel what I'm missing now in my middle-aged
isolation. For others, the nearest equivalent may be looking back fondly on
their time at university, when their immediate surroundings were suffused
with the possibility of interesting casual social encounters and socializing
didn't involve making appointments and getting in a car to visit friends in
distant places.

What I miss most is the possibility in the evening of just dropping in on
a convivial neighbor for a chat and a meal.

Each nod elderly people receive from a neighbor counts towards their RDA of Vitamin T.

Solitary elderly people trying to survive on a state pension are among those most in need of such informal neighborhood contacts. Each nod they receive from a passing neighbor in the street, each chat with a local shop-keeper, counts towards their RDA of Vitamin T.

In our evolutionary past we lived in small groups of 50 to 250 or so people, and we still need that intense level of intercommunication and sense of place and neighborhood. The Rev. John Papworth, who edits *Fourth World Review* (with its slogan of "small nations, small communities, and a human scale"), used to give sermons on the theme of Jesus's commandment to "love your neighbor," while complaining that nowadays most people don't even know who their neighbors are.

There's no word in the English language that quite means "lonely despite having your happy nuclear family around you" — lonely in the sense of feeling without a tribe, isolated, rootless, and alienated. A new word such as *kithless* — as in without kith and kin — is needed. For kithlessness is, I believe, today's most unrecognized feeling. Almost all urban dwellers feel it deep in themselves, but hardly anyone recognizes or verbalizes the feeling.

Some people even go to great lengths to keep apart from their neighbors. They believe that their tribe consists of those who share the same interests as them, in whatever far-flung places they may live, or just the people they work with, or just their cozy nuclear family. No doubt in the past people could feel very trapped in their isolated, stultifying village culture, but now the pendulum has swung the other way, and we have only too many ways of escaping from our locality through travel, work, holidays, telephone, television, and the internet.

But Vitamin T is based on the assumption that we have an inbuilt need for a tribe we live in proximity to, for kith and kin living cooperatively within in a geographical neighborhood.

A strong social network is a predictor of long life.

Doubtless Vitamin T is essential for our health too. There is accumulating evidence that a strong social network is a predictor of long life — and a better predictor than our smoking and drinking habits (see, for instance, <www.globalideasbank.org/wbi/WBI-70.HTML>).

In the future that's rapidly arriving, where computer programmers and web designers and their ilk will be the aristocrats lording it over the rest of us, who will be either out of work or providing them with their luxuries, it will be ever harder to feel part of society, and will only be within cohesive neighborhoods that we'll be able to receive recognition for who we are as people, whatever our job or lack of one may be.

Please note that in this questionnaire, "nuclear family" means "you, your spouse, and your children" and "local" means "within a 15-minute walk from your home." The questions only address encounters in your neighborhood or at work that take place within this 15-minute range and that are outside your nuclear family. It is a neighborhood rating, not a test of how many friends you have in distant places or how happy you are with your partner and children.

Vitamin T questionnaire

- Roughly how many local people (neighbors, local shopkeepers, waiters, hairdressers, local co-workers, etc.) have you chatted with in the last week (apart from your partner and immediate nuclear . family)?
- Roughly how many others have you nodded to or greeted while, for instance, passing them in the street? (For scoring purposes, divide this total by two.)
- How many local people (apart from your partner and immediate nuclear family) would be likely to notice and regret your death if you were to die now (only include those whose deaths you would also notice and regret)? (For scoring purposes, divide this total by three.)
- If you were seriously ill, roughly how many local people (apart from paid caregivers, your partner, and immediate nuclear family) could you count on to visit you, to do your shopping for you, etc.? (For scoring purposes, double this total.)
- How many households locally do you feel you could drop in on for a chat or a meal, almost on impulse, without it being a big deal? (For scoring purposes, multiply this total by five.)
- How many local people are there (apart from your partner and immediate nuclear family) whom you tend to treat as confidantes, people you can discuss and share your innermost fears and worries with? (For scoring purposes, multiply this total by ten.)
- How many local people (apart from your partner and immediate nuclear family) care about your goals in life and actively support you in trying to achieve them? (For scoring purposes, double this total.)
- Last week, how often did you engage in the equivalent of a tribal ritual — e.g., a religious service, a meal with local friends or local co-workers, a drink at the local tavern or coffee shop with friends — occasions, in other words, where there was active participation by all those present? (For scoring purposes, double this total.)
- In general, to what extent do you feel that you are part of a local neighborhood or tribe that cares for each other? (Score on a range

from 0 to 20, where 20 is "Just one big extended family" and 0 is
"no contact at all.")

How about inviting your neighbors for a
social meeting in your home?

Add up your total to arrive at your personal very rough-and-ready percentage of the Recommended Daily Allowance of Vitamin T. If you're over
100 percent, don't worry. There's no danger of overdosing. A friend of mine
rated himself on this questionnaire as regularly over 1,000 percent for one of
the interesting and stimulating periods of his life in which he lived in
Christiania community in Copenhagen. If your score is low, how about taking up John Papworth's suggestion — photocopy a notice and put it into your
neighbors' mailboxes, inviting people for a social meeting either in your
home or in a neutral venue? We have an annual tea party in our street, meeting in a different house each year, which I initiated, and even this small token
event is beginning to make a difference to our sense of neighborhood and the
way we help each other out when we have problems.

I would be interested to receive feedback and suggestions for improvements from anyone who tries this questionnaire out.

Comment from Rabbi Mimi Weisel

As a group of us were sitting together and enjoying dinner on New Year's eve,
we took your Vitamin T quiz and discovered that we have a large dose of
Vitamin T in our lives. We attributed our relatively high score to our explicit, conscious choice to live as observant Jews, a choice that provides each of
us with a great variety of the connections author Nicholas Albery says are
lacking in most urban settings today, even though we live in Los Angeles, one
of the largest, most spread-out cities on earth.

As we are Jews committed to following the laws of our tradition, our
lifestyle fosters community connections outside our immediate families,
thereby providing us with networks for socializing and for nurturing.
Perhaps the best example is our weekly observance of Shabbat, the Jewish
Sabbath. We do not drive or ride in cars on Saturday, so we need to live within walking distance of a synagogue.

Part of our weekly ritual is saying "Shabbat Shalom" to others we pass on
the way to and from the synagogue. On Shabbat we share meals and drop in
on one another so our families can interact. Furthermore, living in a close
neighborhood such as ours also means that an infrastructure to support our
observance is created. There are kosher restaurants and bakeries, Jewish
bookstores and gift shops. Walking into these establishments, one is bound

to run into friends and acquaintances and to create casual relationships with the shop owners.

Being part of an observant Jewish community, we are also involved in synagogue life, which promotes visiting the sick, comforting those who are in mourning, and welcoming others into the community. We work together to support schools, a variety of charitable causes, and social justice issues. We talk together and discuss our concerns for our community, our families, and the world as we sit together at shared meals and celebrations.

Jewish tradition helps us to achieve balance and connection, community ties and support.

My friends and I are aware that many might consider our lifestyle to be restrictive and confining. Nonetheless, though we live in an open society with its plethora of choices and freedoms, all of us have chosen to live a life of observance. Each of us could have opted out of this life choice, yet we have all embraced it. Why? As modern individuals involved in careers and families, we are just as apt as others to be isolated by our computers, cell phones, and cars, or to face the anonymity of the malls and movie theaters. In contrast, Jewish tradition helps us to achieve balance and connection, community ties and support.

Most organized religions offer strong support for creating communal connections. Not only synagogues but also churches and mosques provide networks for caring and friendship on an ongoing basis. My friends and I feel blessed to have these resources as well as the tenets of our tradition, which have resulted in the physical creation of a small community within a large metropolis.

→ *Please send feedback to The Institute for Social Inventions, 20 Heber Road, London NW2 6AA, UK (Phone: Int.+44 [0]20 8208 2853; Fax: Int.+44 [0]20 8452 6434; E-mail: rhino@dial.pipex.com; Web: www.globalideasbank.org).*

→ *The Institute for Social Inventions and <www.DoBe.org> are co-sponsoring International Neighborhood Day (see the entry on "Neighborhood Day" in this book).*

→ *John Papworth, Editor,* **Fourth World Review,** *The Close, 26 High St, Purton, Wiltshire SN5 4AE, UK (Phone: Int.+44 [0]1793 77221; Fax: 01793 772521).*

→ *Rabbi Mimi Weisel, Assistant Dean, Ziegler School of Rabbinic Studies, University of Judaism, 15600 Mulholland Drive, Los Angeles, California 90077 (E-mail: mweisel@uj.edu).*

Voice recognition of suicide cases

Summarized from an article by Ian Sample in the *New Scientist* entitled "Voice from the grave."

RECENT RESEARCH HAS SHOWN THAT THE EARLIEST SIGN that someone is seriously considering committing suicide could be a slight change in the sound of their voice. The change is distinctive, and psychiatrists are planning to use this change in sound as a kind of early warning system to distinguish between those who are actually suicidal and those who are just depressed.

Stephen Silverman, a psychiatrist from Yale University, noticed that he could infer from patients' voices if they were likely to make a suicide attempt. With this unscientific hunch he went to see Mitchell Wilkes, an electronics engineer at Vanderbilt University in Nashville, to see if there was any empirical evidence for such a change in voice sound. They recorded interviews with a number of depressed patients and compared the recordings with others who were not depressed. A further comparison was then made between the recordings and the history of the patients.

After conducting these tests and analyses, Wilkes noted that the voice became "slightly hollow and empty" in suicidal patients, a characteristic that people call "the voice from the grave." More scientifically, he noticed that those who were seriously suicidal used a narrower range of frequencies when pronouncing vowels than those who were merely depressed. Added to this, the voices of the seriously suicidal patients had a noticeably higher pitch.

Changes in muscle-tone quality can occur in times of stress, which might affect the vocal cords.

The reasons for these changes are unclear, although Wilkes believes they could be due to stress-induced physiological changes. Changes in muscle-tone quality can occur in times of stress, which might affect the vocal cords. Wilkes adds that "you get changes in moisture and elasticity of the vocal tract" when anxious or stressed.

The science behind these findings is less important than the findings themselves, though, which could potentially aid helpline volunteers in their assessment of a depressed caller's mental state. The eventual result of this research could be for helplines and emergency rooms to get diagnostic devices. Volunteers could then have a better idea of whether a person is truly suicidal or not — and lives could be saved. As Emma Charvet from The Samaritans says, "If there's any way of finding out earlier the level of someone's risk of suicide, it'd be a great help."

W

Walking club "discussion salons" for schools

VALERIE YULE

A BRILLIANT TEACHER AT MY SCHOOL LED A WALKING CLUB that went on walks, rather than hikes, out in the countryside. Both staff and older students would join in. About 15 to 30 of us would go out by train; we would straggle along some tracks through the countryside, and then stop for a leisurely picnic lunch somewhere.

We had a marvelous non-ageist time, and the discussions did far more for my (I should say *our*) education than what we did in classes.

Informal walking outings for real education

All schools could have these informal walking outings for *real education*. Nobody has to join the club — you just turn up.

➔ *Valerie Yule, 57 Waimarie Drive, Mount Waverley, Victoria, Australia (Phone: Int.+61 [0]13 807 4315; E-mail: vyule@pa.ausom.net.au). She runs the Australian Ideas Bank (http://avoca.vicnet.net.au/~ozideas/).*

Washing-up water good for plants

Summarized from an item by Nigel Hawkes in the London Times entitled "Gardens thrive on dish water".

YOU CAN SAVE WATER BY USING "GRAY WATER" FROM SHOWERS, dish water, washing machines, and dishwashers on your garden plants.

Garden plants respond to the
phosphates in the dish water.

Garden plants (except lettuces) flourish better on dish water than on tap water. They respond to the phosphates in the dish water. Although direct contact with the surfactants in such water can damage plants, these surfactants readily break down in soil.

W

Gardening Which? magazine found that of the five plants they tested, busy lizzies, nemesia, and fuchsias all grew more vigorously in dish water. Runner beans produced a bigger and better tasting crop. The lettuces, however, grew less vigorously and tasted bitter.

→ *For further information go to <www.oasisdesign.net>.*

Web archive for the transcendent experiences of scientists

The following is adapted from the TASTE website <www.issc-taste.org>.

A WEBSITE CALLED THE ARCHIVES OF SCIENTISTS' TRANSCENDENT EXPERIENCES (TASTE) has been designed to allow scientists from all fields to share their personal transcendent experiences. The site is a safe, anonymous, but quality-controlled space that scientists and the general public can have ready access to.

For fear of adverse effects on their career, scientists refrain from making public their transcendent experiences.

For fear of ridicule from their colleagues and of adverse, prejudicial effects on their career, scientists refrain from making public their transcendent experiences. Such fears have, unfortunately, too much of a basis in fact. It is not that there are a lot of scientists deliberately trying to suppress their colleagues; it is just the social conditioning of our times. This website, edited by Professor Charles Tart of the Institute of Transpersonal Psychology and the University of California at Davis, seeks to change this culture.

As Tart puts it: "Over the years, many scientists, once they've realized I'm a safe person to talk to, have told me about unusual and transcendent experiences they've had. Too often, I'm the first and only person they've ever spoken to about their experiences, for fear of ridicule from their colleagues."

Scientists today often occupy a social role similar to that of high priests, telling laypeople and each other what is and is not "real" and, consequently, what is and is not valuable and sane. Unfortunately, the dominant materialistic and reductionist psychosocial climate of contemporary science (which sociologists long ago named "scientism," an attitude different from the essential process of science) rejects and suppresses both the having and the sharing of transcendent, transpersonal, altered, spiritual, or psychic states and experiences.

From Professor Tart's perspective as a psychologist, though, this prejudicial suppression and rejection psychologically harms and distorts both scientists' and laypeople transcendent (and other) potentials. It also inhibits the development of a genuine scientific understanding of the full spectrum of consciousness. A denial of any aspects of our nature, whatever their ultimate reality status, is never psychologically or socially healthy.

TASTE is intended to help change this restrictive and pathological climate. Specifically, TASTE

1. enables individual psychological growth in the contributing scientists by providing a safe means of expression of vital experiences;

2. leads toward a more receptive climate within the scientific professions to the full range of our humanity — which, in turn, would benefit world culture;

3. provides research data on transcendent experiences within a highly articulate and conscientious population, that of scientists;

4. facilitates the development of a full-spectrum science of consciousness by providing both data and psychological support for the study of transcendent experiences; and

5. helps bridge the unfortunate gaps between science and the rest of culture by illustrating the humanity of scientists.

✦ *Charles T. Tart, Institute of Transpersonal Psychology, 744 San Antonio Road, Palo Alto, CA 94303 (Fax: 630 604 3279; E-mail: cttart@ucdavis.edu).*

Web search engines to find compatible partners

Doug Wilson

In the book *Creative Speculations* (on the web at <www.globalideasbank.org/crespec/CS-25.HTML>), Nicholas Albery proposed that people looking for partners could do so for free by answering a web questionnaire and copying and pasting the code generated by their answers onto their home page. Then anyone using an internet search engine could look through many millions of such pages in a few seconds to find their perfect partner. Doug Wilson liked this idea and plans to develop it, as he describes in the following piece.

Here's my version of Nicholas Albery's idea for finding compatible partners using web search engines.

We create a questionnaire, put it in HTML form,
and generate a few codewords.

We create a questionnaire, put it in HTML form with CGI code to do the processing, and use it to generate a few codewords. I think the codewords should all begin with a sequence of unlikely characters, like "XJ6," so that people using a search engine will not get a lot of extraneous hits from ordinary words that happen to contain the rest of the code letters. And I think we need to give people precise instructions on how to use the codes.

W

Specifically, we need to make sure that people don't look for people exactly like themselves. It is well established that people are not compatible with others exactly like themselves. We need to tell them that in no uncertain terms.

My own formula for compatibility is probably a good starting point, and we can refine the process once it is in use by soliciting feedback from the users. My formula is essentially this: similar interests, everything else as different as possible. The reverse is not bad either: different interests, everything else as similar as possible, but these two versions lead to different kinds of relationships.

The fundamental idea I have here is to encode the questions on the questionnaire into a set of codewords, so that the codewords capture almost all of the information. I think the best approach is to start out with codes that are somewhat cryptic so fewer people will try to subvert the system. Eventually people may figure them out.

To start with, I'd suggest something simple: three codewords, two to place at the bottom of your page, and the third used in searches.

The first would encode your interests, and might be 'XJ6Iabzq' with 'XJ6' saying it is a codeword; the letter "I" indicating that it encodes interests; and the "abzq" representing your interests.

The second would encode everything else about your character and personality and might be "XJ6Cjkla" with the "C" indicating it was about your character.

The third would be the *inverse* or opposite of the second; it might be "XJ6Cwxyz," also having a "C."

On the bottom of your page you'd then put: "XJ6Iabzq XJ6Cjkla." To look for compatible people you would seek "XJ6Iabzq XJ6Cwxyz." Same interest; as different as possible in personality.

As I said above, the other works too, so we could generate a fourth word representing the opposite set of interests, but we can investigate that later, just as we can investigate adding more codewords.

It would certainly be possible to generate comprehensible, or at least pronounceable codewords, but for now I suggest being cryptic.

My figures suggest significant levels of compatibility — good enough for genuine friendships — at least at a level of one person in every 1,000.

My figures suggest significant levels of compatibility — good enough for genuine friendships — at least at a level of one person in every 1,000. We could cover that by having 32 different words for interests and 32 different codewords for character/personality, 32 times 32 being 1,024. (More would be better, once we get enough people involved.)

There is really no need to talk to the search engine people or involve the search engines in setting this up at all. We can go ahead and set up the system and let people know about it. As the search engines index the pages, they record strings of symbols as words (except for the few like yahoo.com that do it manually), so as soon as a few pages containing codewords get indexed, people should be able to find them with the search engines in the usual way.

I think we should match by compatibility *only* and discourage people from searching for others of specific ages, races, sexes, sexual preferences, incomes, and all those things. These are, after all, precisely the sort of distinctions that are the subject of the worst prejudices.

Some people may turn out to be so completely compatible with you that you decide to overlook age, race, and marital status, and some may just become good friends — having a lot of good friends is the best way to find a sexual partner anyway.

One problem with the scheme is the potential abuse of matching codes by commercial users wanting to advertise their products. There seems to be no low beneath which advertisers will not go.

One could include a link to a site where a list of known
scams and scammers is maintained.

But I think we can solve this. What I have in mind is to include something like "SYT verify," where verify is a link to a site where a list of known scams and scammers is maintained. You can then just click on "verify" to see if SYT@notascam.com is offering romance or trying to pick your virtual pocket.

→ *Doug Wilson (E-mail: dpwilson@island.net). There are many other "social technology" ideas on Douglas P. Wilson's website <www.island.net/~dpwilson/index.html>.*

The "Wellness" show

Summarized from an article in the *London Guardian*, an interview with Dr. Patch Adams in the *Washington Post Magazine*, and a letter from Dr. Adams to the Institute.

DR. PATCH ADAMS OF ARLINGTON, VIRGINIA, CHARGES NO MONEY, carries no malpractice insurance, and lives with patients in a country farm setting.

His "products" include nutrition,
exercise, wonder, curiosity, and love.

Joy, he says, is more important than any other drug. Dr. Adams promotes his philosophy of healthcare through a stage show in which he plays a 19th-century snake-oil salesman. His "products" include nutrition, exercise, wonder, curiosity, and love.

Dr. Adams lectures regularly at medical schools throughout the US and has begun building a hospital and healthcare center on a 320-acre farm in Pocahontas County, West Virginia. Funding has flowed in since the success of the movie *Patch Adams*, starring Robin Williams. Once the 40-bed hospital is completed, it will be dedicated to providing totally free healthcare to the community at large. Patch Adams' income is based on donations and fees from his "Wellness" show.

"The best therapy is being happy. All the other things doctors can do are at best aids," he says.

"Health is typically defined as the absence of disease. To me, health is a happy, vibrant, exuberant life every single day of your life. Anything less is a certain amount of disease.

We will never think in terms of cure rates. It gives a false sense of security. People are always "in process" until they die. You don't cure depression. You help a person find happiness, according to their own definition, and hopefully you help them to perpetuate that.

When a person comes to me, unless the problem is an arterial bleed, which has to be addressed that second, the first goal is to have a friendship happen out of that relationship. So we spend three to four hours in the first meeting. We might go for a walk. If you like to fish, maybe we will go fishing. If you like to run, we run together, and I'll interview you while we are running. By the end of that time, I hope we have a trust, a friendship starting to develop, and from there we can proceed.

Forget the patient, it had to be fun for us.

From the start, it was obvious to me that we had to have fun in what we were doing. Forget the patient, it had to be fun for us. Life has to be fun! I saw what life was like when I was serious. I had ulcers and I wanted to kill myself. That was me as a serious person. That failed.

When you say, "That doctor has a good bedside manner," what are you really talking about? The element of love and humor that they bring into the room.

But the fact is, until we build our place with beds for our patients and the technology required of a modern medical facility, a model, we will have no impact on the healthcare delivery system in this country, and that's what we're about.

For many years we have tried to challenge the problems of healthcare delivery in the US in a single model:

* We do not charge any money — thus addressing the issue of the power that greed has in our society.
* We carry no malpractice insurance.

Not only hospital but also home — farm, theater, crafts center, recreational facility, in a beautiful material setting

---

* We live together. Staff and patient can feel a home environment that is not only hospital but also home — farm, theater, crafts center, recreational facility, in a beautiful material setting — all to address the issues of boredom, loneliness, and fear that also are hurting most patients.
* We will be a place to study health in relationship to community and how one can learn skills of cooperation and compromise. The whole community is a long-term example of joyful interdependence.
* We find humor so important that we will substitute a silly, playful hospital for serious ones.
* This will be the first interdisciplinary hospital in the US — having respect for and working in cooperation with all healers.
* This will be a hospital whose underlying ethic is that of living healthy lives and not just of conquering sickness.

→ *Patch Adams, MD, The Gesundheit Institute, 6855 Washington Blvd., Arlington, VA 22213 (Phone: 703 525 8169), or volunteer coordinator Kathy Blomquist, The Gesundheit Institute, HC 64, Box 167, Hillsboro, WV 24946 (Phone: 304 653 4338). Patch Adams is trying to raise $25 million for his hospital project. The Gesundheit Institute puts out an occasional newsletter called* **Achoo Service!** *("Good health is a laughing matter – and that's nothing to sneeze at!"). Those wishing to make a donation can send a check made out to The Gesundheit Institute at the above address or can put their names on a list at <www.patchadams.org>.*

→ *The* **Real Patch Adams** *is a documentary produced by Judith Bourque (see <www.therealpatchadams.com>). Bourque is an independent filmmaker who attempts to sidestep the commercial interests usually involved in documentary-making for the major networks. She is keen to create an online bank for constructive, positive documentaries.For more information contact her at <judithbourque@email.com>.*

W

Wildlife areas around hospitals

PAT HARTRIDGE

THIS IDEA WAS BORN DURING TWO GRAY WEEKS IN NOVEMBER 1984 when I was in the isolation unit of the Churchill Hospital, Oxford, awaiting diagnosis of Legionnaires' disease. My stay was enlivened by a robin that perched on a wall outside my window. A string of nuts would probably have produced a bluetit or two, and a bird table would have been better than TV. My home convalescence was enlivened by my recording wildlife from my window.

To encourage birds, bees, and butterflies to come closer to the wards so they can be seen by the patients

---

I think it is a good idea to plan wildlife areas around hospitals that will encourage birds, bees, and butterflies to come closer to the wards so they can be seen by the patients. This can be done by using birdbaths, feeding stations, nest boxes, and plants specially chosen to be attractive to them. The point is to create for the patients an interest outside the daily routine of the ward; to encourage visitors to bring gifts of birdseed rather than flowers when visiting; and to encourage those patients who are keen to record sightings of various species for their own interest and to add to their local nature conservancy records.

For the long-term disabled, there could be visiting speakers on wildlife topics to increase knowledge and to add enjoyment to observation, with, perhaps, the help of volunteers from nearby schools to maintain the sites once they were established.

After putting this idea to the Institute for Social Inventions, I was encouraged to enter it in the annual competition. In order to do this, I had to show that the scheme was viable and I therefore approached local hospitals for their reaction. The Churchill Hospital was particularly enthusiastic, and with the active help of the assistant nursing officer, Mrs. Petursson, the areas to be planted were planned.

My original idea — for two or three gardens to be planted and maintained by volunteers from the hospital and local schools — was defeated by its own success. The site proved so rich in likely sites that a more organized work force was obviously needed, and I got the Berks, Bucks, and Oxon Naturalists' Trust to act as agents for me through their community program. This program eventually ended, and the scheme has since depended on myself and one or two volunteers.

The Wildlife Trusts (formerly the Royal Society for Nature Conservation) produced a project pack giving advice on planning, planting, and labor. Although information regarding grants is now out-of-date, the rest of the pack is still very relevant.

Of the original five wildlife gardens created at the Churchill Hospital, two have had a change of use, one has been built over, and one is being maintained by the hospital garden staff. I maintain the Old Chapel Wildlife Garden, built on the site of a demolished Nissen hut that served as a chapel during the Second World War. It has been a great success and is used regularly by patients, staff, and visitors. It is looking fabulous, with a white wisteria draped over one of the struts that supported the old Nissen hut.

→ *For more information about the idea, or to obtain a copy of the project pack, please contact Pat Hartridge, 49 Old Road, Wheatley, Oxford, OX33 1NX, UK (Phone: Int.+44 [0]1865 874487; E-mail: wildlife@p-hartridge.demon.co.uk; Web: www.hospital-wildlife-gardens.org).*

Work credit system for use in businesses

Nicholas Saunders

The Institute for Social Inventions is looking for a business that is still at the planning stage which might like to take advantage of the work-credit system. Such a system could have an extremely beneficial effect on the standard employer-employee relationship.

In this system (adapted from the American "Walden 2" commune experiments), each task within the day's work is awarded credits, with the value of the credits being decided by the workers themselves, so that the most unpopular jobs receive the highest credits. Among the many advantages are that people can then work nearer to their own preferred individual pace, at work of their own choosing, and be paid according to the real value of their work, with the element of self-assessment resulting in less interference by the employer.

Introduction

This is a system for paying staff more fairly, and one that can be extended to everyone involved in a business, including the customers. The assessment is made by those doing each job in such a way that it is automatically revised at regular intervals. As the assessment comes from the workers, it is unnecessary for a "boss" to evaluate their worth, thus eliminating a cause of tension. As payment is by credits, staff have more freedom to work at their own pace and to choose which jobs they do.

The principle of operation

The work involved in the business is divided into specific jobs. Where it is impractical to distinguish some jobs, these may be combined in one category — for instance, book-keeping and ordering stock may fall under "office work."

W

> A list of the day's jobs is posted along with their
> credit ratings. The staff choose their jobs
> (from those that they are qualified to do).

Specific jobs are allotted a number of credit points each — for instance 12 points for cleaning the work area, ten points for banking the day's takings, and so on. Non-specific jobs are allotted points by time — say, office work at 20 points an hour; driving a van, 15 points per hour. In practice, most of the jobs would be specific, but examples depend on the type of business. Where several people work together, they of course share the credits for the work they do.

The operation in practice

A list of the day's jobs is posted along with their credit ratings. The staff choose their jobs (from those that they are qualified to do) and cross them off the list, taking a note of how many credit points they have earned.

The jobs that are not chosen (i.e., those that are taken when no choice is left) are automatically upgraded in credit rating by having their number of credit points increased by, say, five percent. Of course, common sense would prevent this from happening if there were a particular reason that a job was not chosen on a particular day. There would also be an opportunity for workers to alter the credit points — either at a regular meeting or by each person having a "ration" of points they could change each week.

The total wages allocated per week would be divided by the total number of credit points — so, for instance, each point might be worth a quarter — and each person's wages calculated accordingly.

Extensions of the principle

It would be necessary to establish some form of agreement with staff at the outset about how the total wages are to be calculated. For many businesses — such as a shop — this can conveniently be a proportion of turnover. It would then be necessary to have an agreement with the staff that all work (within set parameters) was to be completed each day, however long (or briefly) they had to work. There would, of course, be no "overtime" as such, but long hours would normally be linked to high turnover. This device of linking total wages to turnover is generally seen to be fair by everyone and is a great advantage when it comes to costing.

> Say that the business is expanding — all the staff will work
> more and more (and earn more and more) until they decide
> that they had rather earn less and work less.

A further extension is for the staff to decide whether to take on more people. Say that the business is expanding — all the staff will work more and more (and earn more and more) until they decide that they had rather earn less and work less. On contraction, the staff could decide if, when, and whom to lay off.

The third — and most fundamental — extension is to include those in the "boss" position. Obviously, fewer people would be qualified to manage than to do basic jobs, but it seems to me that responsibility could also be assessed and rewarded by credit points. And to complete the set-up, why not assess and reward those risking and investing their capital too?

Optional extension: combined workers'/consumers' co-op

Imagine this system in operation in a shop that catered to regular customers. It would then be possible for those who own the business to sell it to the customers so that it became a co-op. Or the same result could come from a group of prospective customers putting in money to set up the business.

The structure appears to incorporate a conflict, on the intellectual level at least — that between the customers' interests and the workers'. But in practice, and with goodwill, I think that this is no real obstacle.

I visualize a committee of owners/customers who would lay down overall principles, employing a group of workers on the work-credit principle. The workers and customers would have joint meetings to agree on a manager and important changes — but apart from that, the staff would have control of the day-to-day and week-to-week running of the business.

Is your business at the planning stage?

I had hoped to use this system in a retail business employing some 12 people which had already been going for some years. However, in this instance there were particular difficulties, perhaps compounded by the fact that the conventional structure was already well established.

The system might therefore suit a business that is still at the planning stage. The types of business that might be most suitable include shopkeeping, distribution and many light industries, and farming.

↦ *Nicholas Saunders died in a car accident in South Africa. Please send feedback to The Institute for Social Inventions, 20 Heber Road, London NW2 6AA, UK (Phone: Int.+44 [0]20 8208 2853; Fax: Int.+44 [0]20 8452 6434; E-mail: rhino@dial.pipex.com).*

www.DoBe.org —
Retribalizing our cities from Beijing to Barcelona

WWW.DOBE.ORG HAS THE POTENTIAL TO REVOLUTIONIZE THE WAY people experience cities. It is a free events website for each and every city in the world, with event announcements posted by its readers. It is strictly for non-consumer events, where people can participate fully. So a stranger arriving in a new city will immediately be able to make real contact with local people, whether by going on a walk or joining a philosophical discussion salon, a writing group, a chess tournament, a football team, a theater group, a dinner party, a cancer self-help group, or whatever the person's fancy may be.

This website is strictly for non-consumer events, for events that people can participate in fully.

The website is not a guide to, for instance, films and plays — it will not include events that involve simply passively consuming — for although it is a great pleasure at times to be merely an anonymous member of an audience, there is also an unmet need in modern city life to get together in small creative groups, to alleviate the isolation and alienation that many people feel.

So films and plays won't be included, but film outings, where a small group goes to see a particular film, with a discussion about the film afterwards in a local cafe, do qualify as participatory. Likewise, a lecture does not qualify, but a lecture with a significant amount of open discussion afterwards can be included. The events, in other words, involve the participants in more than just listening and watching.

Nor is this a website for matchmaking. All events are for groups of three or more. And there are restrictions that exclude sexual or illegal activities or racist or unkind material.

www.DoBe.org is a charitable project and has virtually no budget at all. It has been programmed thanks to the labors of Phil Wilson and Merlyn Albery. It is based on a server in California, set up and maintained by Flemming Funch of the New Civilization Network.

www.DoBe.org now seeks volunteer editors and activists who can help get the website going in each city, who can seed the board with interesting events, and who can persuade people to take part and local media to publicize it. It is trying to interest librarians throughout the world to act as key editors for their area, doing what they can to boost the uptake of creative and community events — everything from opera groups to mother-and-daughter book discussion groups.

Ideally it needs money spent marketing it. But in practice it is no doubt going to have to rely on people passing on the word to their friends and getting them to do the same.

If you can help in any way, either with marketing or editorially, or by helping with the web design or by creating an event, please get in touch.

→*www.DoBe.org, 20 Heber Road, London NW2 6AA, UK (Phone: Int.+44 [0]20 8208 2853; Fax: Int.+44 [0]20 8452 6434; E-mail: rhino@dial.pipex.com; Web: www.DoBe.org).*

X-shape buildings optimize window offices

Summarized from *Barbarians led by Bill Gates: How the world's richest corporation wields its power* by Jennifer Edstrom and Martin Eller (published by Henry Holt and Company Inc), monitored by Roger Knights.

ALL THE BUILDINGS AT MICROSOFT ARE IN THE SHAPE OF AN "X." The cafeterias, mail rooms, and supply room are all in the center of the X. This was a design that Microsoft had copied from IBM. In this way the company could maximize the number of window offices.

Years of service rewarded with more free time

TOM WALKER

A shorter work week need not cost more.

THERE IS A CONSENSUS AMONG BUSINESS ANALYSTS AND LABOR ECONOMISTS that a shorter work week costs more money. That consensus is wrong. It is based on a 30-year-old analysis of even older data. Times have changed.

In some cases, even today a shorter work week may still cost more money, but in many others it could save the employer money, create jobs, and provide an important benefit to all employees.

The changes in labor costs that have occurred over the last quarter century are consistent with what the economic model of supply and demand would predict. But employers haven't responded to the price signals. If they had, there would now be full employment without inflation (and without fudging the numbers).

Arbitrage the market for free time by rewarding years of service with more free time rather than with higher annual income.

When a commodity sells for unequal prices in different markets, an opportunity arises to profit from arbitrage — buying and selling the commodity simultaneously in the different markets. The commodity in question is free time. This proposal would arbitrage the market for free time by rewarding years of service with more free time rather than with higher annual income.

Labor costs at the millennium

In the 1970s and 1980s, rampant inflation brought a new urgency to business concern with labor costs. Greater attention was paid to the structure of those costs.

Labor economists singled out the growing importance of fixed, per-worker expenses — known as quasi-fixed costs — in the total make-up of labor costs. Such quasi-fixed costs were found to create incentives for the use of overtime and to impede the introduction of work sharing.

Since then, however, decades of tightfisted employment strategies have changed the terrain of labor costs. A clue to the contemporary mystery of labor costs and hours of work can be found in many collective agreements as well as in the personnel policies of non-unionized employers. That clue is the schedule of wage rates.

The typical rate schedule provides for service increments within a job classification and pay grades between classifications. The unquestioned assumption is that as an employee moves up the wage rate schedule, the annual paid hours remain constant and his or her annual income increases in proportion to the increasing wage rate.

An equally logical (but unheard of!) alternative would be to keep annual incomes steady while reducing hours of work in direct proportion to the wage increments. That is to say, more free time would be the reward for skill and years of service.

That is not to say, however, that all people, or even most, would prefer having more free time to having more income. It is only to point out that nowhere in the standard collective agreement is it acknowledged that this is a possibility.

For an employee facing a marginal tax rate of, say, 33 percent, one extra day off would be worth one-and-a-half days' income.

Nor does the standard collective agreement offer any comparison of the relative benefits of such a trade-off between free time and income. For an employee facing a marginal tax rate of, say, 33 percent, one extra day off would be worth one-and-a-half days' income.

Who pays for the overhead cost of labor?

The wage rate schedule doesn't entirely explain why the structure of labor costs has changed the way it has over the past 30 years. Such an explanation was given in the 1920s by the American economist John Maurice Clark.

Clark argued that when employers try to shift the costs of cyclical fluctuations in demand to their work force, those costs ultimately return in another form. To illustrate the fallacy of treating labor as a variable cost, Clark asked, "If all industry were integrated and owned by workers, what would be the relation of constant to variable expense?" His answer was that "it would be clear to worker-owners that the real cost of labor could not be materially reduced by unemployment."

At first blush, Clark's hypothetical worker-owned, integrated industry may seem remote indeed from today's actual economy. Accounting at the level of the firm for the social costs of unemployment would seem to pose insurmountable technical problems — not to mention protests from investors.

As luck would have it, though, there is already in place a rough-and-ready surrogate for social cost accounting: the progressive income tax. The difference between a firm's gross-of-tax payroll costs and its workers' net-of-tax compensation provides a convenient index of the extent to which the firm has tried (but ultimately failed) to shift its overhead cost for labor to the worker.

In many firms, while employers kept a gimlet eye on fixed labor costs and tried to cut costs by trimming the work force, the average seniority and pay classification of remaining permanent workers crept steadily upward. As long-term employees rose on the pay scale, their incomes pressed inexorably onward into higher tax brackets.

How to profit from high taxes and labor market polarization

The strategy for arbitraging labor market polarization and high taxation is simple. The secret is to move in the direction of equalizing annual incomes and to reward skill and seniority with more free time.

Move in the direction of equalizing annual incomes and reward skill and seniority with more free time.

Not every employee would want to make such a radical trade of income for free time. But there's no need to impose it or to offer new incentives. Marginal income tax rates already create a substantial premium on free time for high-income earners. Many would jump at the opportunity, if given the option and the information.

The changeover to rewarding service and skill with free time doesn't have to be done all at once. It can be introduced a little at a time. In the meantime, employers might begin to wonder about the motivation of employees who choose to drone on incessantly for diminishing returns.

Governments have a role to play by acting as model employers and by refusing to subsidize the growth of inequality further. Pension fund managers could scrutinize investments for their potential to pay reduced work time/income equality dividends. Entrepreneurs could buy up high-wage, long-hours-bloated companies and negotiate a new free-time deal with employees.

→ *Tom Walker can be reached by e-mail at <timework@vcn.bc.ca> and on the web at <www.vcn.bc.ca/timework>.*

Young@Heart — Political theater from the over 65s

BOB CILMAN

Summarized from program notes by Bob Cilman for the London Lyric Theater production of *Road to Heaven*.

YOUNG@HEART BEGAN AS A LARK. It was a way to break up the tedium at a low-income meal site for the elderly in Northampton, Massachusetts. The food, sort of the typical government issue, was not great, but there was a stage with a piano and a woman who wanted to accompany a chorus. It seemed like the right thing to do. I was the director of the meal site, and my artistic resume was shaky at best. I was in a short-lived cover band called the Self Righteous Brothers, with a small yet fanatical following. For theater experience I had spent a year as an actor, stage manager, and general manager for a theater that had managed to alienate just about every artist in town (before I worked with it).

I found a woman to direct this new elderly chorus, but she only lasted three months because her choice of music was too condescending for the elders. I decided to take over the directing because I loved the excitement of the people in the group and they seemed very willing to try anything.

After less than a year we decided to stage a production at the meal site where they ate and rehearsed. Roy Faudree, from No Theater, was intrigued by the project and agreed to work with us. That was a thrill for me, because Roy created the most wonderful and inventive art in our community.

That first production was more memorable for the sensation and buzz it created in town than for any great artistic merit. The show sold out four times and brought in a broad cross section of younger and older people from the community. The star attraction was an 85-year-old woman, Anna Main, who developed into a stand-up comic with plenty of filthy jokes that only she could get away with. We knew from the beginning that if the songs weren't going over, we could give them Anna and she would keep it entertaining. Right from the start the chorus had the reputation of being different from most elderly groups and a bit outrageous. In the second year, things became even more outrageous when two female impersonators, Ralph Intorcio and Warren Clark, showed up along with Eileen Hall, a Brit with unique vaudeville routines.

I've always been asked about the significance of this work for old people. To explain what it is, I first have to make clear what it isn't. The chorus was never intended to be a social service to aid the elderly. I am sure there are benefits derived by the people involved and that this all adds years to their lives. If so, great, but that has never been the reason for doing the work. There has always been a very strong political element to the art. Northampton, Massachusetts, like most New England towns, is divided between the people who have lived there all of their lives and the newer people, who have moved to town in the past 25 years. Young@Heart has helped bridge that gap with the theater we've been performing for the past 18 years.

Some examples: In 1984, we created *Boola Boola Bimini Bop*, which combined Young@Heart with a group of young breakdancers from one of the housing projects in town. The breakdancers created routines to songs the older people liked to sing. It was the first in a long line of shows that featured a clash of cultures. The benefits to that production went well beyond the performance. There is a bus route in town that goes to all the public housing throughout the city. Members of both groups were based in housing projects and had often seen each other on the bus. Before the show they were wary of each other; after the show they were sitting together on the bus.

In 1988 the show *Oh No, A Condo* examined the rampant gentrification in town. The seniors, displaced from their housing project by a condominium developer, meet up with Cambodians in the local park, who have recently been displaced from their country, and with some punks who rule the park. By the end of the production the seniors are singing traditional

Cambodian folk songs, the Cambodians are singing "Let Me Call You Sweetheart," and the punks are dancing to Irving Berlin.

In 1991 the chorus put on two major productions: *The Devil in Ms. Main* and *Louis Lou I*. The first combined the chorus with young Puerto Rican dancers and an African American gospel choir. The highlight was Anna Main (95 at the time) and her unique take-off on Madonna's "Vogue." In *Louis Lou I* the chorus was reunited with Roy Faudree. The production, a retelling of the French Revolution using the songs of Sinatra, was a departure from the traditional Y@H narrative. The show, a stunning visual piece, was a revolution for the chorus in that it changed our thinking on how we can present ourselves on stage.

In 1994 the chorus created *Flaming Saddles*, a big campy production with the Pioneer Valley Gay Men's Chorus. Old cowboy songs were combined with disco, and the old people and the gay people in the audience were screaming together in appreciation.

When we were invited to the R Festival in Rotterdam in 1997, we created *Road to Heaven*, a compilation of some of the best work from all of these shows. We dedicated the work to Anna Main and Warren Clark and all the other chorus members who had died. The performance in London in 2000 was the sixth time in the past three years we've been to Europe with this production. Chorus members have discovered that there is something interesting about the music they begged their kids to turn off. For those of us who were brought up with the music, it's amazing how it is transformed when older people sing it.

Throughout most of our 18 years, Y@H has presented concerts in public schools for students of all ages. These programs have followed the concert format as described above. Currently we are touring a show called *From Radio Days to Rap ... and Back*, which is a musical tour of the songs and styles that were popular from 1930 until now. We have performed this show in over 100 schools throughout Western Massachusetts. The show is fun and very interactive, with students performing with the chorus. Some of the student performances are spontaneous and some are planned in advance by our director and the school's music teacher. What makes the performances unique is that the students are joined in the audience by senior citizens from their own community. Typically, the seniors are invited to attend school concerts (during school hours) by local Councils on Ageing as well as by the students themselves.

→ *Young@Heart (E-mail: rcilman@hotmail.com; Web: www.youngatheartchorus.com).*

Z

Zip Art — Software that makes everyone an artist

PAUL FRIEDLANDER

The Institute for Social Inventions has tried out the free Zip Art software described by Paul Friedlander in the following piece and can confirm that it is a magical way for users to become abstract artists producing stunning patterns, able to control their shapes and colors and to collage them together. The result, when printed out, can be a picture worth framing. Zip Art could inculcate in philistines a love of art. It is software that every school should have, certainly every art school, and could be adapted for use by children with severe physical handicaps.

AS AN ARTIST, when I first tried using computer graphics I had the impression that something was missing. Just as a word processor is like a typewriter and filing cabinet combined, a typical graphics package is a drawing board, pens, and airbrush — very useful, but the computer is not being used to its full potential. I wanted to do something that used the power of the computer and just looked magical. I decided to write my own software. Zip Art is the result.

Once you start using it, you will soon be creating surprisingly subtle and beautiful images. Intricate forms appear effortlessly with each mouse movement. It looks as if your computer has come alive.

Intricate forms appear effortlessly with each mouse movement. It looks as if your computer has come alive.

This is quite unlike any other drawing package on the market. It does not filter, morph, or modify existing images with readymade textures and patterns. The rich variety and subtlety of forms are "painted" onto the screen with your mouse, with which you control the size, shape, and position of the patterns and merge them into one another.

Zip Art has ten readymade color palettes, a color editor for creating your own color palettes, a choice of backgrounds and pen widths, literally hundreds of different drawing tools, and numerous other special effects, including animation. There are two animation demos, a tutorial, and help files.

Each tool produces beautiful forms
based upon mathematical algorithms.

It is easy to learn, intuitive, and simple to use. You draw using a choice of special graphical tools. Each tool produces beautiful forms based upon mathematical algorithms, but the user needs to know nothing about the math, which the computer carries out automatically "behind the scenes."

You are creating new pictures, interacting in real time with the computer's "calculating engine." The computer records your actions and at the touch of a button, the drawing can be replayed, taking you from a blank screen through each step you have drawn to the current state of your picture.

It is so easy that five-year-olds will fall in love with it instantly.

Zip Art is both a toy and a serious graphical tool. It is so easy that five-year-olds will fall in love with it instantly; parents and teachers will realize how stimulating it is for the creative potential of their children. Adults who enjoy art will love it too. Anyone using Zip Art will be creating their own original images, which they can print or save as bitmaps.

For artists and graphics professionals, Zip Art offers a host of features allowing the rapid production of highly polished images that can be used "as is" or exported to other software environments and seamlessly embedded into any number of other uses.

➜ *Paul Friedlander, 43 Narcissus Road, London NW6 1TZ, UK (Phone: Int.+44 [0]20 7 794 8665; E-mail: praskovi@clara.net).*

➜ *A Pentium is recommended to run Zip Art. It must be running Windows 95 or Windows NT. There is no Mac version available. A full version can be downloaded for free from <http://home.clara.net/praskovi/text/zippage.html>.*

Zoo-Zoo Vouchers

A LOCAL CURRENCY SCHEME reported by the American Schumacher Society concerns Zoo-Zoo, a natural foods restaurant in Oregon, now defunct, but for many years flourishing as a workers' cooperative. On one occasion the workers decided to expand and move to larger premises. To finance the move, they held benefits and persuaded friends to lend them money, but this still left them $10,000 short. They raised this amount by preselling future meals, issuing $10 food vouchers stamped "Help the Zoo now," with varied "Valid after" dates to prevent people from redeeming them in one rush.

They raised $10,000 by preselling future meals,
issuing $10 food vouchers.

Even the carpenters working on the new premises accepted part payment in Zoo-Zoo food vouchers, and customers bought more than they would need to give to friends. Zoo-Zoo food voucher customers were their best advertisers, bringing friends who paid in dollars.

Five businesses in Great Barrington, Massachusetts, have since copied Zoo-Zoo's example, with help from the Schumacher Society. One restaurant owner — spurned by the banks when he asked for a loan that would allow him to move across the road when his lease expired — issued 500 of his own Deli Dollars. Each note sold for $9 and bought $10 worth of food as long as customers waited at least six months to redeem it.

→ *Susan Witt, E.F. Schumacher Society, Box 76, RD 3, Great Barrington MA 01230 (Phone: 413 528 1737).*

If you have enjoyed *The World's Greatest Ideas*,
you might also enjoy other

BOOKS TO BUILD A NEW SOCIETY

Our books provide positive solutions for people who
want to make a difference. We specialize in:

Sustainable Living • Ecological Design and Planning
Natural Building & Appropriate Technology • New Forestry
Environment and Justice • Conscientious Commerce
Progressive Leadership • Resistance and Community • Nonviolence
Educational and Parenting Resources

For a full list of NSP's titles, please call **1-800-567-6772** *or check out our web site at:*
www.newsociety.com

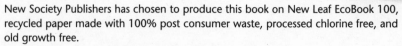

New Society Publishers

ENVIRONMENTAL BENEFITS STATEMENT

New Society Publishers has chosen to produce this book on New Leaf EcoBook 100,
recycled paper made with 100% post consumer waste, processed chlorine free, and
old growth free.

For every 5,000 books printed, New Society saves the following resources:[1]

28	Trees
2,527	Pounds of Solid Waste
2,781	Gallons of Water
3,627	Kilowatt Hours of Electricity
4,594	Pounds of Greenhouse Gases
20	Pounds of HAPs, VOCs, and AOX Combined
7	Cubic Yards of Landfill Space

---

[1]Environmental benefits are calculated based on research done by the Environmental Defense Fund and
other members of the Paper Task Force who study the environmental impacts of the paper industry.
For more information on this environmental benefits statement, or to inquire about environmentally
friendly papers, please contact New Leaf Paper – info@newleafpaper.com Tel: 888 • 989 • 5323.

NEW SOCIETY PUBLISHERS